MARK DEVENPORT was born in Oxford in 1961. He was educated at Cheney Comprehensive School in Oxford and at Sidney Sussex College, Cambridge, where he graduated with a first-class degree in history. He has spent most of his career working for the BBC and was the BBC's Ireland Correspondent between 1994 and 1999. With David Sharrock he wrote *Man of War, Man of Peace* (Pan Macmillan, 1998), a biography of Gerry Adams. He is now the BBC UN Correspondent and currently lives in New York.

FLASH FRAMES

twelve years reporting Belfast

MARK DEVENPORT

THE
BLACKSTAFF
PRESS
BELFAST

for Melinda

First published in 2000 by
The Blackstaff Press Limited
Blackstaff House, Wildflower Way, Apollo Road
Belfast BT12 6TA, Northern Ireland

This publication was made possible with the kind co-operation
of the British Broadcasting Corporation

Mark Devenport has asserted his right under
the Copyright, Designs and Patents Act 1988 to be identified as
the author of this work.

Typeset by Techniset Typesetters, Newton-le-Willows, Merseyside

Printed in Ireland by Betaprint

A CIP catalogue record for this book
is available from the British Library

ISBN 0-85640-674-0

www.blackstaffpress.com

Contents

PREFACE
AND ACKNOWLEDGEMENTS

If you are a student of Northern Ireland politics or history looking for a handy guide to the twists and turns of the peace process then don't buy this book. There are lots of better ones on the market. If you are going on a long flight, however, or recuperating from a serious illness, it might just be worth your while. I will not, though, refund your money if the in-flight entertainment is more exciting or Chapter 25 annoys you so much that you suffer a relapse. This is an unashamedly anecdotal account of one journalist's time in Belfast. It could not have been compiled without the help – down the years – of innumerable friends and colleagues whose reward should be copious mentions in the text. I'd like to thank in particular Shane Harrison, Stephen Grimason, Barra McGrory and my brother Peter for their suggested amendments, Cathy Grieve and Gwyneth Jones for help with names and dates, and Trevor Ferris and Peter Cooper for providing pictures for the cover.

Everything from now on in actually happened, although on occasion I may have got carried away with the adjectives. Everyone is real although in a couple of cases I have changed their names for reasons best known to myself. All the mistakes are mine, and if my track record is anything to go by I am sure you will find loads of them, despite the great work of everyone at Blackstaff. I am very grateful to the BBC for allowing me to write this book. I am even more grateful to June Gamble from BBC Northern Ireland's Information Research Department for helping me with various obscure details. The account starts at the beginning and finishes at the end, but it isn't always chronological as that would make things far too easy for the reader.

United Nations – Once Again

SPRING 1999

Covering the aftermath of a bombing is nothing new, and working straight through the night feeding the many programmes of the BBC is also par for the course. But this is different. First, I am not in Newtownards but in New York. Second, the bomb in question did not explode a few hundred yards off, somewhere on the other side of a stretch of white tape. Instead it destroyed an embassy thousands of miles away. Third, the aggrieved party isn't Catholic or Protestant, but his Excellency the Ambassador Extraordinary and Plenipotentiary, the Permanent Representative of the People's Republic of China.

Mr Qin Huasun is livid and who can blame him? NATO missiles have just struck his country's embassy in Belgrade, reducing the building to rubble, killing three Chinese journalists and injuring a number of the People's Republic's diplomats. The tragedy comes at the height of the 1999 bombing campaign ordered by Bill Clinton, Tony Blair et al. in order to bring the Serbian regime of Slobodan Milosevic to heel and ensure the return of thousands of ethnic Albanians forced from their homes in Kosovo. Here at the United Nations, the Chinese are determined to make their official anger with the West absolutely clear. For the members of the UN Security Council and those of us covering it that means a lengthy emergency session, a lot of hot and heavy speeches and a night without sleep. China dubs NATO's attack a 'war crime'. The Russians chime in, claiming the West is intent on destroying the whole world order. An exotic collection of ambassadors from Cuba, Iraq, Serbia and all points east queue up to kick the US-led alliance whilst it is down.

The cast list is very different but there are, nevertheless, some familiar elements for a correspondent rather more used to the Northern Ireland peace process. Just as they do at Stormont, reporters huddle around politicians and their spin doctors trying to glean the latest details. Each provider of news has their own unique gravitational attraction making the corridor look a little like a planetary system. One relatively small player can attract a large number of satellite hacks happy to circle around in the absence of anything else. However, when one of the stars of the UN comes into view – say the haughty Russian ambassador – the journalists peel off at speed and enter an alternative orbit.

In the days after the missile attack the very words which preoccupy the Chinese and the British and the Americans also bring back memories of the terminological minefield that reporters in Northern Ireland are used to picking their way through. Will they condemn the bombing? Why can't they condemn it if civilians have been killed? Will those responsible be brought to justice? Is it enough merely to express shock and sadness? How many mistakes can you make, before you have to stop what you are doing altogether? Are there some things you simply can't say sorry for? These questions aren't directed at the IRA or the UVF, but at NATO, still, at this stage, prosecuting its air strikes against the forces of Slobodan Milosevic.

On the night of the attack the NATO ambassadors look uncomfortable, repeating their regrets in a variety of ways. I half expect them to tell us that this tragedy should provide us all with an impetus for redoubling our efforts in moving the peace process forward. But nobody expects the word 'condemnation' to pass the ambassadors' lips, or to find its way into any formal UN statement. The United States, Britain and France are, after all, permanent members of the Security Council and each wields a veto. They will not condemn the pilots and planners acting under their orders, however horrendous their blunder. But China has a veto too, so for a while there's deadlock.

Day in, day out, a committee of experts convenes to pore over suggested texts. It strikes me that Gerry Adams could have used these sophisticated draftsmen when he was being pressed to condemn IRA attacks. Maybe, on second thoughts, NATO could do with Gerry's able assistants. There are only so many words in the English language the diplomats can employ. In the face of NATO opposition, China starts to compromise. 'Condemn' comes down to 'strongly deplore'. The Americans suggest 'lament', a proposal ridiculed by the Chinese as 'religious and archaic'. The argument over terminology seems petty and academic, but it's holding up all the work of the Security Council and for a while the future of wholly unconnected UN peacekeeping missions is under threat. Eventually the war of words is resolved. The draftsmen and the ambassadors shake hands on a profession of 'profound regret, deep distress and concern'. Grudgingly, diplomatic honour is satisfied. China buries its dead. More bombs fall, killing more civilians, before Belgrade throws in the towel. The world moves on.

I have moved on too. Or have I? Five time zones and a wide ocean away Belfast still exerts its pull. I never intended to be anything more than a passing 'blow-in'. But now my friends, my professional experience and a fair slab of my life are rooted in Northern Ireland. Even pacing the corridor outside the UN Security Council, I instinctively see the world through a Northern Irish looking-glass. The place just won't let go. Which is why, I suppose, I am writing this book. Why *Flash Frames?* Because in the world of television journalism, a flash frame is a subliminal image – a momentary picture which seems jarring and out of place. During television editing we make sure we iron out those images, in order to ensure a smooth watch for the viewer. But in the pages ahead I try to summon up some of those flash frames – episodes and images which generally didn't make it into my day-to-day reporting during twelve years in Belfast, but which stuck in my mind then and still influence the way I see the world today.

1

'Blow-In'

SPRING 1986–WINTER 1986

'I presume from looking at the rota that you must be Devenport.' The editor screwed up his eyes, focused on the sheet of paper in his hand and then turned back to me. 'Have you ever done any TV reporting before?' he asked. 'No,' I replied, 'but I have done a course.' 'Well theory is one thing, practice is another,' the editor, Graham McKenzie, continued. 'The Ulster Motor Show launches today. I want three minutes for the end of my show. The camera crews are that way.'

With a gnawing feeling in my stomach I went to find Bill Brown senior, a veteran news cameraman for whom a light feature on a motor show was just another soft job in the middle of a busy hard news week. 'Done this before?' he asked, as we got into the crew car. I decided that honesty was the best policy. 'I haven't a clue about what to do,' I confessed. 'Half the trainees on my course got a chance to do a mock TV report but I wasn't one of them. Also I don't drive – I know less than zero about cars, and, by the way, I forgot to check where the Motor Show is being held.' He rolled his eyes, smiled at the sound recordist, Mickey Payne, and said, 'I think we can find our way to the show. We'll see you right.'

We wandered around the King's Hall in south Belfast filming in a scatter-gun fashion anything that appeared before our eyes. It seemed sensible to seek out the newest car, the most expensive car, the one with the slickest light show. 'You've got to do a piece-to-camera,' Bill told me. So I found myself draped over the bonnet of a sports car holding forth in front of an audience of maybe fifty people. I am glad I cannot remember what I said. A few minutes later Bill spotted the Northern Ireland goalkeeper, Pat Jennings, strolling down an aisle. 'Quick, grab him,' my cameraman urged me. We buttonholed Pat. I seem to remember hitting him with a tough question along the lines of 'How are you enjoying yourself?' Pat, always

4

courteous, obliged with a usable twenty-second comment.

A couple of hours later Graham McKenzie poked his head around the door of the editing suite. 'Does he know what he's doing?' he enquired of my picture editor, Davey Dillon. 'He seems to,' Davey replied hesitantly, adding when the editor was out of earshot, 'Or at least I hope you do.' It was, I admit, an exercise in the professionals around me covering up for my ignorance and incompetence. At around five minutes to six that evening the piece went on air – it was never going to win any awards, but on the other hand it was three minutes long and I didn't libel anyone. My career in TV journalism had begun.

I arrived in Belfast by chance. There was a lot of competition amongst the BBC's trainee journalists to go to Northern Ireland because it was regarded as the one area in the UK where you were guaranteed a lot of news. That didn't mean that a trainee was going to be sent out to cover an atrocity or a high-level political meeting, but the rapid pace of life in the Belfast newsroom had a knock-on effect. Business or social stories which would have been the lead in an English region were halfway down the running order on an average day, and junior staff got a chance to go out on real stories which they would never have been allowed near in the south of England. Some regions I visited actually rehearsed their news shows in full a couple of hours before going to air. In Belfast, where reacting swiftly to unpredictable incidents was the name of the game, the notion of a full dress rehearsal was absurd. Hence the appeal to cub reporters.

Because of Belfast's reputation the attachments to the Northern Ireland newsroom, offered as part of my BBC journalism training course, were filled far in advance. Not especially competitive, I shrugged my shoulders and looked elsewhere. But then just before the attachment was due to begin, my course tutor approached me – one of the other trainees couldn't go to Belfast, so a vacancy had come up. Would I go?

A few days later I found myself at Belfast International Airport at Alder-grove. It was the spring of 1986. Because of the lack of warning I hadn't read up much about the recent developments in the Northern Ireland conflict. I was vaguely aware that unionists were annoyed about something called the Anglo-Irish Agreement which Margaret Thatcher had signed a few months previously. But beyond that I felt both ignorant and miserable. The latter emotion had nothing to with work, rather it was the result of a recent break-up with my girlfriend back in London.

Help was at hand, however, in the shape of Terence McKee, a gifted guitarist and teacher from Maghera in County Derry and the only person I knew in Northern Ireland. Terence went to university with my eldest brother and volunteered to go to the airport to pick me up. We drove out past the fortified checkpoint on the airport access road. I stared, like any tourist visiting Northern Ireland for the first time, at the police carrying sub-machine guns, an unsettling sight for any English person used to unarmed bobbies on the beat. As we made our way to my bed and breakfast in the university area of south Belfast we passed convoys of RUC and army Land Rovers, with soldiers leaning out of the back doors, training their rifles on anyone they passed.

These images were balanced, though, by Terence chatting away amiably in the driver's seat. After dropping off my bags he asked if I wanted to visit some friends of his who lived in east Belfast. I quickly agreed and soon found myself sitting in their kitchen drinking Irish whiskey with a houseful of some of the brightest, funniest people I had met in a long time. Marie Jones and Eleanor Methven, both actresses with Belfast's Charabanc Theatre Company, regarded me with good-natured amusement. 'So let me get this straight,' Marie cross-questioned me. 'You have come here to report on us, and your reports will be going out to people here in Belfast, and you've never been here before and you don't really know anything about this place?' 'Absolutely right,' I confirmed. 'Well good luck to you,' she laughed.

But I must have some preconceptions, they enquired. And so I confessed a few – most common to the average Englishman, some rather more personal. Like any English person I suppose I regarded Northern Ireland with a mixture of bewilderment and fear. The place wasn't far away, and, on paper at least, was part of the same country as the one I had grown up in. But the images on the TV screens were wholly alien. The place remained mired in an ethnic, religious conflict which appeared frankly out of date in modern Western Europe.

At the same time I had made friends with a couple of people from Belfast at college so I knew nothing was really as simple as it seemed. One friend had a breakdown which was connected to a bombing he had witnessed many years before. Through him and other student friends, I had gleaned some sense of how deeply people's emotions ran in Northern Ireland, and, more importantly, the certainty that they were people just like me, who spent most of their time thinking about music, films and holidays rather than brooding on an age-old quarrel.

I don't think I went into it as I sat drinking whiskey with Marie and Eleanor, but I also had some personal baggage. Despite my exclusively English-sounding name, my family is Catholic with distant Irish roots. My great-great-grandfather Thomas Devenport was a labourer who left Dublin around the time of the potato famine in the 1840s and sought work at a coal mine in the north-east of England. According to family mythology some Protestant 'Orangemen' amongst the miners objected to the arrival of an outsider, but 'Dublin Tom' offered to fight the best man amongst them, beat him and hold him over a fire until he screamed. The same mythology claims that Thomas Devenport was one of the pall-bearers at the funeral of Daniel O'Connell, the champion of Catholic emancipation.

Rather than staying in an Irish ghetto my forebears integrated with the society around them. Sectarianism remained a problem in the north of England until the early decades of the twentieth century – my dad always told me that my grandfather, Chris Devenport, a brilliant mining engineer, had been stymied in his career because of religious discrimination by Freemasons, who were then active in the mining industry. But by the time I appeared on the scene in the 1960s the idea that anyone might judge me according to my faith seemed frankly bizarre. It was just as well, as 'Dublin Tom' passed on to me neither his physique nor his aptitude for fighting! I went to a Catholic primary school and then to a state comprehensive school. At no stage did our family ever think of ourselves as anything but English. My Catholic background may have been a factor in my leaning towards a 'soft nationalist' perspective on Ireland. But by and large my attitude was the typical somewhat patronising English one – 'When on earth will those people see sense?'

During my entrance interview at university, a history professor asked me what my solution to 'the Irish problem' would be. I replied that it would require another Gladstone – a leader who was prepared to sacrifice his own career to achieve a settlement. The unspoken implication was that something radical needed to be done to 'pacify Ireland', as Gladstone put it, whereas all modern British prime ministers had refused to look beyond 'holding the line' during their immediate term of office. The answer seemed to satisfy my interrogator, although it was just the kind of pat, back of the exercise book solution to the troubles which came to annoy me after a few years reporting the realities on the ground. As a student I thought I knew all about Northern Ireland. But in fact I was horrendously ill-informed. The hunger strikes took place whilst I was at university, but my recollection of them is extremely hazy.

Even the most dramatic and harrowing moments of the troubles didn't permeate my student bubble.

After my uncertain debut at the Ulster Motor Show I graduated to flower shows, new attractions at Belfast zoo and visits to the city by the latest teen pop sensation. It was hardly front-page news but it gave me a chance to learn the art of putting television packages together, making sure they made sense, weren't too long and – most important – made the deadline. Also it gave me the opportunity to watch some of the BBC's best reporters in action – the Belfast newsroom boasted journalists like Denis Murray, Tom Coulter, Noel Thompson, David Shukman, Lance Price and Margaret Gilmore, who were to go on to report for *BBC National News,* security experts Austin Hunter and Chris Moore, and Iain Webster, a future *TV News* editor whose ability to put together a good-looking feature was recognised by all. As the local news magazine, *Inside Ulster*, hit the air the reporters would often gather around the screen and engage in a no-holds-barred, yet generally well-intentioned, slagging match – pulling apart a package's weaknesses, but giving praise where it was due. It wasn't a bad way to learn on the job.

Whilst I filled up the back end of the programme most of my colleagues had more sombre matters to cover. These were months of rising anger amongst loyalists and unionists over the Anglo-Irish Agreement. Unionists regarded the 'Anglo-Irish diktat', as they called it, as an abrogation of democracy because it hadn't been put to a vote amongst the people of Northern Ireland. Dublin and London argued that as two sovereign governments they could decide what level of co-operation they wanted to engage in without having to hold a referendum in one small part of the UK, albeit the territory most affected by the treaty. The unionist anger spilled over onto the streets in rioting in loyalist areas. The RUC stood in the front line – a difficult job for a force which was more than 90 per cent Protestant. Night after night our camera crews went out to cover the aftermath of arson attacks on police officers' homes, which tended to be located in Protestant areas not only because of the religion of the officers but because there they felt safer from the constant threat of an IRA attack. The loyalist campaign of intimidation was designed to break the RUC's resolve and make its officers feel like traitors to their own community.

One weekend at Terence McKee's parents' home in Maghera I sat down for a meal with his extended family. His elderly uncles probed me about the BBC's reporting of the Anglo-Irish Agreement. It didn't take long for me to detect that they weren't exactly enthused about the deal, nor the corporation's coverage of the political scene. For a long while I held my tongue, deciding that silent neutrality was the best policy. But eventually I cracked, telling Terence's Uncle Joe, 'The one thing it's hard for English people to understand is why people who claim that they are loyal to us seem to be spending all their time lately going around attacking policemen who are meant to be defending British law and order. It's a strange kind of loyalty.' He drew himself up in his chair and administered a sardonic put-down: 'Well I am sure we older folk don't know as much as you young people, I am sure you have all the answers.' Another uncle, Evan, acting as umpire, brought him to order: 'I don't think we should be bothering our guest with all this political talk.' It was only after the meal that I learned Joe had been a Unionist MP at Stormont, Northern Ireland's old parliament which the British government closed in 1972.

During the same visit I overheard another guest asking Terence's father, Charles, whether he thought there were any Catholics who were Christians. Having long since left my family's Catholicism behind, I was not offended by this remark, but I was bemused, as I hadn't previously been exposed to the evangelical outlook which regards only those who live 'by the book' as true 'Christians'. Mr McKee senior, an extremely enlightened Presbyterian, replied that he thought many Catholics were indeed Christians.

The McKee household was a warm and welcoming home where I felt I could say more or less whatever I felt. But in the tense atmosphere after the Agreement there were plenty of places where you had to watch what you said or did. Terence played guitar in a band which did a gig one night in a pub in County Antrim. After the last rendition of Eric Clapton's 'Wonderful Tonight' they broke into, on instructions from the management, a quick burst of the national anthem. Back at home in England the refrain would probably have reduced any self-respecting pub rock audience to a fit of giggles. Here, though, there seemed to be a competition to spring to your feet more quickly than the person next to you. Staying seated was not an option.

I moved from my B and B to a house in east Belfast just off the lower Newtownards Road, then a regular location for anti-Anglo-Irish Agreement rallies. My English accent generally provoked a warm response. Queuing for a bus into work I started chatting with one old lady who asked what had brought me to Belfast. I decided to be a little coy and said I was a student over on a course. She talked about how much she loved England and English people – the only problem is that 'They don't get the right picture of the loyalist people over here, they don't realise we are just like them. That's because of those IRA-loving people at the BBC, you know, they only tell the English what they want them to hear.' I felt glad I hadn't owned up to my profession straight away.

One weekend my girlfriend from London came over to visit. I suppose I still entertained some hopes that we might rebuild our relationship. But Belfast seemed determined to ensure that wouldn't happen. It rained all the time. I didn't have any transport and so couldn't show her all the beautiful places, like the astonishing Antrim coast, which I had already discovered. One night we went for a drink in the famous and picturesque Crown bar with a friend, a Protestant clergyman called Robert. Robert had a car so at the end of the evening I suggested we might go for a drive and show my girlfriend a bit of Belfast away from the city centre. It was eleven o'clock at night and the idea was patently stupid, but we went anyway. All was fine as we drove up the Catholic Falls Road and peered at the brightly coloured green, white and gold republican murals lit up by the street lights. But as we approached the Protestant Shankill the city seemed darker – a lot of lights had been put out during previous bouts of trouble – and we were in the only car on the road. As we drove slowly towards the Shankill recreation centre I noticed some activity ahead of us off to the side of the road. I shouted something to my friend and then we saw a group of youths in balaclavas push a car out into the road in front of us.

What happened next took only a few seconds but I remember seeing it in slow motion, almost as if I were watching a film. One teenager, with a hood pulled down over his face, flicked his wrist and a tiny spark appeared in the darkness. The spark of the match he'd struck disappeared inside the car and then there was a whoosh and the vehicle was enveloped in flames – the youths had doused it in petrol. Whilst I stared, Robert applied his foot sharply to the brake pedal. We pulled to a halt just a few yards away from the burning vehicle. We were now the next obvious target to add to the burning barricade. As the teenagers turned towards us, Robert slammed the car into reverse and hit the accelerator. We rocketed backwards up the Shankill Road. As we beat the retreat, another vehicle, a police Land Rover, roared past us on the wrong side of the road in the opposite direction. The hooded youths scattered into the side streets.

I apologised profusely, both to Robert and to my girlfriend in the back seat, for suggesting the drive in the first place. It had been classic 'troubles tourism' but none of us had intended to get quite so close. Making our way back to the centre of the city along the Crumlin Road, we stopped off at the Mater Hospital where I phoned the BBC newsroom to tell them what had happened. The reporter on duty, Liam Creagh, asked me what on earth I had been doing on the Shankill at that time of night. Well might he ask, I thought.

The loyalist protests against the Anglo-Irish Agreement continued and intensified. They began to have an impact even on the lighter kind of stories which I had been covering. The unionists on Belfast City Council refused to set a rate as part of their protest campaign and this threatened to close down a number of community groups reliant on local government funds. Some moderate unionists felt very doubtful about this, as they watched drop-in centres and other organisations in loyalist areas closing their doors. The then Lord Mayor, Alderman John Carson, appeared at a news conference which welcomed a move by central government, stepping in to strike a rate and thereby saving these groups. I pointed out that the Mayor, an Ulster Unionist, now seemed to be out of step with his own party's policy. Alderman Carson responded by attacking the boycott of council business, a brave decision which resulted in his loss of the party whip.

The height of the anti-Anglo-Irish Agreement campaign was the so-called 'Loyalist Day of Action' on 3 March 1986 which threatened to close down Northern Ireland for a day. Most people in Belfast had strong memories of the Ulster Workers' Council strike in May 1974 which brought down the attempt at partnership government between unionists and nationalists forged as a result of the Sunningdale Agreement of December 1973. The fear was that any government initiative which unionist leaders found unpalatable would go the same way – brought down by the unionists flexing their muscles on the streets. The day before the Day of Action I went to a city centre shop doing healthy business selling Calor gas heaters and cookers to people worried that the loyalist influence over the workers at the main Ballylumford power station would result in a wholesale loss of electricity. I interviewed a spokesman for the charity Age Concern about what senior citizens should do to keep warm in the event of power cuts.

On the day itself I spent most of the time inside the BBC, keeping people updated on the latest developments through a series of local TV summaries. The problem was keeping pace with events as reports of rallies and isolated violence kept coming in all the time. With the mid-afternoon summary approaching, I realised I didn't have time to put my voice track down on the latest pictures and hit the air on time. The only way was to read my scribbled script over the pictures live on air. I hurried down to the studio and took a seat next to the presenter Seán Rafferty, whose calm assurance helped me control my nerves. As we rehearsed the opening, the studio plunged into darkness. The loyalist power workers had done their bit. An emergency generator kicked in, so we could go on air. But we still didn't have any lights. At those homes which still had electricity for their television sets, the news summary must have looked weird. The 'Northern Ireland News' logo was illuminated but the viewer could only just make out Seán's silhouette as he sat in the dark reading his script off the light of the camera autocue. Next to him, I sat in complete darkness and couldn't make out the scribble on my notepad. One of the studio assistants saw my frantic waving and instantly put two and two together. As Seán finished 'the latest now from Mark Devenport' someone appeared behind me and shone a torch over my shoulder. I started reading my script by the torchlight as the images of a massive loyalist rally outside Belfast City Hall hit the screen.

Most of the people at the rally were peaceful, but inevitably some indulged in violence. We showed some slightly absurd pictures of demonstrators breaking the windows in city centre shops with a hail of golf balls. My job remained to stay inside, but at one stage we had a problem when some of the camera crews who had filmed good footage couldn't get back to Broadcasting House because of the loyalist roadblocks. They weren't far away so I volunteered to head out on my bicycle to try to pick the tape up. At this stage no one would have recognised me from the television and, on a bike wearing jeans, I looked like any curious youth. I pedalled past the barricades and crowds on the Albert Bridge Road in east Belfast trying to look nonchalant and scanning the street for our crew. Nobody bothered me – the atmosphere was that strange mix of latent violence and street festival which would become familiar to me. A lot of the teenagers were out on the streets because it was simply more fun than any of the available alternatives. I cycled on, but my still incomplete knowledge of Belfast geography let me down and the newsroom runner, Sandy, who rode a motorbike, picked up the vital video long before I got to the right place.

The Day of Action came and went. Under the direction of its trenchant Chief Constable, Sir John Hermon, the RUC held the line, and some unionist politicians began to ponder their alternatives, given the determination of London and Dublin not to back down. People went back to their day jobs, and in his Protestant working-class parish my clergyman friend Robert continued to work tirelessly responding to his parishioners' everyday problems. His flock rewarded him with fierce loyalty. But there was an aspect to Robert's life which he didn't advertise to the churchgoers. Robert was gay, something which would always be tough for a clergyman to be open about, but which seemed doubly difficult to cope with in Northern Ireland, where social attitudes on subjects like this appeared to trail England by at least a couple of decades. Northern Ireland had, memorably, been the home of the 'Save Ulster from Sodomy' campaign led by the Democratic Unionist leader, the Reverend Ian Paisley, when homosexual sex in Northern Ireland was belatedly legalised.

One day I was having a cup of tea with Robert when I noticed he was wearing sunglasses, which looked extremely odd given that Belfast weather was being what Belfast weather usually is. 'Why the shades?' I asked and got an evasive reply. I peered more closely and realised Robert had a nasty black eye. I didn't buy his initial attempts at explaining it away so finally he told me the truth. He had been working evenings at the gay helpline in Belfast where he had been counselling a young Catholic married man who had decided he was gay. The caller kept ringing back again and again. He seemed genuinely disturbed and Robert took seriously his talk of attempting suicide. Under pressure, Robert broke the rules and went to meet the caller. He discovered Paul, a man in his twenties who lived in a tough working-class Catholic enclave, the offspring of a big family of travellers who hadn't taken kindly to his talk of being gay. Whilst Robert tried to advise Paul about the best way to handle his emotions, Paul's brothers burst in. Promptly concluding Robert was the source of all the trouble, they beat him up and then beat up Paul for good measure. Hence the black eye.

Unbelievably, I discovered Robert intended to go back, as Paul had kept calling and threatening suicide. I told him to look in the mirror and leave well alone, but I knew that he would follow the dictates of his conscience. Within a couple of hours we were in the car heading towards Paul's house. I decided I should ride shotgun, which was a faintly absurd gesture, given my particular combination of cowardice and a featherweight build. We knocked, and getting no answer we pushed the door and found it open. We edged warily down the hall and made our way into the front room, which was in almost complete darkness.

Inside we came across Paul, on his haunches, rocking back and forth letting out an occasional wail. In the opposite corner of the room the one source of light came from the stub of a single candle which had been burning for some time. Arranged around the candle were four crossed knives. 'Don't touch them, don't touch them!' shrieked the superstitious Paul. 'I'm cursed, I'm cursed.'

It turned out the curse had been the work of Paul's own mother, who had no time for a son who thought he was 'bent'. Robert knelt down beside the candle and began to say a prayer. Making the sign of the cross, he carefully took the knives away, one by one. 'There, the curse is broken,' he pronounced, summoning up all his most clerical tones for the benefit of Paul. The impromptu exorcism over and done with, we all settled down for a cup of tea.

The time came to return to London, where my few months in Belfast seemed like an exotic adventure. Yet none of the training attachments which I later completed seemed half as fulfilling. As my course approached its end I saw an advertisement for a television journalist in Belfast. I mulled it over. My best friends and family were all in England, but a year or so in Northern Ireland might not be so bad. One night I went to the Drill Hall at Goodge Street in central London to see a play by my friends in the Charabanc Theatre Company. *Somewhere over the Balcony* was a gritty portrayal of life in west Belfast's Divis flats, written with the sharp good humour and brilliant ear for Belfast slang which I had marvelled at when I met the playwright Marie Jones in her kitchen on my first day in Northern Ireland. The jokes came thick and fast and, while they might not have picked up all the references, the London audience gave the play a rousing reception. 'Me, I wouldn't want a united Ireland,' quipped actress Rosena Brown in her role as a Divis housewife. 'I couldn't afford it.'

After the play Marie, Eleanor, Carol Moore and the rest of the theatre company were as good crack as ever. I told them I was thinking about taking a more long-term job in Belfast. 'Well that's good timing,' said Eleanor, 'because a room just came free in our house.' I didn't need to hear any more to make my mind up.

2

A Question of Identity

Life at Ravenhill Park was as lively as I imagined it would be – the only problem being that I operated on a different life cycle to everyone else. Being theatre people they got up late, did their work in the evening then partied until the early hours. I am by no means an early riser. But all too often my shift pattern at the BBC entailed getting up hideously early to write the breakfast TV news summaries. On more than one occasion I stumbled bleary-eyed around the kitchen fixing breakfast whilst the others stared at me in a bemused fashion and decided my appearance was a signal they'd better think about going to bed.

At this stage I still didn't drive, so on the cold winter mornings it was quite an effort to jump on my bicycle and pedal into work. Every day I cycled across the bridge over the Lagan and down the predominantly Catholic lower Ormeau Road towards BBC Broadcasting House. The lower Ormeau was and is a tough little enclave. One night a couple of youths strolled out into the road and took a swing at me as I passed by. Fortunately I don't think they were too sober or too serious as I swerved and got out of the way. A friend of mine was punched for being 'a Brit' in the same area, which was ironic as he was brought up in County Louth.

To my right, as I cycled into work, I could see the Hatfield bar where a man was shot dead one night as part of a feud inside the republican splinter group the INLA. To my left was a house where some gunmen from the loyalist UVF had burst in and shot dead a Catholic youth. As I passed by I would stare at the front garden and think about the attackers running down the path.

One lunchtime I was padlocking my bicycle to a lamp-post at Shaftesbury Square in the centre of Belfast when a man tapped me on the shoulder. As the plain-clothes cop flashed his identification card I wondered momentarily if some new offence had been created of abandoning a bike close to an RUC station. 'Have you got ten minutes free – do you want to earn a fiver?' he asked.

Melodramatic thoughts flashed through my head. Why was a detective offering me money? Did I bear an uncanny resemblance to some IRA man in west Belfast? Did the security forces want me to report on any information I gathered professionally? A blunt and negative reply formed swiftly in my head.

At the same time I could hardly call myself a reporter if I didn't find out what this was all about. 'Just head around to Donegall Pass police station,' the detective told me, 'and say I sent you.' Once inside the heavily fortified station I found myself together with a dozen equally puzzled men, all of us in our twenties or thereabouts.

A few minutes later another detective strolled through the door and thanked us for our patience. 'Boys, what we want you to do is to help us with a very important matter. We've got a couple of suspects for a crime we're investigating and we want to see if some witnesses recognise them. So we've got to hold an identity parade just like you see in the movies. It won't take a few minutes and then you'll be on your way. Oh and boys, it's murder and it's terrorist.'

His last words provoked a clearly audible intake of breath from everyone. Like me, most of the others appeared to be wondering what on earth they had got themselves into. Any contact with paramilitaries, no matter how slight, was something the average person walking around Shaftesbury Square could do without.

We walked into a big room with a shiny floor. The detective asked us all to take our shoes off. Then other police officers brought in two suspects, accompanied by their lawyer. The lawyer gave us the once-over to see if he approved of the motley collection. The suspects took their shoes off then stood alongside us. I was surprised at how young and how small they were. The lawyer moved them around, presumably trying to achieve an order in the line which would make them look less obtrusive. Perhaps because I am short, one of the suspects, who was about the same height, was placed next to me.

There then followed a few embarrassed minutes whilst the police officers checked if the witnesses were ready. The suspect looked at me. I looked back. He had hair that could have been mousy but perhaps had been dyed, and, if I remember correctly, an earring. What do you say to a terrorist murder suspect? Answer: not very much. Before the witnesses came in he mumbled to me, 'When they come past just go like that', and made a wincing or twitching movement with his face. I guessed he thought this would put the witnesses off. Whatever he was up to, I decided the best course of action was to pretend to be deaf.

The witnesses were brought into the room one by one. It was only as they walked up and down in front of us that I realised this was a rather more primitive set-up than in the movies. The witnesses weren't behind a sheet of one-way glass or looking through a peephole. They were there, in touching distance, inches away. If it felt a bit unnerving to me, how frightening must it have been for them? If they picked a suspect out then their own identity could be revealed to a paramilitary organisation. No joke in Belfast in the 1980s when intimidation of witnesses was swift, brutal and all too effective.

Three witnesses walked up and down before apologising to the detectives. They didn't recognise anyone. But then the final witness, a young girl with jet-black hair and big dark eyes, came in. She walked up and down twice, then came back to my part of the line. She stared hard at me and the suspect standing next to me. Whilst I knew I had nothing to be concerned about, the old cliché was true. I was scared of being picked out. But then she stepped forward and touched the suspect beside me on his shoulder. 'It was him,' she said, without blinking, and walked away.

I didn't steal a glance to see the suspect's reaction. Instead, fearful that any move could invalidate the process, I kept staring straight ahead. But when the witnesses left and we started to put on our shoes, he appeared remarkably relaxed. A fiver in my pocket, I returned to my shopping trip. He returned to the cells.

I didn't put a name to the suspect until a few days later when I read reports that one Robert Irwin had appeared in court. The girl with the jet-black hair was called Rosario McCartan. She lived at the house which I cycled past every day on the lower Ormeau Road. Rosario had been at home around eight o'clock on the night of 7 May 1987 when she looked out of the window. Her brother Gary was standing in the hallway combing his hair preparing to go out to see his fiancée. Rosario let out a piercing scream – two men with machine guns were coming up the McCartans' path. They burst through the door and opened fire. The bullets hit Gary in the stomach. The gunmen tried to force their way onwards into the living room where the rest of the family were watching the television. But Gary's father, Seamus, slammed the door in their faces. The gunmen sprayed the door with gunfire then ran off. Gary stumbled in and collapsed in his father's arms. The seventeen-year-old, already the father of a baby daughter, was taken to Belfast City Hospital where he died an hour later. The McCartans would never celebrate Gary's marriage that September as they had planned.

Some time later the loyalist Ulster Volunteer Force admitted the murder. They claimed Gary McCartan had been a member of the Provisional IRA. The claim was a lie as the police quickly confirmed. In fact Gary's mother, Joyce, was well known throughout Belfast as a woman committed to peace and energetic in her pursuit of cross-community work. Living in an exposed position on a main road close to a sectarian borderline, the McCartans suffered especially badly during the troubles. Before Gary's murder, Joyce had already lost twelve relatives. Whilst Joyce wanted her son's killers brought to justice, her reaction after his death was typical. 'I hope no one else dies because my baby has been taken,' she told reporters. 'I feel pity for those who shot him. Their minds are warped but one day they will meet their maker. Our family don't breed hatred. Hatred only destroys. But I will never accept or understand why it happened to Gary. I'm heartbroken. My heart goes out to the others who have lost sons and daughters, no matter what side they are from or if they are policemen or soldiers.'

After doing my duty in the line-up I continued to cycle past the McCartans' house. Each time I thought about Rosario seeing her brother die and wondered what would happen to the suspect who had stood beside me. When the case came to court the following year Robert Irwin pleaded not guilty. His barrister argued that whilst Rosario might have been convinced in her own mind that she had picked the right man, there were too many inconsistencies in her evidence for the court to rely on it.

Robert Irwin's dyed hair featured strongly in the legal argument. Immediately after the shooting Rosario had described the murderer as having dirty fair hair and a moustache. But when he stood in the identity parade, his lawyer said, he in fact had dark hair and no moustache. In court he also had dark hair. The police said he had told them that he had recently dyed his hair. Robert Irwin maintained that he had in fact dyed his hair six years before.

The case was heard by a no-jury Diplock court, introduced in Northern Ireland because of the habitual intimidation of jurors dealing with terrorist cases. The judge pondered the arguments, and decided there were too many doubts to rely on the identification alone. He said that whilst Rosario McCartan had given her evidence in good faith, the inconsistencies in her descriptions of the killer meant he could not convict the man in the dock. Inside the Crumlin Road courthouse, Robert Irwin's friends cheered when the acquittal was announced.

Joyce McCartan didn't let the death of her 'baby' deflect her from her cross-community work. She developed a network of women's groups linking working-class Catholic areas, like her own lower Ormeau district, with their Protestant counterparts in places like Ballybeen on the outskirts of east Belfast. Mrs McCartan consistently stood for peace, even when in 1992 loyalists murdered five of her neighbours in a coldly executed sectarian attack on a bookmaker's just across the road from the McCartan family home.

Joyce McCartan's no-nonsense grass-roots approach to community work received high-profile recognition in November 1995 when America's first lady, Hillary Clinton, called in on the chip shop her community group ran on the lower Ormeau Road. The cup of tea Joyce and Hillary shared at the Lamplighter might have been carefully choreographed, under the gaze of television cameras, but Joyce's story seemed to genuinely touch Mrs Clinton. She didn't dwell on her personal loss but talked, as ever, about the issues like debt, unemployment and poverty which were closest to her heart.

Joyce died in January 1996 after a short illness. When Mrs Clinton returned to Northern Ireland the following year she gave a lecture at the University of Ulster in Joyce's memory. Before she died Joyce came into the BBC one evening to be a guest on a current affairs programme I was working for. On air, she talked again about what people in working-class communities could do to overcome sectarianism. But she also exposed her lasting hurt over Gary's death. She said her daughter Rosario had moved out of the area for fear of reprisals against her as a key witness.

Joyce stayed for a coffee after the programme and I found myself telling her about how I had come face to face with her daughter on the line-up years before. She told me she thought of Gary every day and how upset she had been that the court refused to rely on Rosario's evidence. 'But still, at least now he's been got for this other business.'

It was only then that it clicked. A few days previously a group of four loyalists had been arrested by the police in a car sitting at a junction on the Falls Road. Amongst those arrested were the son of an independent unionist councillor, Joe Coggle junior, and Robert Irwin. When the police moved in, one of the four, worried he was going to be shot, put his hands up and shouted,

'We're Prods! We're Prods!', an instinctive reaction which betrayed the loyalist paramilitaries' belief that the RUC would be more trigger-happy if dealing with IRA men. When Robert Irwin got out of the car he was holding a home-made sub-machine gun and he accidentally fired a shot which hit the pavement between where two of the arresting officers were standing. Luckily for Irwin the policemen weren't trigger-happy and they arrested him and his three companions, recovering in the process the sub-machine gun, two assault rifles, a semi-automatic pistol, 150 bullets, three balaclavas, gloves and a radio handset.

This time there was no room for clever legal arguments. The judge described Robert Irwin and his gang as 'determined and ruthless terrorists who were bent on murder'. They got eighteen years for conspiracy to murder. Mr Justice Kelly said they had been caught 'red-handed ... Their weapons were deadly and the total firepower immense. No explanation has been given which would raise the slightest doubt to the strong inference that they were on this road with their arsenal of weapons ready to commit murder.' The police never found who Irwin and his companions were looking for that night on the Falls Road. But the terrible experience of the McCartan family suggested that in the gunman's eyes, any Catholic would do.

3

When the Phone Rang

SPRING 1987–WINTER 1987

I didn't make a habit of taking part in identity parades. The daily grind involved writing scripts in the newsroom and, if I was lucky, getting out on the road with a camera crew to shoot a story. Belfast was much the same as any other news operation in that you started on lighter features for the back end of the evening programme, and as you won respect you slowly but surely got given harder-edged stories.

Two other trainees off my course also got jobs in Northern Ireland. From the word go I assumed they were both on a fast track. Alex Thomson worked for BBC Radio Ulster current affairs programmes, before moving to the TV current affairs show *Spotlight*. Alex would later move to ITN and become a familiar face on *Channel Four News*. Kevin Connolly got a job as a Radio Ulster news reporter, before heading down to Dublin, then landing more BBC foreign correspondencies than I care to count. Even as trainees Alex and Kevin already looked like the finished article. Kevin would amaze me by going live onto Radio Ulster news summaries on a breaking story and delivering a flawless straight dispatch without a script of any sort – the listener would never have been able to tell it was a brilliant ad lib. Having Alex and Kevin around was good socially, although I avoided trying to match them drink for drink. After one horrendous night during a trip to Berlin, when we ended up at four in the morning trying to teach a group of French conscript soldiers to sing 'The Wild Rover', I realised I was well out of my league.

Kevin was fond of putting the occasional bet on the horses. One morning he came into the newsroom talking about a hot tip he'd received, but before he could do anything about it word came in of a shooting and he had to rush off. On his way out Kevin thrust a fiver into my hand and made me promise I'd get to the bookmaker's on his behalf. I never bet myself, but obediently trudged along the Dublin Road to the local branch of Eastwoods, only to find it was too early and the shop was shut. I walked back to the newsroom and made up my mind to try to sneak off again in an hour or so. But ten minutes later reports of another incident came in and now it was my turn to grab a camera crew and head off. I promptly forgot about the bet until that afternoon when an eager Connolly burst into the editing suite.

'Where is it?'

'Where's what?'

'The slip, of course . . .'

The punchline might seem predictable now but that didn't prevent the use of a few choice phrases on the day Kevin contemplated the winner that got away.

Despite this, we kept talking, and one evening a few weeks later we got tickets to see the England soccer team play Northern Ireland at Windsor Park. With the kick-off about an hour away I finished my shift in the newsroom and was just leaving the desk when the phone rang. There, on the other end of the line, was the IRA. 'There's a bomb at Windsor Park,' said a youngish-sounding man who seemed just as nervous making his call as I was receiving it. 'Windsor Park, the football ground?' I asked. 'Yes,' the bomber replied. 'Where England are playing Northern Ireland tonight?' 'Yes,' he confirmed. 'But I'm just on my way there, I've got a ticket to see that match,' I went on without thinking. 'So?' said the bomber, apparently put out because I had departed from the normal routine.

I went on to get details of the vehicle the device was hidden in, then asked him for his codeword. This time he decided to depart from the norm. 'Never mind about the fucking codeword,' he said, 'just get on with it.' Following the standard rules for bomb warnings, I phoned the police, who set about clearing the area.

Kevin and I set off to the match – amidst the crowds we couldn't work out whether the bomb alert had been for real. But after the match, as we made our way back along the Donegall Road, it was pretty obvious a big security operation had been under way. We stopped and asked a police officer what was up. 'The army had to carry out a controlled explosion on a car up the road,' the policeman told us. 'You mustn't have heard it with all the roaring in the ground.' 'Was it a hoax?' I enquired, thinking of my telephone conversation. 'From what the lads are saying it seemed real enough – it would have made a pretty mess amongst this crowd if we hadn't got the warning.' We explained we were journalists and he told us we had better contact the RUC press office for the details, but he was prepared to share one tip for two Englishmen on the Donegall Road. 'If I were you boys, by the way, with your accents, I'd keep my voice down.' England had won the match and it would have been foolish to rub it in.

When the phone rang in the Belfast newsroom it could be something urgent, something offensive, something humorous or something moving. Another terrorist call I took came not from the IRA, but from the loyalist Ulster Freedom Fighters. The caller gave a codeword but he had such a strong Belfast accent that I couldn't make out what he was saying. 'Can you spell that for me, please?' Slowly he spelled it out U-L-I-D-I-A. Ulidia. Still baffled, I asked, 'Ulidia, what's that?' 'It's the ancient word for Ulster, you ought to know that if you're going to work here.' I would have chuckled about this impromptu history lesson if it hadn't been for the fact that the person on the other end of the line had just admitted responsibility for the sectarian murder of a bread delivery man in County Tyrone.

Other callers didn't represent anyone but themselves. Yet they weren't bashful about accusing us of being mouthpieces of the government or yes-men for this or that politician, often following through with a suitable array of expletives. The favoured method for dealing with such calls was to listen politely for thirty seconds or so and then to ask the caller for his or her television licence fee number. There seemed to be a correlation between willingness to give off stink to the BBC and forgetfulness in paying for a television licence. On one occasion a man who didn't like an explanation I gave him launched into a tirade, 'You're nothing but an IRA man, you're a traitor, if I had my way with you sort of people ...' I butted in telling him that my father had not fought the Nazis for him to start lecturing me on treachery. What my father's war record had to do with anything was extremely questionable. But it seemed to shut him up, which was the object of the exercise.

During one period of widespread unrest in republican areas, a loyalist street corner gang felt left out of the coverage. Again the phone rang and this time the caller was in a phone box in Protestant east Belfast. 'Hello, is that the BBC? ... This is the Woodstock Road Tartan gang ... you've been reporting on the radio there that all the Catholics are out rioting, well will you report that we're having a bit of a riot too ... will you put that on your radio?' Intrigued, I enquired just how the Woodstock Road Tartan intended to spend their night. 'Well some of the boys have collected up some rocks and some of the other boys have made a couple of petrol bombs and we're expecting the peelers soon and we're going to have a wee riot.' He described the preparations as if he'd just been organising a barbecue. I told him that most of our reporters were already out elsewhere around the city but that if we got the chance we would check his patch out.

For every memorable telephone conversation on the desk, there were scores of mundane ones, many with our colleagues elsewhere in the BBC. The vast majority of these calls were informed and professional, and often I would look at the computer to see that some poorly written copy I had put over to London had been sharpened up by a far better scribe. But, inevitably in any big organisation, some of the enquiries were plain daft. I remember one morning when reports came in shortly before ten that a soldier had been shot in west Belfast. I got on the phone to London and ensured the incident made it onto the ten o'clock national TV news summary as well as the regional one I was writing. But the summary had only just come off air when the phone went and I found myself talking to the journalist writing the eleven o'clock news. 'I'm just preparing my script for eleven and I want to know if I can say, "A soldier has been injured . . ."' I explained that details were very scarce and I would update him nearer the time of his summary, but the sub-editor didn't seem to understand that such a story could change in a number of ways. I explained that by eleven the soldier might be dead, or it might become clear he had only slight injuries or some extra information might become available which would change the story in some other way. 'What sort of soldier was he?' the caller persisted. A British one. 'Which regiment?' I don't know, it's only just happened. 'What exactly was he doing in west Belfast in the first place?' At this stage, I lost it, and told my interrogator that the private was doing his shopping, then promptly put the phone down. My colleague Angelina Fusco overheard the call and thoughts flashed through her head of an eleven o'clock national news leading on a soldier shot whilst on a shopping spree. I picked up the phone and called the national news desk back – the injured soldier, I confirmed, was on foot patrol, their usual role in west Belfast.

The telephone wasn't the only means of communication we employed. In the days before mobile phones became commonplace, all BBC reporters on the road were issued with walkie-talkies which could transmit and receive across the greater Belfast area. The handsets were big grey units that looked a little too military for comfort when you were strolling around a strongly republican area, looking for the scene of an incident, sometimes before the police and army got there. A producer called me as I walked warily around the nationalist Twinbrook estate, searching for a house where shots had been heard during yet another vicious INLA feud. Whispering conspiratorially into the walkie-talkie inside my raincoat didn't do much to help my enquiries.

One afternoon on the Springfield Road the IRA threw an impact grenade tipped with high-explosive Semtex at an RUC Land Rover. The device missed and lay unexploded in the middle of the road. Kept back by the usual length of white tape, I waited with my cameraman to film the army's bomb disposal squad dealing with the device. Local people lined the street to watch the spectacle. The clientele who emptied out of one bar derived immense amusement from the newsroom's occasional walkie-talkie broadcasts to me. One drinker decided this was a suitable time to complain about the recent budget hike on alcohol – he addressed the only symbol of the state ready to hand, namely myself. The graffiti on the brick wall beside us added to the surreal atmosphere. Parodying an often aired advertisement for a toilet cleaner, it read 'RUC beware – Semtex kills even more known germs than Vortex.'

As we watched the army bring out the 'wheelbarrow', the robot device used to great effect to examine and defuse bombs, I realised that a senior officer was heading purposefully in my direction. 'I am going to have to order you to turn your radio off,' he told me, 'it's interfering with our transmissions.' I was more than happy to oblige as the newsroom had kept buzzing me every five minutes, even though I had nothing new to report. The officer stalked off, but my brief conversation with him, combined with my English accent, only served to convince the locals, especially the customary gaggle of children, that I had to be a soldier.

'Mister, you're one of them, we know you are.'

'No, I'm not.'

'Yes, you are.'

'No, I'm not.'

A pause followed, then one boy chimed in with 'Mister, make it go right.' This was a reference to the wheelbarrow, which was now trundling towards its target. The children were convinced that my grey handset could control the robot's every movement. 'Mister, make it go left.'

'I can't make it go left, right or anywhere else.'

'Mister, you are one of them.'

'No, I'm not.'

'Mister, prove you're not one of them.'

'First of all, I don't have to prove anything to you. Second, it's obvious I'm not in the army or the police – just look at me, I'm too small to be a policeman.'

That kept them thinking for a while, but as the wheelbarrow went right a bit, then left a bit, without any assistance from my walkie-talkie, the 'wee skitters' – to use west Belfast slang – renewed their attack. 'Mister, what do you call policemen. We call them peelers. We call them black bastards.'

I decided to shock them, as the best way to avoid tackling head-on, in the middle of the Springfield Road, the rights and wrongs of the RUC. 'Well, where I come from the kids call the police "pigs".'

'Pigs! They're not pigs, them's Pigs.' One boy pointed towards the army personnel carriers pulled up further down the street.

'Not where I come from, they're not,' I insisted.

I thought the interrogation had come to a natural end. But as some of the boys ran off, I was left with one little girl looking up at me. 'Mister, are all peelers bad men?' she asked, with a shocking naivety which convinced me she had imbibed the idea with her mother's milk. Aware of the many pairs of ears still around me I spoke quietly. 'There might be a few who are bad men, but most of them aren't. They're people, just like you and me.' Finally, she had flushed me out for the woolly liberal I really am.

4

Learning Lessons

SPRING 1987–SUMMER 1988

Whilst the unionists spent the mid to late eighties venting their wrath on the government over the Anglo-Irish Agreement, the IRA concentrated on smuggling in massive new stockpiles of arms from Libya, then using them to mount a new onslaught on the police, the army and a long list of other targets which it defined as 'legitimate'. The first substantial bombing I had to cover destroyed part of a hotel on the Antrim Road in north Belfast. We careered up through the traffic, dumped the car and ran towards the scene. Stopped by some policemen from carrying on up the road, we nipped down a driveway and saw the car park of the hotel full of smoke – at least one vehicle was still in flames. But as the cameraman tried to start to film through a hedge, another policeman arrived and ordered us off.

Things seemed to go from bad to worse. Unprepared for the confusion and the tension, I wasted a lot of time running around the perimeter of the incident. When we found our way to those most affected by the bombing I talked at length to them, then politely asked if they would be prepared to give an interview for the television. Everyone said no. I ended up with a brief clip of a local householder whose home had been slightly damaged. I got back late and edited my report nervously and inefficiently. It made its slot, but only just. I watched the opposition with a heavy heart – there was the bride whose wedding reception had been ruined, there were the guests and staff who had been given a matter of seconds to run for their lives, there were the pictures of the hotel car park, the flames, the smoke, the panic.

Afterwards my boss wanted to know what had happened. I didn't have much of an explanation. I had broken all the rules, and failed miserably. But it was a learning experience. If you are going to report on a fast-moving situation, speed and self-control are absolute necessities. If your way is barred you do your best to find another route in. You don't waste time running around like a headless chicken. Being sensitive and understanding to those traumatised by an incident is essential. But there are ways and ways of approaching people, and inviting someone to do something utterly out of the ordinary is often the best way to ensure they say no. You can't guarantee you'll get all you want; however, you can try to be at least as good as your counterparts.

The next time I had to respond to a bombing was in Lisburn, home to the army's headquarters in Northern Ireland. The IRA had placed a device under a policeman's car which exploded just as he drove down a town centre street. The scene looked gruesome – the officer's body lay stretched across the bonnet of his vehicle, covered by a piece of tarpaulin. I told my cameraman to stay on my shoulder and film whatever happened. Instead of talking to people off camera for an age, then asking them to do a formal interview, we put the preamble on camera. Most people were quite happy to describe what they saw, what they heard, and, yes, that most derided but often most important of questions, how they felt. Some people saw the camera and asked not to be on television, in which case we respected their wishes. But not making an issue of it made all the difference. Back in the edit suite we had all the pictures and all the interviews we could have wanted. I still had a lot to learn to match my more experienced colleagues, but this time I wasn't scared to watch the other side.

So what? Thinking about it now my sense of defeat or achievement as a reporter appears utterly irrelevant, even somehow offensive. What of the widow of the policeman, to whom the relative merits of the BBC or Ulster Television's reports that night mattered not at all? What of the bride, whose memories of her marriage would now always be tinged with terror? Yet to be honest these are not always a journalist's most immediate concerns. For me, these were early days and it was hard to get matters in a proper perspective. Perhaps becoming more confident about the practicalities of reporting provided the space at a later stage to reflect on what was happening in a more mature manner. Perhaps a little bit of ageing helped. But back then it appeared a simple matter of professional survival – treating life and death incidents like a job, any job, was a way of coping.

To approach news events in that way, however, is to invite misunderstanding. One weekend I got called out to head down to County Fermanagh for the funeral of two Protestant building workers murdered by the IRA whilst they worked on the roof of a small rural police station. I had been due to have the weekend off and was phoned only at the last minute. I arrived late, but at least the cameraman got there before me. I interviewed the local bishop in the country graveyard. As he condemned the murder of the two men, who were both nearing retirement, he leaned on his crook and the wind made his vestments billow. The scene looked impressively sombre on the screen that night.

When I got back home I went on a bit about my weekend having been ruined. There were a couple of visitors from Dublin whom I didn't know. Later that night we sat at the kitchen table together sharing a drink. One of the guests seemed obviously republican in his sympathies, and as the evening went on I detected that he didn't like me. The English accent and the BBC background seemed to be part of it. But he also appeared to take offence at the matter-of-fact way I spoke about my busy day. He wanted more obvious respect shown for the dead, even though he appeared to approve, at least to some extent, of the cause which their killers used to justify their actions. More drink was taken, then out of the blue he punched me in the face. Chairs flew across the room – the others pulled him away. He stumbled out of the door vowing not to come back.

For the next few days I nursed a black eye and a bruised ego. If I had been too unthinking about the people whom I dealt with on a day-to-day basis in my reports then it had been a useful short sharp shock. I wasn't sure, however, that an armchair republican was the best person to teach me the lesson.

The incidents we covered in the late eighties weren't all one-way traffic from the IRA. The security forces had their successes too. One weekend in August 1988 I went to the border to help cover the extradition of an IRA prison escaper Robert Russell. The handover was expected to take place in the early hours of the morning at the main crossing point on the Dublin to Belfast road. We had only a vague idea of the time and precise location where the Garda Síochána intended to hand Russell over to the RUC, so we had a number of cameras and reporters trailing his convoy up from Dublin and waiting at points where he might be brought across. A large crowd of Irish republicans also converged on the border from north and south in order to protest against the extradition. We abandoned our vehicles close to the Carrickdale hotel, which is just south of the border, and made our way through a growing and rather noisy anti-extradition protest.

A colleague stayed with the protest in case it became violent, but I and my cameraman walked on several hundred yards past the first police line to the point of the border itself, which was one of the possible locations for Russell's handover. We tried to keep warm in the bitter cold of the pitch-black night, but after several hours had passed every bone in our bodies was frozen. I cracked and asked a policeman if I could make my way back to our car to retrieve some hot coffee and sandwiches we had packed. I trudged along the road, listening to the republican protest get ever noisier. Having negotiated my way through the police lines and pushed through the protesters, I found the car and loaded up with the goodies. I set off north again, clutching two large vacuum flasks and a pile of sandwiches. Getting back through the protest was more difficult as tempers were starting to fray. The shouts of 'No extradition' had turned to 'I-I-IRA' repeated ever more quickly and aggressively.

Just as I strolled back through the no man's land between the protesters and the police I saw the first volley of projectiles – sticks, stones and bottles – hurtle over my head and towards the police line. Before I had time to realise I was in the worst possible place, I heard a thick Dublin voice bellow from the police side 'At 'em, boys.' With that, the Garda riot squad went into action. Suddenly some of the biggest officers in the Irish police force were charging directly towards me, a wall of police with truncheons out. There was nowhere to escape to, so I decided the only option was to throw myself at the hedge and fencing on the side of the road. The flasks and sandwiches flew up in the air. I landed in a thorny bush, and watched as the riot squad clashed with the pro-testers. The Gardaí didn't appear intent on taking prisoners – I saw a couple of small young-looking women being beaten violently with batons. The hail of bottles came to a stop, the protesters turned and ran.

I extricated myself from the thorns, picked up the remains of my food and drink and hobbled back to my cameraman. Our wait went on, but it was all in vain. A short while later we saw the flash of the lights of a helicopter. The Irish police convoy had peeled off the main road about a mile away from the border and taken their prisoner to another nearby crossing point. There the RUC and army had picked him up by putting their helicopter down in a field, thus avoiding the determined protesters. Russell shouted 'Tiocfaidh Ár Lá' – the IRA slogan 'Our Day Will Come' – as he was extradited. The camera crew which had chased the convoy from Dublin was on hand to get the essential picture.

The stretch of south Armagh border road where Robert Russell was handed over had been the scene of many attacks during the troubles. Running from Newry to Dundalk, the road is kept under surveillance by British army lookout posts on several surrounding hills. But in the mid-eighties the IRA proved time and again that this was its backyard and despite the army towers and helicopter patrols it appeared able to attack at will. In April 1987 a roadside bomb destroyed the car carrying the senior Northern Ireland judge Lord Justice Maurice Gibson and his wife, Cecily – sending them to 'the final court of justice', as the bombers put it in a deliberately ironic twist of one of the judge's own speeches in a previous case.

I didn't cover the murder of the Gibsons, but I did go to the border for another attack in July 1988 when the IRA tried to kill another Northern Ireland judge, Mr Justice Iain Higgins. The bombers tracked the judge all the way from Dublin airport where he had returned together with his wife and daughter on an Aer Lingus flight from the United States. But somewhere along the line the IRA's carefully prepared plan went wrong and it confused the judge's Land Rover with another jeep-type vehicle – a Shogun belonging to the Hanna family from Hillsborough in County Down, who were returning from a holiday at Disneyworld in Florida. The Hannas arrived in Dublin on the same flight as the judge. Just as their Shogun crossed the border into Northern Ireland, a massive device hidden in a derelict building detonated, completely destroying the vehicle and instantly killing Robert and Maureen Hanna and their six-year-old son, David.

The police and army mounted a major security operation, and for broadcasters there were the same two challenges posed by every such incident – getting pictures of the scene and getting some interviews to tell the story. The security forces cordoned off such a large area that finding a vantage point proved difficult. We drove around and about in ever decreasing circles to see if any high ground could possibly afford a view. A narrow lane runs parallel to the main Newry to Dundalk road but hedges and trees cut off all direct lines of sight. At one point I thought that hopping over a five-bar gate and walking a few yards into a field might do the job. Generally speaking this wasn't something you did lightly near the scene of an incident just in case the bombers had left any secondary devices behind for the security forces. But just as I shouted to my cameraman that we might be in luck and put my foot on the first rung of the gate, the long grass in the field in front of me rustled and a whole company of expertly camouflaged soldiers stood up. The commanding officer greeted me with a polite 'Hello, sir, can we be of assistance?' which was code for 'we intend to be of no assistance'. We made our excuses and left.

Typically when it came to border incidents nobody had seen anything and nobody would talk about anything. It simply wasn't worth anyone's while to say something, no matter how bland, which might be construed wrongly by the IRA. We, the media, were able to go home to Belfast, but local people would have to live with the consequences. Eventually the daughter of a local family of travellers took pity on me and gave me a back to camera interview, describing the scene of the explosion shortly after the bombing. Later the army allowed camera crews in to take close-up pictures of the grisly site.

The murder of the Hanna family was just one in a long line of 'mistakes' which the IRA committed throughout the mid to late eighties. The notion of being able to conduct a 'clean' guerrilla war in which only 'legitimate' military and security targets were hit remained a fallacy throughout the troubles. Despite some so-called 'spectaculars' when the bombers successfully destroyed prestigious or carefully guarded targets, the catalogue of indefensible atrocities continued. Who for instance could have possibly authorised the idea of putting a bomb underneath a school bus as it set about its rounds in rural County Fermanagh? Yes, the bus driver may have been a part-time soldier in the Ulster Defence Regiment. But who in the IRA didn't pause to think that attacking this so-called 'legitimate' target inevitably carried the enormous risk of injuring dozens of children?

In the event the booby trap bomb went off just as the school bus passed another in the town of Lisnaskea on the morning of 28 June 1988. With a sense of disbelief, we set off on the road to Fermanagh to try to get the pictures back in time for the lunchtime news. At the scene, getting pictures and interviews was easy – the damaged bus was in full view and local politicians, policemen and school officials queued up to talk. But then someone told me the grandmother of a girl badly injured in the explosion lived up on a hill which overlooked the site of the bombing. We made our way up to the house and I sat down and had a cup of tea with Gillian Latimer's grandmother, Lucy McCoy. Shocked and bewildered, the elderly Mrs McCoy didn't want to talk on camera, not because she didn't like the media or felt angry, but simply because she didn't think she had anything worth saying. I felt very sorry for her, not only concerned about her granddaughter's condition, but thrust into the unexpected and pressurised situation of suddenly having the BBC and a host of other reporters knocking at her door.

We had taken the unusual step of hiring a helicopter to pick up an early tape of our film and get it back to Belfast in time for the lunchtime news. So together with Mrs McCoy, I was able to watch my colleague Denis Murray report on the incident which had taken place just a few yards away. She corrected Gillian's age, which early reports had got wrong, and once again said, 'I'm sorry I can't tell you anything', before carrying on, 'I am worried about the driver though. Even though he was really badly hurt himself, he was able to crawl back through the bus and give Gillian mouth-to-mouth resuscitation, you know, he was very brave.' I told her that if she told me that and no more it would make a lot of difference to people across the world trying to understand what had happened and how the driver and the children had reacted. A few moments later, together with John Irvine, then with Ulster Television, I recorded a brief interview on Mrs McCoy's doorstep. Her unadorned account had far more impact than all the words of condemnation from the politicians. Two years later, the driver, Ernie Wilson from Enniskillen, was awarded the British Empire Medal for his courage and quick thinking in saving Gillian Latimer's life.

5

Accidents Will Happen

SPRING 1987–SUMMER 1988

The decision to send a helicopter to the bus bombing at Lisnaskea was a recognition of its particular horror. But in general the BBC couldn't afford such an expense to bring its pictures back from incidents across Northern Ireland. In more recent years mobile 'Fast Response Vehicles' have transformed news coverage. Dispatching the vehicle soon after you get the camera crew on the road means you can transmit pictures from at or near the scene – it dramatically cuts down the time it takes to get a newsworthy image to air. But when I began in Belfast there weren't any Fast Response Vehicles. For years the BBC didn't even have the ability to transmit pictures from Northern Ireland's second city, Derry. In practical terms this meant that a reporter's time at the scene of any news story was sharply restricted and that a death defying drive towards a bombing or shooting was matched by an equally hairy drive back.

During my first year in Belfast I couldn't engage in either of these activities for the fairly straightforward reason that I couldn't drive. Pedalling to and from work was okay so long as I remained newsroom-based but presented an obvious obstacle to a career as a reporter. My colleague David Shukman told me to take my test and get a little car of my own and I would be 'flying'. I took lessons, terrorising the pedestrians on a series of quiet streets in east Belfast, but found it all a bit difficult as I didn't have a car to practise in. I failed my first test, which coincided with my birthday. At the party that evening my housemates pinned a note on the front door urging guests to respect my feelings and 'don't ask'. As the months went on I had to rely on getting lifts to stories in the back of camera crew cars. This had its advantages, as I mused in the early hours of one morning when we hit 120 miles an hour en route to a bomb attack in Carrickmore in County Tyrone. Some of the cameramen could handle a car much better than I ever would. But it could also be a complete pain, as became clear on the way back from a story in Derry when my camera crew were diverted to a shooting on the far side of Lough Neagh and I found myself stranded far away from the edit suite where I should have been.

Second time around the examiner proved more humane than his predecessor, and my driving slightly less incompetent. I had wheels. There remained the problem that in Northern Ireland for the first year after passing your test you have to carry an 'R' plate which stands for 'Restricted', limiting the driver to a maximum speed of forty-five miles an hour. At the same time I had a job which put a premium on rushing to and from far-off places. Something had to give.

Having been brought up in the shadow of Morris Motors in Oxford, I invested in a Mini as my first car. I enjoyed driving it around Belfast, but the choice turned out to be a triumph of sentiment over practicality. I found myself hurtling around Northern Ireland's country lanes at top speeds with my foot pressed hard to the floor on the accelerator pedal. Still I didn't seem to get anywhere in the time necessary. I remember rushing back from the scene of an IRA attack on an army patrol just north of Dungannon and very nearly turning the car over as I came around a sharp corner.

Maybe the Mini's lack of power was a blessing in disguise – as a new driver I found bigger, more high-powered vehicles like the camera crew's cars hard to handle. One day we had to cover an IRA funeral in Lurgan and Bill Brown senior, who was famous for his near-suicidal driving, decided to teach me a few manoeuvres in case we got into any tight spots. I wasn't entirely convinced that the sight of Bill and myself doing handbrake turns in a strongly nationalist area nearby was guaranteed to give us the low profile we wanted to keep. When the funeral got under way Bill and the sound recordist hopped out leaving me driving their Audi in a slow-moving cortège which followed the funeral procession. I scanned the mourners keeping an eye out for the crew but I lost them in the crowd. As I looked from left to right there was suddenly an enormous crunch. The cortège had come to a halt, but I hadn't. My heavily built Audi had run smack into the Toyota Corolla in front, demolishing its boot. Covered in embarrassment I got out and admitted liability. Quite correctly the driver in front wanted to wait until the police arrived at the scene. But we were in the middle of a major IRA funeral and the likelihood of the RUC rushing to attend a call to a traffic accident seemed remote. All the while the clock ticked towards my deadline. Eventually I agreed with the other driver that we should both head for a police checkpoint on the edge of the estate.

This was bad enough but it proved to be no more than a dress rehearsal for my next even more farcical accident. Early one evening reports came in from Newtownbutler in County Fermanagh that the IRA had mounted a mortar attack on the local police station. We couldn't possibly gather the pictures in time for the teatime local news but the *Nine O'Clock News* was champing at the bit. For reasons I can't remember I opted to travel with the camera crew. Since it would be getting dark when we arrived a lighting man, Alastair Maxwell, also travelled with us in a separate car. Getting to Newtownbutler from Belfast is a long and tortuous business. It's one of those parts of Northern Ireland which is best reached by driving through County Monaghan south of the border. In those days you had to be careful which route you took as many smaller roads were designated as 'unapproved border crossings' because the army didn't have a checkpoint on them. In order to make it more difficult for the IRA to bring arms across the border the security forces cratered these roads so it was impossible for most traffic to pass. The cratering often seemed more symbolic than practical as it appeared that IRA guns and explosives always managed to find their way across the long and porous border.

Once we reached Newtownbutler we ran into all the usual difficulties at the scene of any incident. The security forces had closed the surrounding roads and it took a lot of negotiating and circuitous driving to find a way in. Eventually we pulled up in the main street still a good distance away from the scene of the attack. The mortars had caused a fair bit of damage to the RUC station but fortunately no one had been hurt. The main street provided a tale of two pavements. On one side of the street stood a crowd, mostly teenagers and by deduction overwhelmingly Catholic. It was a hot summer's evening and the youths were thoroughly enjoying the occasion, their general view being that the IRA had given the British soldiers something to think about and something to keep them busy. 'Sure no one was hurt anyway,' laughed one teenager. On the other side of the street were the Protestants who had decided to stay indoors rather than join in the festivities. Nevertheless the attack had provided them with a social occasion of sorts. I made my way into one house where a family were providing temporary shelter for neighbours who had been moved out of their homes closer to the scene of the blast whilst the army searched for secondary devices. The locals sat around alternatively tut-tutting about the dreadful terrorists and complimenting the woman of the house on the quality of her chocolate cake. Back out on the street one bizarre element which lent added complexity to this social mix was the presence of a large family of young Sikhs who appeared to run a local shop. Probably because of their age, the Sikhs had obviously decided it was more fun to be on the side of the Catholics so the turbanned teenagers joined in the relatively good-natured jeering of the soldiers on duty.

The minutes were ticking by and I felt anxious that we wouldn't make our vital feed to the *Nine O'Clock News*. We had some reasonable pictures of the soldiers patrolling the surrounding area which would do for the *Nine*, but logic dictated that the camera crew should hang on as they would be allowed closer to see the damage at the station and the trailer the mortars had been fired from once the army finished its follow-up operation. Logic also dictated that the lighting man should stay as the light was failing. I realised I had made a serious mistake by not bringing a third car. We pondered the problem and decided that lighting man Alastair Maxwell could lend me his car, take some of his kit out and travel back, once the extra pictures had been gathered, with the rest of the crew. I would drive like a madman for Belfast. I jumped into the car, wished them the best and set off at full pelt.

I hadn't got far outside Newtownbutler when I came to a junction. I felt sure the left fork was the one to take but the signposts were a bit ambiguous. I put the foot down, charging the car along the country lane. After a mile or two I felt dismayed as I saw a 'dead end' sign. I was on an unapproved road and there was a large crater somewhere up ahead. I would have to turn and retrace my route. There was only one possible place to turn – a gate leading into a field full of cows. I pulled into it, went to put the car into reverse and then . . . couldn't find reverse. This was ridiculous. Alastair had pointed out a couple of unusual things about his car before I set off but we hadn't antici-pated I might head towards Belfast in reverse. With a little bit more driving experience I am sure I wouldn't have been so daft but at this stage I had never come across a car with a hidden release which you had to trigger to engage reverse.

Like Robert the Bruce's spider, I tried, tried and tried again. But each attempt to go backwards resulted in me edging forwards. The gate and the cows came closer, whilst the prospect of ever making the *Nine O'Clock News* moved further away. Cold beads of sweat formed on my brow. Visions of being drummed out of the BBC for arrant incompetence formed in my brain. Eventually I decided the time for lateral thinking had arrived: if I couldn't get out of my predicament by going backwards then I had better work out how I could solve the problem by moving forwards. Fortunately the cows had got bored of my antics and had moved en masse to the far side of the field. So, leaving the engine running I opened the gate. It looked possible that if I stayed in first gear I would be able to drive into the field, turn on the side of a hillock and get out again. I had no choice.

I revved the engine and hit the accelerator. I calculated that if I completed the whole manoeuvre at a smart pace I might escape without getting bogged down in the field. Overjoyed I watched the field, the hillock, the cows rotate around me. Now I was heading for the gate, for freedom, for – just possibly – a successful picture feed to London. Then moments before I reached my nirvana I heard a loud crunch. I continued out of the gate and a little way along the road but the constant thudding noise from the offside front wheel told me something was horribly wrong. The car came to a halt. I got out and discovered that not only was my front tyre flat, but the wheel itself was buckled, and the bodywork around the wheel arch appallingly twisted.

I strolled disconsolately back towards the scene of the disaster and discovered, hidden in the long grass, a large block of concrete. The cows regarded me curiously as I shut the gate on them and made my way back to the car. I struggled hopelessly with a wrench trying to move the nuts on the buckled wheel. The birds chirruped in the trees and, quite simply, I felt like crying. Then I heard the sound of a vehicle in the distance. Along came a little school bus – the driver, now off duty, was taking his vehicle home.

About twenty minutes later I couldn't hide my embarrassment as I slunk back into the house in Newtownbutler's main street to find my crew very comfortably ensconced on the sofa, happily munching away on the seemingly inexhaustible supply of chocolate cake. I rang the Belfast newsroom, preparing to take the full blame on my shoulders. 'Don't worry,' said Noreen Erskine on the desk. 'The *Nine O'Clock News* have just been on the phone. Given that there were no injuries they decided not to run the story. We're happy just to get the pictures back for the local breakfast news summaries.'

Alastair made quick work of replacing the wheel and limped his car back to Belfast for repairs. The crew finished the last crumbs of their chocolate cake, took the pictures we had been hanging on for, then gave me a lift home. Subdued, I sat in the back seat of the car, vowing to have no more accidents and pondering the slagging undoubtedly coming my way.

6

'We Should Have Burned Them'

AUTUMN 1987–SPRING 1988

One weekend near the end of my first full year in Belfast I came back into my house and flicked on the television. There were pictures of people picking their way through rubble, trying to dig survivors out of a morass of timber and masonry. It was Remembrance Sunday, November 1987, and the amateur video being broadcast had been taken at Enniskillen where an IRA bomb had detonated killing eleven people. Although I wasn't on duty I immediately went to work and assisted with the special programmes which BBC Northern Ireland put out about the bombing. On this occasion my input was all back at base. Along with the rest of my colleagues I had to choke back the emotion as we aired the extraordinary interview obtained by my colleagues Charlie Warmington and Chris Moore in which Gordon Wilson described with love, compassion and forgiveness his last moments together with his daughter Marie.

The attacks continued and they were by no means all carried out by the IRA. The loyalist paramilitaries ratcheted up their campaign making Catholics in certain enclaves scared to walk the street. I covered a funeral of one loyalist victim in Ardoyne in north Belfast, where the sermon was given by the then Bishop of Down and Connor Cahal Daly, who went on to become Cardinal and head of the Catholic church in Ireland. Bishop Daly called for more security in Catholic areas and I remember putting to him the dilemma for the RUC that if its officers went into these areas at the times and in the numbers he wanted they would be sitting ducks for the IRA. The bishop answered that he understood these concerns but still thought more needed to be done to reassure his faithful. For Bishop Daly a probing question from a BBC journalist was the least of his worries. The cleric was involved in an all-out battle for the hearts and minds of west Belfast Catholics with Gerry Adams and the leadership of Sinn Féin. Dr Daly didn't let any occasion pass without spelling out his views on IRA violence. Even at the funeral of the loyalist victim he devoted a substantial portion of his sermon to a condemnation of the IRA, which, he argued, bore a responsibility too because of its failure to break the cycle of violence. Many of the massgoers weren't impressed by the bishop's logic, wanting to hear him criticise the other side, but not their own. As I waited for Dr Daly to record his interview, he greeted the mourners leaving the church. One woman stared at him, then, standing just a few inches away, spat a mouthful of spittle at him full in the face. Dr Daly didn't respond, but wiped the spit away and carried on greeting other parishioners.

Some months were relatively quiet and then a period would come along when everything went haywire. In the spring of 1988 one particularly vicious cycle of events began with the death of three unarmed IRA members in Gibraltar, shot dead by the SAS as they plotted to plant a bomb in the centre of the British colony. The killings prompted street riots in republican areas. We toured the troubled districts at night filming out of the window of our car, trying to get close enough to capture a distant image of burning cars and barricades, but not getting so close that we would end up adding to the bonfire.

When the funerals of the IRA members took place I didn't get sent to Milltown cemetery, instead I voiced short summary reports from the newsroom. So I wasn't there when the loyalist Michael Stone mounted his one-man gun and grenade attack. All my colleagues dived for cover – I would have been down there too – but BBC cameraman Peter Cooper, whom I had the good fortune to work with a great deal whilst I was in Belfast, stood his ground. Peter is known as being 'steady as a rock' amongst the most trying circumstances and as a result he captured the terrifyingly vivid footage of Stone firing carefully aimed shots at the mourners from his handgun whilst a group of apparently insanely brave youths kept chasing after him. They caught Stone just as he got to the nearby M1 motorway and would almost certainly have killed him if the loyalist hadn't been freed by a group of RUC officers. Later in jail Stone passed a message back to Peter Cooper which froze the blood in his veins. Peter had been under the impression that Stone had been firing in his general direction but not that he was the target. But Stone told a couple of my colleagues, 'Say sorry to Peter Cooper for me – I shouldn't have aimed at him, I thought that thing on his shoulder was a weapon.'

After the cemetery attack, in which Stone claimed three victims, I saw some journalists over from London celebrating with a large magnum of champagne. They weren't happy about the killings, just wanting to mark a journalistic 'job well done'. But the gesture seemed insensitive and didn't impress me or my colleagues based in Belfast, who were all too aware that nothing happens in Northern Ireland without a reaction. The next weekend three funerals were scheduled to take place and as the second reporter on duty I discussed with my more experienced colleague Austin Hunter how we should divide them up. Austin said he would take the first one, the funeral of John Murray, aged twenty-six. I could do the second, which was the funeral of Kevin Brady, a thirty-year-old IRA member killed by Stone. Then Austin would have time to run up to the third funeral, that of twenty-year-old Tommy McErlean.

Our plans were thrown into disarray when overnight a loyalist gunman shot dead a Catholic man in County Fermanagh in the far west. Austin headed off to the murder, leaving us to sort things out in Belfast. I agreed with a colleague that I should do funerals one and three, and she should go to the IRA funeral I had been due to cover. At the time it seemed like a sensible logistical decision but it was to have fateful results.

The first funeral, whilst harrowing, passed off quietly. I recall thinking it strange that the priest, a very traditional Catholic, gave a sermon which concentrated on 'the significance of the sacraments', at no stage mentioning the shocking circumstances in which John Murray had died. I then went to the City Cemetery in west Belfast where Mr Murray's burial took place. On this occasion I chose to travel with the camera crew so I could drive their car ahead should they need to get out and take any pictures of the cortège, but once again this decision proved problematic when the newsroom ordered them to go to the scene of a sectarian arson attack. I had to get the pictures of the Murray funeral back to the office, so accepted a lift from Pauline Reynolds, a colleague who worked for the nationalist *Irish News*. As we made our way across town my walkie-talkie erupted into life. 'Can you get back to west Belfast?' the producer Eddie Fleming asked me urgently. 'There's been some kind of an incident at the IRA funeral, we need you back up there.' I looked apologetically at Pauline and asked if there was any way she could deposit me back where we'd just come from. She agreed as she too wanted to see what was going on. Both of us immediately jumped to the conclusion that there must have been another loyalist attack on a republican funeral.

When I arrived at the scene, near the Andersonstown leisure centre, I detected one of the most poisonous atmospheres I had ever experienced. Riot police stretched across the road poised in apparent expectation of a confrontation with some of the hundreds of mourners who were now inside Milltown cemetery.

I approached a priest, whom I would later recognise as Father Alex Reid. 'I'm sorry, Father, I've just arrived, can you tell me what happened here?' He just walked away.

Two urchins came up, apparently gleeful. 'They were Brits, they were Brits.'

'Who were?' I asked.

'The ones that tried to attack us.'

'Not loyalists?'

'Royal Signals, Royal Signals – we saw their ID cards . . .'

In Northern Ireland I was well used to both conspiracies and conspiracy theories but this seemed hard to comprehend. What were two members of the Signals Regiment doing in the middle of an IRA funeral, let alone attacking mourners? Collusion by some soldiers with loyalists had been well documented throughout the troubles but this seemed pure madness.

We found our way to a house which offered a view – albeit obscured – of the patch of rough ground where the security forces were recovering two bodies. As we tried to get some pictures of what was going on, more urchins crowded around.

'You're English, aren't you?' one said.

I didn't respond.

'They got what they deserved,' the youth continued, adding for my benefit, 'We should have burned them.'

Borrowing a telephone, I contacted the newsroom and began to dictate the latest details. My news copy identified the victims as military personnel. 'The RUC says the men were pulled from their silver Volkswagen Passat car, taken to the corner of Casement Park, severely beaten and partially stripped. They were then put into a black taxi and taken to waste ground where they were shot dead.' 'Got that?' I checked with the copy taker. 'There's more . . . The bodies are still at the waste ground. One is virtually naked, the other has had most clothes removed. Both bodies are badly beaten. The silver Volkswagen Passat is burned out.'

I never figured out what happened in west Belfast that day. When the RUC spokesman walked towards us with the first official statement he began by saying that the soldiers' car became surrounded by a crowd outside the shops on the Andersonstown Road. But how and why did it get there? I did not buy the notion that this was an attack on the IRA funeral as the two corporals weren't well enough armed, nor that it was an intelligence gathering exercise as the security forces could learn everything they wanted to know from the helicopters which hovered not far overhead, or by placing covert operatives inside the crowd of mourners. A bit of showmanship on the part of the driver which went horribly wrong appears to be a plausible explanation, or a fatal confusion of local geography. But, that said, the car had to cover a long stretch of road between passing the republican stewards ahead of the cortège and driving at speed into the crowd of mourners. All that is certain is that the mourners must have initially thought they were under loyalist attack and that once they disarmed the two men and established their military identity they had no intention of stopping. By the time IRA gunmen stepped in to administer a *coup de grâce* the two corporals had already been subjected to one of the most frightening examples of mob brutality seen in the entire course of the troubles.

At the time there were moments when I wondered what might have been if our logistical arrangements had been different. My colleague, who did cover the mob attack, performed brilliantly, ensuring that a group of republican heavies who tried to confiscate the vital video tape did not succeed. I wouldn't have relished witnessing the terrible incident, but it would have been the biggest story of my career to date. It wasn't very long, however, before I was thanking my good fortune that I had missed this particular story. The television footage which shocked audiences the world over proved central to the RUC's investigation of those who had carried out the attack. But to use it as evidence the police had to put in the dock a series of BBC employees to verify that it was the genuine video taken on the day in question.

To avoid being seen in republican areas as a willing arm of the RUC's intelligence gathering, the BBC took the view that it should oppose the use of any film until forced to hand it over. The Director-General, Michael Checkland, told the newspapers that 'If we allow automatic free access to our material, the next victims could be our staff.' Given the gravity of the crimes under consideration it seemed inevitable the police would pursue the matter further. On 23 March 1988 RUC detectives seized the material from the BBC and ITN quoting two pieces of anti-terrorism legislation, the Prevention of Terrorism Act and the Emergency Provisions Act, as their legal basis for the raids. The BBC believed the stance it had taken, although short-lived, was correct in principle. But an illustration of the 'no-win' position we were in came a few weeks later when I was sent to the scene of an IRA booby trap bombing which killed a naval recruiting officer as he drove through a staunchly loyalist area of east Belfast. Some youths had witnessed the bombing and I approached them to see if they might record an interview.

'You're from the BBC, aren't you?' they replied. 'You're the ones who wouldn't hand over the film of the corporals.'

I tried to explain that we had a duty to defend our independence from the government, but it was all in vain.

'Fuck off out of here or we'll kill you,' the youths responded.

Later, either because they'd calmed down or because he had rather better diplomatic skills than me, my colleague Denis Murray, by then the BBC's Ireland Correspondent, was able to persuade my would-be killers to record an interview.

As the court case came closer, I grew ever more grateful that I had missed the story. Associates of the many accused − the IRA denied it was its members − decided the prosecution might be derailed if the video evidence could be rendered ineligible. The only way to do that was to mount a campaign of intimidation against the journalists who, under a subpoena, had to testify the video was genuine. A chillingly well-organised campaign of intimidation took place, as several of my colleagues were told over the telephone that it wasn't in their interests to testify. Some BBC staff left Northern Ireland and never returned.

As it turned out I was free to cover some of the early stages of the lengthy case of those charged in connection with the murder of the two corporals. I remember attending a packed session at Belfast Magistrates' Court when Terence 'Cleeky' Clarke, a close associate of Gerry Adams, appeared. Afterwards I caught a word with Clarke's solicitor, Paddy McGrory, who strolled out of the court in the company of another prominent criminal lawyer, Pat Finucane. The loyalist Ulster Freedom Fighters murdered Pat Finucane less than a year later. Paddy had used his speech in court to launch a sharp attack on the 'scurrilous English press' who he claimed had already tried and convicted his client. As I earnestly checked a point with him, Pat Finucane joked, 'Paddy, should you be having anything to do with the scurrilous English press?' Paddy, with a typical glint in his eye, replied, 'This man thinks that because he stands my son the occasional pint, he can touch me for information. What he doesn't realise is that he won't get any until he stands ME a pint.' Paddy was one of the most engaging characters I came across in Northern Ireland, but more of him later.

7

Focusing on Funerals

SPRING 1988–WINTER 1995

Viewers in Britain got used to seeing pictures of funerals during that dark period in March 1988 but the public in Northern Ireland had to watch them all year round. Sometimes I felt very uneasy about turning up at what, by rights, should have been very private occasions for those who lost loved ones. At one funeral at St Agnes's on the Andersonstown Road in west Belfast I hovered at the back of a church to check how far through the mass the priest had got before nipping out to the car to tell the cameraman to get ready to roll. 'Don't you ever feel bad about doing this?' the cameraman asked me. 'It may have escaped your attention,' I replied, 'but you are in the same car as I am.'

We were certain many mourners found our presence ghoulish, but for our bosses it was a question of fairness. Some funerals – like those of the three IRA members killed at Gibraltar – were inevitably going to be news events making international headlines. So who were we as the local media to decide that one victim of the troubles was worthy of less note than any other? Logic dictated that if were going to cover one troubles-related funeral we should cover them all. Looking back I think we could perhaps have better advertised a willingness not to go, if such a request was made in a reasonable manner. Almost always reporters tried to liaise with the minister or priest who would be conducting the funeral. But understandably some families weren't interested in having anything to do with the media, whether it was giving an interview or asking us to stay away. Whilst most clerics were helpful a few didn't try to hide their contempt of us.

In the end we were often filming where we weren't wanted. Personally I always tried to show the respect I would have wished to get if it had been a member of my family who was being buried. I saw one reporter doing a 'piece to camera' as a cortège passed alongside him and wasn't impressed – a cortège, in my view, isn't just a convenient backdrop for someone's portentous

45

television turn. During some funerals the option of doing such a thing did not exist. Reporters particularly dreaded being sent to loyalist paramilitary funerals. These events obviously had great news value as the size of the gatherings and the nature of the paramilitary trappings indicated the level of support and community respect for these organisations in certain hardline areas. But the loyalists, by and large, hated the media with a vengeance and made it clear that our presence wasn't welcome. In June 1988 I had to cover the funeral of an Ulster Volunteer Force member, Robert Seymour, whom the IRA shot dead in a video shop on the Woodstock Road in east Belfast. Every Belfast-based crew refused to go to the event after threats were issued by the UVF so I had to work with a crew over from London. I decided the only way we would get any footage and survive would be if we filmed out of the car sunroof. I ambled around the Cregagh Road area beforehand where the funeral was taking place to try to work out which way the cortège would head. The area was packed but there wasn't a single journalist or camera crew in sight. I spotted an RUC officer and sidled up to him.

'Hello, officer,' I said, continuing under my breath, 'I am from the BBC and I have got a camera crew around the corner. Do you think if they joined me and got out their gear you could guarantee our safety?'

'I can't guarantee your safety right now,' he replied. 'If I were you I'd get off this road immediately.'

In the end I found a long side road where it seemed conceivable that we could get a distant shot of the cortège for a few seconds. The cameraman quickly poked his camera out of the sunroof and started to roll. I saw a large group of men in black suits detach themselves and head towards us at speed.

'I don't like this – let's get out of here,' I said to the driver.

Ahead of the welcoming party came a smaller man in an anorak. He fixed me with a stare and said, 'If you respect us, we shall respect you.'

'Absolutely, we're out of here,' I shouted as our car roared off. Our twelve seconds of steady footage featured on the local news summary that night.

It wasn't only the loyalists who could give you a hard time on these occasions. Republicans were normally much more media-savvy, and in a series of funerals where there were confrontations with the RUC they used the media's presence in a highly sophisticated manner, sometimes pushing women to the forefront of fights in order to ensure the pictures conveyed an image of RUC officers battering the innocents. But in some areas dyed-in-the-wool republicans had as dim a view of the cameras as any loyalist. I recall being surrounded by a group of mourners at the funeral of two of the three IRA men killed by soldiers during a thwarted ambush on a part-time Ulster Defence Regiment soldier at Drumnakilly in County Tyrone in August 1988. Gathered outside the church in the staunch republican village of Loughmacrory, the mourners wanted to know why the BBC didn't report more instances of army brutality. I told them that if they gave me the evidence I would be happy to pass it on to my newsroom, but the IRA funeral we were all attending was an important story in its own right which I was trying to cover. Some of the mourners, who didn't like my accent or my BBC background, jostled me as I talked. As they accused me of censorship, a few yards away other mourners, presumably IRA stewards, were physically stopping my camera crew filming as an IRA speaker made an oration at the side of the funeral plot. On this occasion Gerry Adams did his best to control some of the aggression shown towards the media but it was clear that in this area of Tyrone even his writ didn't run completely.

Years later, in May 1995, I had to film the funeral of Mickey Mooney, a notorious drug dealer from the Short Strand, a small Catholic enclave in east Belfast. Mooney had been shot dead by an IRA front organisation which called itself Direct Action Against Drugs. The use of the front name enabled the IRA to maintain the fiction that its ceasefire remained intact. Mickey Mooney's mourners included a lot of his associates who didn't want their faces on the television for either Direct Action Against Drugs or, indeed, the RUC to see. Once again discretion seemed the better part of valour so we filmed what we thought was a reasonable distance away from the cortège as it wound its way into the church grounds in the Short Strand. This time, though, we hadn't banked on a flanking movement. As Peter Cooper continued filming the last mourners heading into the church, I heard a roar and looked up to see four heavy-looking blokes vaulting the six-foot-high church fence beside me. Horrified, I shouted to Peter and headed for our car, but it was too late. The four swooped on him and started pushing him around and kicking him. Our producer, Cathy Grieve, who is far more handy in a dodgy situation than I shall ever be, let out a shout and a scream. A single policeman a few yards away hesitated, not wanting to wade in on his own and hoping the fracas might blow itself out. Eventually we got Peter into the car and drove off, with the four heavies kicking and punching the vehicle.

A few days later a contact told me he'd met one of our assailants in a pub where he'd been having a belly laugh about running us out of the dealers' patch. 'See that little bugger Devenport,' he told my contact, 'you should have seen him run.' A few months later the man in question, Paul 'Saul' Devine, had nothing to laugh about. In December 1995 he became another of Direct Action Against Drugs' victims.

8

Ballygawley and the Ban

SUMMER 1988–SPRING 1993

At midnight that Friday night I remember letting out a little cheer. I had been the late reporter but after midnight I was no longer on call. I thought about what I had planned for the next day. About twenty minutes passed before the phone rang. The duty editor explained that although I'd officially clocked off he wanted me to go to Ballygawley, about three-quarters of an hour's drive to the west. Reports were coming in of an explosion and it looked like a big one. It was August 1988.

We drove past Ballygawley and kept going in the direction of Omagh until we came to a white tape stretched across the road. In the black night it proved impossible to see a thing. Going around the other side proved no more use. We sat and waited looking anxiously at our watches, aware from conversations with our newsrooms that the casualties were high, but equally aware that we had no pictures to offer the breakfast news outlets whose deadlines were by now getting very close. Suddenly a series of reporters decided en masse that in the absence of images they had better record 'pieces to camera' giving all the details they knew. In the darkness half a dozen bright spots of light beamed out as the crews lit up their 'turns' and the 'turns' struggled against the background of each other's voices to sound fluent and authoritative. One colleague had some trouble with her lines, an ailment which afflicts every reporter once in a while. But by the time she reached her fifteenth take I think we all knew the words of her script better than she did. A soldier, heavily camouflaged and dug into a nearby verge, wasn't amused. The lighting man's beam shone right on him rendering all his efforts at concealment absolutely pointless. When take sixteen started the soldier decided he had had enough. 'If you don't put that fucking light out, I'll shoot it out!' he shouted. The beam lowered and the seventeenth take proved sufficient.

Then out of the darkness came the Ulster Unionist MP Ken Maginnis accompanied by my colleague Denis Murray and two local farmers. Both the farmers were big men, but both were literally shaking in reaction to what they had seen. They told us what it had been like before the police closed the road, of trying to help the injured, of walking around in the dark before realising they were wading through bits of bodies. The IRA had concealed its bomb in a trailer left beside the road and had scored a direct hit on a bus travelling from Aldergrove airport to the army barracks at Omagh. Eight young soldiers died. The farmers gave moving accounts of their attempts to help the survivors. But we still had no pictures to match the horror of the accounts we were hearing.

Ken Maginnis cracked. He'd been on the phone to the Prime Minister, Margaret Thatcher, telling her what had happened and he said she wanted the world to see and hear it too. He lifted the tape, and marched us through, despite the protests of the RUC officers on duty. We drew close enough to see the wreckage of the bus thrown across the road and the debris still strewn all around. The injured had long since been taken away, and the darkness spared us the sight of any remains of the dead which had not yet been gathered up. It was highly unusual to be so close without having a police escort. Suddenly a senior army officer saw us and charged over.

'This area is still sealed off. What the bloody hell do you think you are doing?'

Ken stepped in. 'They are here with me, they're not close enough to damage any of your evidence.'

'And whose authority do you think you're working under?'

'I am the local MP and I am operating under the authority of the Prime Minister – she wants the world to see what the IRA did here tonight.'

The military commander didn't appear best pleased by this unusual high-level interference. But after a bit more huffing and puffing we had gathered enough pictures to tell the story. We all retreated back behind the tape and waited for daylight to reveal more.

Apart from telling Margaret Thatcher exactly what happened at Ballygawley that night, Ken Maginnis spent a lot of time telling her what he thought she should do about it. With his Ulster Defence Regiment background Ken has always been a politician who believes in cutting the Gordian knot. At this stage he was the most impassioned advocate of what he called selective internment – detention without trial just as in the early 1970s, although different, Ken argued, because it would be based on superior intelligence and would be targeted on small groups of individuals rather than whole communities. Many sceptics reckoned such a policy would inevitably provoke all the same difficulties it had first time around, but Ken wasn't convinced. Neither, it appeared for a time, was Margaret Thatcher who, enraged by Ballygawley, sought some measures which might root out the bombers.

In the event the Prime Minister didn't opt for internment. Instead, after taking advice from her security chiefs, she unveiled a package of measures designed to make it more difficult for the paramilitaries and their political associates to function. The package included strict restrictions on the right to silence to make it harder for terrorist suspects simply to stare at the walls of their interrogation rooms when being cross-questioned by the police. The government reduced the remission given to prisoners in Northern Ireland. All candidates in council elections were required to sign a pledge of support for non-violence. At the sharp end, the SAS appeared to be given a freer rein – the killing of the IRA men whose funeral I covered at Loughmacrory came only ten days after the Ballygawley bus bombing, and shortly after Ken Maginnis had presented Mrs Thatcher with a list of leading IRA members in County Tyrone.

But there was no doubt which of the responses to Ballygawley touched us journalists most directly – the infamous broadcasting ban. For Mrs Thatcher the ban provided a convenient way of dealing with two of her pet hates in one go. It went without saying that the Ballygawley bombers posed a threat to the nation. But the Prime Minister regarded with no less hostility the 'dangerously liberal' television reporters who insisted on putting their noses into areas of national security which ministers believed were none of their business. Mrs Thatcher had not been impressed by the broadcasters' refusal to hand over immediately its footage of the attack on the two corporals in Andersonstown in March 1988, and shortly afterwards hints had appeared in the press that action might be taken to curtail media coverage of IRA 'stunts' like the firing of volleys over coffins at paramilitary funerals. The government also vented its wrath over Thames TV's *Death on the Rock* programme on the Gibraltar killings and a parallel investigation by my colleagues Alex Thomson and Bruce Batten, then working for BBC Northern Ireland's *Spotlight* current affairs series. Both programmes examined the threat posed by the unarmed IRA squad and whether the SAS could have arrested the three rather than opening fire.

The then Home Secretary Douglas Hurd announced the ban to the House of Commons on 19 October 1988. The ban took the form of a notice under the BBC's Licence and Agreement and under the Broadcasting Act, which covers independent broadcasters, rather than a distinct piece of legislation in its own right. The notice required broadcasters to refrain from transmitting statements from representatives of illegal paramilitary organisations, although such interviews had been practically never broadcast since the 1970s. It also banned interviews with representatives of the loyalist UDA, the republican splinter group Republican Sinn Féin and Sinn Féin itself, which at this stage had one elected MP, Gerry Adams, and more than fifty elected councillors. It went further in banning statements by any person 'which support or invite support for these organisations'. Douglas Hurd acknowledged that 'broadcasters have a dangerous and unenviable task in reporting events in Northern Ireland' and claimed the ban was not intended as a criticism of journalists. He justified it by arguing that terrorists had 'drawn support and sustenance from having access to the radio and television' and by making reference to the similar restrictions which the Irish Republic already had in force. He claimed the ban was 'not a restriction on reporting' because we could still report the words of those concerned, although we could not carry their voices.

Mrs Thatcher argued the ban would choke off what the government called 'the oxygen of publicity' for terrorist sympathisers. But given the base of support Sinn Féin already had within the Catholic community, the restrictions had only a marginal impact. I suspect, though, that the prime minister felt vindicated if the ban at least made things more awkward for her enemies in the media. On the first day it was in force I had to cover a news conference by a community group in the lower Ormeau, a strongly nationalist area of south Belfast. Like local people in many other urban areas throughout Britain and Ireland the group was concerned about the danger posed by the amount of fast traffic passing along the main road into the centre of the city. It decided to mount a campaign against the widening of the Ormeau Road and in favour of more speed restrictions. This was innocuous stuff politically, but on that first day we hadn't a clue quite how the broadcasting ban would apply in practice. Our initial guidance, prepared before the ban was formally announced, was very broad indeed – one note warned about quoting newspaper articles about the IRA or reporting statements made from the dock by paramilitary suspects during court cases. These warnings were later withdrawn after broadcast executives held talks with the Home Office to clarify the details of the ban, but not before I found myself apologising to my interviewee on the Ormeau

Road story for having to check with him whether he was a member of Sinn Féin. It made me feel ashamed to be a British journalist.

I remember pondering at one stage whether this should be a resigning matter. I had always believed that journalism should be a mirror held up to society. Now we were being told that some elements had to be airbrushed out of the picture. Philosophically I didn't have a problem with some groups being deemed dangerous and illegal, therefore causing us a legal problem in broadcasting their words. Most journalists do not feel any divine right to interview known murderers announcing their plans to kill more people in the future and then not to expect any comeback from the authorities. But I did profoundly disagree with the notion that certain individuals were fit to walk the streets, to organise politically and to stand for election, yet were not fit to appear in sound and vision on the radio and television. Whilst the Home Secretary might claim the ban wasn't a restriction on reporting, creating such a category of people unfit to appear on television inevitably made our screens a distorting mirror.

The thought of making a solitary stand didn't last very long. I was too far down the pecking order for such a gesture to affect anything other than my own insignificant career. Also even if I sought out another branch of journalism I would still inevitably be working in a country which had the ban as a part of its system. I agreed with Kevin Boyle of the pressure group Article 19 who told the *Independent* the day after the ban, 'Although the situation in South Africa is vastly different from the situation in Northern Ireland, the means now being used by the British government to stifle debate – political censorship – is the same as the means used in South Africa.'

The National Union of Journalists discussed what to do about the ban. In Belfast we wanted to stand up for the principles of free speech whilst at the same time remaining sensitive that our words were likely to be deliberately misinterpreted by unionists as evidence of 'leftie journalists' being 'soft on the IRA'. Similar arguments were played out in NUJ chapels elsewhere – the BBC voted in favour of a protest strike, whilst ITN voted against. Eventually the NUJ abandoned the strike, partly because it wasn't sure about the solidity of support for the action and partly because broadcast managers made the point that the union's basic argument was not with its employers but with the government. BBC and ITN management made it clear that whenever an interviewee's words could not be carried because of the ban they would broadcast on-screen 'health warnings'. Senior executives also committed themselves to attending an NUJ-organised lobby of parliament. I volunteered to be one of a number of NUJ delegates who travelled over to Westminster to lobby MPs on the matter. On the eve of the trip the BBC Director-General, John Birt, came over to Belfast to have a word with a small group of reporters, including myself, about how the ban affected us in practice. I told him about the ridiculous incident with the road safety campaigners and the McCarthyite implications if we had to ask interviewees 'Are you or have you ever been a member of Sinn Féin?'

Once at the Commons I realised what a short straw I had picked. As a Northern Ireland delegate it was my responsibility to lobby Ulster MPs, and it seemed that day that there were only unionists around, all of them firmly in favour of the ban. As the MPs trooped out to do combat I realised that a reporter from Radio 4's PM programme was beside me, microphone in hand, ready to record my exchanges for the benefit of a national audience. I found DUP leader Ian Paisley in a buoyant mood. He made it clear from the word go that there would be no meeting of minds, as his only criticism of Mrs Thatcher's security measures had been that she hadn't seen fit to bring back capital punishment. Probably the most difficult exchange, however, was with Ken Maginnis, whom I had stood alongside at Ballygawley just a few weeks before. Well used to being interrogated by me, Ken relished the opportunity of turning the tables. With a twinkle in his eye, he said, 'Now let me ask you a few questions, Mr Devenport . . .' before launching into an elaborate analogy which involved wondering exactly how I would feel if someone saw fit to put my sister's rapist on the national news. As Ken's rhetorical enquiry continued I glanced down at the PM microphone and tried to remember the politician's dictum: under no circumstances get drawn into answering questions. I replied with a quick 'Well that's as may be . . .' then continued with a prepared speech which, aimed rather pointlessly at Unionist or Conservative ears, concentrated on our inability to cross-question Sinn Féin about its attitude to violence if its responses could not be heard. The exchange ended, the microphone went off and Ken chuckled telling me how much he'd enjoyed putting me on the spot.

I got a few more positive responses including a letter from the Labour MP in my home constituency who seemed genuinely annoyed to have missed meeting me. A constituent lobbying about something so esoteric as the broadcasting ban would have enlivened his usual round of business. On the way back to Belfast I made my way into Gate 49, the old rather dreary waiting area at

Heathrow into which Northern Ireland shuttle passengers were herded. I plonked down in a seat ready to forget about politics when I realised I was sitting next to James Molyneaux, the Ulster Unionist leader, whom I had unsuccessfully tried to lobby. Mr Molyneaux apologised for not being able to see me and in typically diffident style studiously avoided talking about the issue of the ban at all, instead heading off onto a lengthy perambulation around his career during the Second World War. After about ten minutes another familiar figure strolled into Gate 49 and took the seat on the other side of me. This time, though, the newcomer had no qualms about telling me exactly how and why he believed I was wrong, wrong and wrong. The Reverend Willie McCrea, then the Mid-Ulster MP for the DUP, has never been known for his shyness in proffering his opinions.

The lobby was a one-off, which, frankly, achieved little in practice. The NUJ's attempts to seek a judicial review of the ban also failed. The real business of fighting censorship was vigilance at work, trying to remember exactly how you would have reported matters before the restrictions were brought into force and trying to work in exactly the same way, only getting contributions which would have been carried in an interviewee's own words voiced over by an actor. This technique, employed by all television journalists, enraged unionists who saw it as a way of circumventing the ban, which, of course, it was.

We would try to stretch the boundaries, exploring exactly when an interviewee was speaking in a personal capacity and could therefore be used in his or her own voice or was speaking on behalf of a specified organisation, or in support of violence, when they would be covered by the ban. In one film I interviewed Gerry 'Mad Dog' Doherty, a former Sinn Féin councillor. Early in the troubles he had been jailed for blowing up the Derry Guildhall. A few years later when he had served his time he returned to the Guildhall to take his seat as an elected councillor. He therefore personified the republican 'ballot box and Armalite' strategy. We broadcast Doherty's account of carrying a dustbin stuffed with explosives into the Guildhall in his own voice, as this was his personal account of his own experiences which didn't include any value judgements about the rights or wrongs of using violence. But when I started questioning him about the possibility of an IRA ceasefire we resorted to an actor's voice, as he was now espousing his Sinn Féin views. The juxtaposition of the two techniques within a few minutes rendered the ban absurd – not as absurd, however, as when, around the same time, the broadcaster Peter

Taylor applied the ban to the IRA prisoners' representative inside the top-security Maze jail complaining in his official capacity about the dwindling size of the prison canteen sausage rolls.

Although most of the time I believe broadcasters did a good job in carrying out their journalistic duty, it would be wrong not to admit that the restrictions probably did have an insidious impact. Sinn Féin's Danny Morrison told journalist Ed Moloney that in the four months before the ban the party's press office took around five hundred calls, whilst in the four months afterwards that dropped to about one hundred enquiries. Sometimes the sheer hassle of having to find an actor to do the voice-over would put you off making the effort unless it was clearly necessary. Moreover the jarring effect of someone appearing on the screen with their words being spoken 'out of sync' offended against a programme maker's sensibilities. In March 1993 I made a current affairs programme about the portrayal of Northern Ireland and the troubles in a series of recently released films. I took a group of politicians to the cinema to play film critics for the evening – it was intended as a light amusing sequence for viewers who wouldn't imagine that venerable figures like the Ulster Unionist MP Willie Ross could possibly go to see the cutting edge film *The Crying Game*. Afterwards, though, the nationalist *Andersonstown News* in west Belfast strongly criticised me for not including Sinn Féin in the outing. In practical terms, of course, persuading a couple of unionists to share popcorn with a republican wasn't, in those pre-ceasefire days, in the realms of reality. But I believe the newspaper got it right when it said that Sinn Féin should have been involved in a film considering how the IRA and other paramilitaries were portrayed in the cinema. Thinking over my decision making, I suspect it was precisely because I was trying to create something which would be aesthetically pleasing that I missed out Sinn Féin, and indeed the loyalists. The lip flapping necessitated by the ban wasn't the most appealing cinematic technique.

That said, the programme about the movie business had its moments. I particularly enjoyed bumping into an elderly Dublin resident in Merrion Square whilst we were taking some pictures of a statue of the old IRA leader and founder of the Irish state, Michael Collins. As the cameraman took various arty shots, the old lady engaged me in conversation.

'That's Michael Collins, you know,' she said, continuing to my surprise, 'I remember him as if it was yesterday. I was a little girl in those days and we used to go out to watch all the funerals. I shall always picture him there at Arthur

Griffith's funeral, a fine figure of a man, he looked like a film star, so he did.'

Now that she had naturally encroached on my cinematic theme, I felt the need to question her a bit further. 'It's fascinating you should think Collins looked like a film star because there are quite a few people at the moment who are hoping to make a film all about his life. In fact Kevin Costner wants to play him, what do you think of that?'

The elderly lady looked at me blankly, before asking, 'Who's Kevin Costner?'

Costner never did get to play Collins – Liam Neeson eventually landed the part. However, my new acquaintance, Theresa Dievers, did become a star of sorts as we invited her in front of the camera to share her memories of Michael Collins with our audience.

9

Beyond the Ban

SPRING 1989–WINTER 1997

Whenever media studies students came to see me or my colleagues to discuss broadcasting in Northern Ireland they inevitably concentrated on the ban. I suppose it was only natural, but it gave a partial view of the many pressures on journalists operating in a conflict situation. My trip to the cinema was by no means the only time when we had to decide who to include and who not to include in a film cast list. When you were working on a straight news report, which generally involved going to the scene of an incident and talking to anyone relevant you could find within a tight timetable, this was not so much of an issue. But when you were putting together a longer current affairs report who to include and who to exclude became crucial.

By the end of 1988 I became tired of doing news reports of two and a half minutes and felt inclined to make longer films. After a couple of tries I got an attachment to BBC Northern Ireland's *Spotlight* programme. *Spotlight* produced half-hour-long films which could be investigative or analytical or could just tell a story which required a bit of time to tell properly. It had a long and impressive track record – previous reporters included Jeremy Paxman and Gavin Esler. More recently the programme had annoyed the government with its investigation of the Gibraltar killings. I was glad to join the team, led by Andrew Colman, a quiet man whose silences at meetings concealed rock-solid editorial judgement and an enthusiast's desire to pursue any story which he thought might shake up the status quo.

At *Spotlight* we required co-operation from all sides and were subjected to pressure from all sides. In particular, unionists, the government and the RUC would play the game of refusing to participate in films if you were also interviewing Sinn Féin. Getting the two sides into a studio together at the same time was out of the question. Even within prefilmed reports negotiations could be ridiculously sensitive. Sometimes you had to make decisions over the course of a series, deciding that police participation would be crucial to one project, but you could afford to junk an interview with a minister on another occasion. It felt especially irksome when you realised that the bullying tactics were more stringent with the Belfast regional programmes than with our London counterparts, like *Panorama*. The interest groups seemed less prepared to try it on with broadcasters who needed them rather less regularly than the local programmes.

We did our best to resist unfair pressure, whatever direction it came from, and frequently scored successes by refusing to let topics drop and forcing, by our persistence, some comment from the unwilling. Inevitably, though, it was a case of 'some you win, some you lose'.

Besides the government-imposed ban the BBC had its own guidelines, developed after more than two decades reporting in an editorial minefield. Most of these, like the rule that junior staff should refer upwards when they got into difficult decision-making territory, were simply common sense. But on occasion I did have difficulty with the interpretation of some rules. Whilst making one *Spotlight* film about the IRA man Joe Doherty, I ran foul of what I believed to be a poor application of the guidelines. Doherty escaped from the Crumlin Road jail in 1981 after shooting dead an SAS soldier in north Belfast the previous year. He flew to the United States and worked for a while as a barman before FBI agents arrested him. Doherty became a cause célèbre amongst Irish Americans in New York, where the corner outside his jail, the Manhattan Correctional Center, was renamed after him. Doherty won his battle against extradition, although the Americans later deported him.

The BBC had a guideline that it 'does not talk to terrorists'. The rule was developed to stop masked men calling news conferences and using the media as a vehicle to make generalised threats about what they intended to do, a practice indulged in during the early days of the troubles which vindicated the government's 'oxygen of publicity' arguments. At the time we were making our film about Joe Doherty, however, he was under lock and key inside the Manhattan Correctional Center and therefore not in any position to make such threats. Nevertheless senior BBC editors decided he was a convicted murderer who, by dint of escaping, had not served his allotted time in a UK jail. So they invoked the 'don't talk to terrorists' guideline and forbade me from talking to Doherty. I was able to go inside the New York jail to take fresh pictures of the prisoner and to chat to him informally. But when it came to detailed cross-questioning the best I could do was to interview his redoubtable lawyer, Mary Pike.

Again, I felt like a journalist from South Africa during apartheid or Eastern Europe under communism as I tried to explain to Mary Pike why I wouldn't be interviewing her client. The decision certainly damaged the film but not at all to Joe Doherty's detriment. During our researches we had uncovered a new witness to the 1980 shooting on the Antrim Road, whose account substantially differed from that given by Doherty to the US court which heard his extradition case. The witness made the shooting appear far less like the 'it was either him or me' situation Joe Doherty had described to the US judge and much more like a clinical execution. Doherty would no doubt have contested this version, but I could not cross-question him about the new account. In the event we were able to include excerpts of interviews given by the IRA man to American television reporters, dubbed over to stay within the terms of the broadcasting ban. However, these comments mostly consisted of Doherty comparing himself with George Washington and probably left the casual viewer with the impression that I had not bothered asking any tough questions. Against the odds, we still managed to make a half-decent film.

Pressures on journalists tend to be viewed as exclusively 'top-down', whether it be from management or government. But any reporter will tell you that the constraints and manipulation can also come from the 'bottom up', especially in an area where politics happens on the streets. One afternoon, during the peace process of the 1990s, I covered a republican protest outside Belfast City Hall demanding early release for IRA prisoners. At an agreed signal the protesters abandoned their picket line and sat down in Donegall Square at the height of the rush hour, daring the RUC officers on duty to drag them off in full view of the assembled cameras. My colleagues and I had our work cut out keeping up with the inevitable rough-and-tumble which followed. But it was only when I stepped back for a couple of seconds that I noticed a woman protester pushing a pram with a baby boy in it. She was closely observing where the worst fighting was taking place and then pushing her child right into the middle of it, strategically placing him between the trouble and the television cameras. The baby, obviously upset by the turmoil around him, screamed. There, ready-made, we had an image of innocence surrounded by police brutality. But back in the editing suite, we junked the picture.

This was one small sneaky attempt at manipulation. Other kinds of pressure were more direct and more brutal. Belfast-based journalists know a great deal of street gossip about the paramilitaries and the politicians. But much of it never hits the air. Of course, the difficulty of proving such stories to the satisfaction of a potential libel jury is a major disincentive. But the preference of most human beings, including journalists, to keep their lives and limbs intact is a bigger concern. That Billy Wright of Portadown and 'King Rat' of the UVF (later the LVF) were one and the same person was not the best-kept secret in Northern Ireland. But this was rarely spelled out explicitly before Wright's death in the Maze jail in December 1997 because most journalists based in Northern Ireland knew that pursuing such matters too closely would soon get dangerous. The full story of loyalist involvement in the drugs trade has not been told for similar reasons. One publication which often pushed the boat out on both these topics was the tabloid *Sunday World* – it was rewarded by attacks on its Belfast offices. On television, reporters' visibility increased their vulnerability. Sometimes it seemed easier for a broadcaster based in England to conduct an investigation then 'get offside'. That said, *Spotlight* did carry out a number of extremely courageous investigations, of which one documentary about the 'Official IRA' made by my colleagues Shane Harrison and Paul Larkin Coyle springs to mind, alongside two programmes by Jeremy Adams, one on the INLA and the other on the vicious practice of cockfighting.

But academics and their students always returned to the ban, because it was unique to Northern Ireland, and because it had made headlines. Ultimately the ban perished because of its own absurdity, highlighted by the broadcasters' determination to continue pursuing the story regardless of the restrictions. As Danny Morrison's log of calls to the Falls Road press office indicated, the ban probably had an adverse impact on Sinn Féin in the short term. But the government wilfully ignored all the other factors which buoyed up Sinn Féin's support base, be they loyalist violence, insensitive security force behaviour, or the growing Catholic population, young and increasingly assertive about its rights. Moreover the official attempts to isolate the republicans ultimately served only to encourage a skilful leader like Gerry Adams to find other avenues to widen his movement's political base by opening up contacts with John Hume and new strands of support within Irish America. With the development of the peace process in the nineties, Sinn Féin was increasingly centre stage and the coffers of the handful of actors we employed to 'do Gerry' started to bulge. Programmes demanded extensive interviews with the Sinn Féin representatives, leading to bizarre situations, such as one where I had to re-enact an encounter with Martin McGuinness with my actor friend Conor, so the interview could be turned around at length for the radio. I tried to be suitably probing and combative, as I had been during the real interview. He sounded appropriately unperturbed. As we continued into the small hours, Conor broke off his Sinn Féin-speak to tell me I worked too much and should 'get a life'.

When the IRA called its ceasefire in August 1994 I had to go on Radio 5 and paraphrase Gerry Adams's speech to the historic rally in Andersonstown in west Belfast. It felt quite bizarre for a BBC journalist to be giving a simulta- neous translation of a man who was already speaking in English, making the key comments regarding what was undoubtedly the most important news story of the day, if not the year. As I continued to commentate I felt it could not be long before the ban died a natural death. Within a month it was lifted. I am still occasionally questioned by Americans about the government's logic in introducing the restrictions. Whilst I can explain the context of Ballygawley and other violent attacks in contributing to ministers' decision making, I have no inclination to excuse the short-sightedness of the government in besmirch- ing my country's reputation as a home of free speech. As the *New York Times* concluded at the time the ban was introduced, it was bizarre for a Conserva- tive government to tarnish a British national asset more valuable than the crown jewels.

10

Under the Spotlight

SPRING 1989–WINTER 1989

As a news reporter I had been used to working on my own, but at *Spotlight* films were made in collaboration with a producer. When it was going well this arrangement provided a unique spark enabling both journalists to bounce ideas off each other. When it was going badly you ended up bickering like an old married couple. The pressure of the immediate deadline had been removed, but this was only for it to be replaced by a more constant long-term obsession as you spent weeks developing story ideas and jealously protecting them from competitors. It was all too easy for what seemed like a sure-fire programme to disappear a couple of weeks before it was due to be broadcast when the newspapers or the local television and radio news got hold of the story and told all there was to tell.

My first current affairs programme concerned the newspaper industry in Northern Ireland and especially the unionist morning paper, the *News Letter*, which was up for sale. One of the interviewees was a somewhat distracted Ian Paisley, who had forgotten about our appointment. I waited inside his office for him to turn up and when he came in he looked puzzled. Although we had met many times before he asked me, 'Who are you and what are you doing in my office?' After I explained that we had arranged an interview, he asked, 'Where's the crew?' I told him they had set up outside and he responded with a brusque 'bad boy' and what I imagine was intended to be a jovial cuff around the ear, which in fact knocked me back across the room. For some reason, Dr Paisley didn't like doing interviews outside, but after a bit of persuading he relented and seemed deeply impressed by my ability to balance on the unsteady camera equipment box which the cameraman had decided I should stand on in order to even up our disparate heights.

On this first programme, which we called 'Tabloids and Takeovers', I made several typical news reporter errors, interviewing my principal characters, such as the Bangor-born editor David Montgomery, at insufficient length and with inadequate rigour to provide the basis for a half-hour film. Only some highly creative editing by my producer and picture editor saved the day. My next film, however, allowed me to maximise my news reporting experience as it was a quick turnaround on the subject of the loyalist paramilitary Ulster Resistance, a terrorist group which in its early days had links with Ian Paisley's DUP. Three members of the group were arrested in Paris in the act of handing over to South African diplomats a demonstration missile launcher used with the Belfast-made Shorts Blowpipe missile. The belief was that the group had already received arms from South Africa and was looking for more. *Spotlight*'s other reporters, Shane Harrison and Noel Thompson, headed to Dublin and London to record interviews whilst I stayed in Belfast to piece the programme together with producer Bruce Batten through the course of a long night. Shane is one of my best friends, but I wouldn't like to be interviewed by him. He is superbly clinical in carrying out an interrogation until he's satisfied that he has exposed precisely every point he wants to reveal. During the 'Ulster Resistance' film the then Irish opposition leader Alan Dukes made a point about the loyalists and the DUP, but didn't spell it out in sufficient detail for our purposes. Shane uttered one word, 'elaborate', making it sound almost like the Dalek catchphrase 'exterminate'. Dukes, a little taken aback, started again and gave us a perfect response.

I stayed five years at *Spotlight* and covered more stories for the programme than I can remember. My strengths, I think, were a good head for potential programme subjects and an ability to knit unlikely elements together into an apparently seamless whole. My weaknesses, amongst many, included an over-consensual style of interviewing (unlike Shane!) and a lack of stamina in pursuing investigations. In this last regard I have to take off my hat to producer Paul Larkin Coyle who proved to me on several occasions the rewards of chasing after apparently lost causes. By his relentless determination he unearthed several stories including his exposure of the Official IRA and his revelation of new details about collusion between soldiers and loyalist paramilitaries.

Before becoming a journalist Paul had been a seaman in the Danish merchant navy. He combined a thick Salford accent with an ability to speak several Scandinavian languages fluently. He was equally passionate about Irish politics, Manchester United, Catholic theology and obscure points of Scandinavian philosophy or literature. Perpetually insomniac, he would travel on filming trips with a suitcase loaded full of books to keep him going overnight.

Whilst a lot of *Spotlight*'s programming inevitably concerned the troubles we did try to provide the viewers with other subject matter so they didn't get bored. One film I made with Paul concerned people from Northern Ireland who emigrated to London and found the streets were not necessarily paved with gold. The film was essentially a public service-type warning to those thinking of following the same route. But being a current affairs programme, we also wanted to explore a number of other issues, one being the level of discrimination experienced by Irish people living in England. We found case studies of Ulster folk living in hostels and above pubs, but not the archetypal homeless person living on the streets. So one night before we began filming Paul and I went down to 'Cardboard City' where scores of people slept in boxes under Waterloo Bridge. I didn't feel especially nervous as, with his merchant navy background, Paul was a particularly handy person to have alongside you if you ever got into any trouble. But once we arrived my producer brightly said, 'Right, you go that way and I'll go this way', and I realised I was very much on my own.

Strolling up to homeless people and saying, ''Scuse me, mate, are any of you from Northern Ireland?' appeared to be the Ulster-based reporter's equivalent to the foreign correspondent's much-derided question, 'Has anyone here been raped who speaks English?' I put on my best down-at-heel Cockney accent and started chatting. Much to my amazement within a couple of minutes somebody pointed me to 'Johnno', a man believed to hail from Belfast, and I ambled over to engage the small, bearded character in conversation. Johnno turned out to be very friendly and talked freely about his expectations when he headed for London and how they hadn't been matched by reality. He earned money doing casual work on building sites but it wasn't frequent enough to enable him to get a proper room. Johnno wasn't keen on the idea of appearing on television because he didn't want his relatives back home to see what had become of him, but I was hopeful that with a bit of persuasion he might do something with the promise that we would conceal his identity.

Then I asked the question about discrimination. 'So mate, umm, what do you think of the English then, do you have any hassle with them?'

Johnno didn't hesitate. 'The English, they're great, no problems at all. It's the Scottish bastards I can't stand.' To my surprise he whipped out a fierce-looking hunting knife from his trouser belt. 'See, if you'd been Scottish, I would have knifed you.'

I agreed vociferously that I too had never been able to stand the Scottish. I didn't mean a word of it, but if you ever find yourself under Waterloo Bridge making small talk with a man with a hunting knife I advise you to agree with him too.

11

Life in the Dub

Around the time I switched from the news to *Spotlight* I moved out of my shared house in Ravenhill Park. Living there had been a great introduction to Belfast and apart from the Charabanc actresses I had met lots of other people associated with the 'Ravenhill mob', most notably Paddy McGrory's son, Barra, and his schoolmate Sean who remain close friends to this day. But all good things must end. The others were going their separate ways, with the exception of my housemates Marie Jones and Ian McElhinney, who were married and had a newborn baby boy, Matthew. They decided to buy the house from the landlord and that seemed as good a cue as any to look for somewhere new. We did have a brief transitional period when we all got used to having a baby around the house, but it didn't last long. I remember one afternoon when we scurried up the stairs to check on Matthew crying, only to find him silently asleep. After doing this a couple more times we were all surprised to hear some strangers comforting 'our' baby and getting the child to stop crying. We discovered we were tuned in to next door's baby alarm.

At about the same stage I met my girlfriend Patricia. Very wisely she decided shortly after meeting me to fly off around the world. Not taking the hint that her desire to linger in South America might mean something, I carried on a long-distance relationship by letter. In August 1989 I was writing to her about the riots in Belfast to mark the anniversary of internment in which the RUC killed a fifteen-year-old boy with a plastic bullet. More trouble was expected later in the month with the twentieth anniversary of the arrival of the troops. My letters expressed my frustration and pessimism about the situation in Northern Ireland, summed up by the death of a boy not even born when the troops went in or when internment was introduced.

In November I reported my annoyance that the Ulster Unionist MP Ken Maginnis had had to cancel an interview on 'the right to silence' during police interrogations, forcing me to replace him at the last moment with 'a Conservative/Unionist lawyer called David Trimble'. From the way I phrased it I guess I hadn't heard much about the future Nobel prizewinner before fixing an interview with him at Queen's University.

During 1989 momentous events were taking place elsewhere in Europe. After the unnaturally static period of the cold war, the rate of change was remarkable. I described to Patricia watching the pictures of people streaming through the Berlin Wall and knocking it down themselves. The pace of events appeared only to emphasise the unchanging nature of politics in Northern Ireland. Few would have predicted that the dramatic developments far away might have a knock-on effect closer to home.

Whilst writing my letters and aerogrammes, I had to find somewhere new to live so I moved in with my *Spotlight* colleague Shane Harrison. Over the next couple of years we shared a series of different houses in south Belfast, but the one I have the most distinct memories of was a little cottage in Dub Lane near the playing fields on the upper Malone Road. Although both Shane and I are fairly diminutive characters the dimensions of Dub cottage proved a test even for us, making it difficult to stand up straight in most of the rooms. Writing in downtown New York, though, I can categorically state that the cottage's proximity to green fields and leafy walks more than made up for this.

Neither Shane nor I could be described as the most domesticated of creatures. One day I came home to find Shane, unusually house-proud, wandering around watering the plants. Overzealous, he had also watered the pot-pourri for good measure. I should say that Shane insists it was in fact me who watered the pot-pourri and he who discovered it, which only goes to show that if you put two BBC reporters on the same story they will come up with entirely contrasting versions of the truth. Ever afterwards, however, we both stayed true to Ian Paisley's dictum of 'No Pot-pourri!'

It's a testament to how small Belfast is that straight across the road from the leafy middle-class Dub Lane was a tough loyalist estate called Taughmonagh. The only contact the residents of the Dub generally had with the inhabitants of Taughmonagh was on the few evenings when some youths from the estate came across and tried to steal our cars. However, on occasion, normally involving work, I would stray into the UDA stronghold. One time I interviewed a young single mother from the estate whilst researching a programme about a Brook Advisory Clinic which was due to open in Belfast against considerable opposition from fundamentalist Christians and anti-abortion activists. 'Pamela' had got pregnant by a soldier when only about sixteen. She had hoped to stay together with him but he had left and she had decided to move away from her home area rather than face what she still thought of as the 'shame' of being a single mother. The facts of life for Pamela were very different from my lifestyle just across the road. Whilst her mother gave her a lot of help she inevitably spent most of the time looking after her child. If she did get a chance to go out, without a car a trip downtown amounted to a mammoth expedition. Instead she found herself with little choice but to shop in the local stores which were small, overpriced and had a limited range. On the social front the only real option was a club, which at the time Pamela visited it tended to be frequented by UDA members and supporters.

As a young single woman Pamela was an object of suspicion to the other women on the estate. When she went on her own to the club they immediately assumed she was out to 'steal' their men. With drink taken, a group of women cornered her and accused her of being 'on the pull'. She denied it, but they wouldn't take no for an answer. A fight started and, small and outnumbered, she was beaten up fairly badly. Someone called the police, who came and surveyed the aftermath. During a subsequent visit one of the officers persuaded 'Pamela' to make a statement. It was then that the trouble started getting worse. People either gave her the cold shoulder or shouted obscenities at her in the street. The man who delivered the coal, who everyone knew was 'well connected' with the paramilitaries, told her she would be wise if she didn't have anything to do with the police. Pamela got the message and dropped her complaint. That didn't stop some of the men from the club coming around after they'd finished a late drinking session. They would bang on her doors and throw stones up at her window, waking the baby, shouting up to her that they'd be happy to oblige if she 'wanted a little something'.

If you are in work, especially well-paid work, Northern Ireland is a wonderful place to live. Housing costs were for many years far lower than in the rest of the UK or Ireland, the roads are less crowded, commuting time to work is shorter, and the countryside is beautiful and accessible. My life, nipping in and out of the city's pubs, restaurants and night spots, may have seemed humdrum, but in fact it was a highly privileged existence. For the thousands of Northern Irish people who are out of work or subsisting on low wages reality can be very different.

12

Mata Hari

AUTUMN 1988–WINTER 1998

Whilst working one of my last shifts as a local news reporter in October 1988 I had to head up to east Belfast to cover the booby trap bomb murder of a senior official in the Prison Officers' Association called Brian Armour. His damaged car lay on a patch of waste ground just off the Beersbridge Road. Local people told us they had heard a massive bang then found a grey-haired man half-slumped out of his car. Ambulances were quickly at the scene but there was nothing anyone could do. Brian Armour, aged forty-eight, had been intending to drop off some papers to a colleague before heading to England for a meeting of the Prison Officers' Association. Driving through Belfast he braked suddenly to avoid some dogs fighting in the road. The jolt dislodged a piece of dirt which had jammed in the mercury tilt switch the IRA had fitted below his car. The switch closed triggering an explosion which threw the car fifty metres in the air. The DUP leader Ian Paisley made his way to the scene and recorded an interview with me in which he said the bombers had murdered a man trying to 'protect society against those who would destroy it'. A few days later I covered Mr Armour's funeral which set off from his home in east Belfast. The prison service pipe band played as mourners braced themselves against a biting wind. At no point as I reported on these events did I ever think that I might have known one of the people responsible for Brian Armour's murder.

That remained the case until the summer of 1990 when Christopher John Hanna appeared in court charged with involvement in Brian Armour's murder. Hanna, a prison officer, confessed to passing on information about his colleagues to the IRA. The police believed Hanna had been the victim of a 'honey trap', tempted by a woman working for the IRA into giving away dangerous details. The police hadn't been able to gather enough evidence to bring charges against the woman who they believed had been working for the bombers. So instead they took the unprecedented move of making things difficult for her, by naming Rosena Brown in court.

I had never known Rosena especially well, but as one of the actresses who worked together with my housemates in the Charabanc Theatre Company I had met her a number of times. Rosena was in her forties but remained an obviously attractive woman. Her strawberry blond hair fringed a striking face and a mouth which generally seemed to be hovering somewhere between a smile and a belly laugh. She impressed me as an earthy working-class woman with an infectious sense of humour who had raised a large brood of children and still had sufficient drive to try to carve out a new career in the theatre. On one occasion we had both been part of a group who had driven down south for a boozy weekend in Dublin. Once she suggested I should go over to her home area in the Divis flats in west Belfast and she could introduce me to people there. Now, as a would-be investigative journalist, I kicked myself that I had never taken her up on the offer.

In court RUC officers testified that they had taken photographs of Rosena meeting Christopher Hanna at a graveyard in Lisburn. They believed she was a top IRA intelligence agent and after arresting Hanna, they decided to pick up Rosena Brown. The police carried out the arrest in dramatic style, walking on to a film set in Derry where she was acting in a film called *Hush A Bye Baby* alongside the pop star Sinéad O'Connor. Back at the Castlereagh interrogation centre detectives cross-questioned her about her relationship with Hanna. They put the photographs they had taken in the graveyard under her nose and told her she may as well talk as they also had tape recordings of her conversations which would clearly link her to the IRA.

Rosena Brown didn't talk, not until she consulted her lawyer. Then she surprised the detectives by telling them that she wanted to make a statement. The police brandished their pens and she began.

'I can confirm that I know this man and I have met this man.' She sat back.

'That's it?' said one policeman.

'That's it,' she replied and went back to staring at the wall.

The tape recordings the police had threatened her with were never produced in court. Without a proper case against her, the RUC decided to use the privilege accorded to the legal proceedings to spell out its view of her real role. Rosena's name was all over the papers – her career on stage seemed at an end.

Having long since moved out of my theatrical household, I did not expect to see much of Rosena again. But a few months later I found myself unable to sleep on a night ferry as it made its way across a choppy sea sailing from Cairnryan in Scotland to Larne in County Antrim. I decided to stretch my legs and made my way to the cafeteria. Looking around for a seat I was surprised to see Rosena Brown. We both did a double take, then I sat down and joined her for a coffee. We talked in a circuitous manner around the details which had emerged in court. I didn't expect straight answers. One day, Rosena joked, I would be able to tell her story 'but that won't be until the war's over'. She confirmed that she hadn't left Belfast as everyone had supposed, but instead had stayed in 'safe' areas in the north and west of the city.

With discussions about the IRA off limits, we turned to more personal matters. I told her what was happening in my life. She talked about the depression she'd felt when her marriage broke up, her husband leaving her alone with seven children. But things had turned out all right. She had a new partner who was younger than her but the age gap didn't seem to matter. He was Davey Adams, cousin of the Sinn Féin President, Gerry Adams.

Before we went our separate ways Rosena told me another personal story. Years before she had worked in a shirt factory where both Protestants and Catholics were employed. These were the days before the troubles began and one of the Protestant men took an interest in her. They went out, but only for one date. She had now gone on to be identified in court as an IRA intelligence agent. He was Tommy 'Tucker' Lyttle who for a few years in the late eighties headed up the loyalist paramilitary Ulster Defence Association.

In the course of a quite separate interview on collusion between loyalists and the security forces, Tommy Lyttle once told me that if there were a few 'traces' on me, a few mentions in security files that I had been seen together with IRA people, 'that didn't necessarily mean Mark Devenport should be killed'. I breathed a sigh of relief for that as I said goodbye to Rosena Brown.

The next time I saw her, in the summer of 1992, I had to hand over my personal belongings to a prison guard before being allowed into a jail visiting room. Rosena was on remand at Maghaberry prison, charged with conspiracy to murder members of the security forces. Larne, the port we'd been sailing towards last time we met, again featured in the story. Rosena had been driving towards the town, accompanied by two younger men. Armed police had pulled over the car, ordering all three out of the vehicle on to the verge. As Rosena Brown took off her white woollen hat, a ginger wig she'd been wearing fell away too. Inside the car the RUC discovered a booby trap bomb. One of

Rosena's companions, stretched out on the verge with a gun trained at his head, shouted, 'It's all right, you're safe. It's not primed.'

Caught in the act, Rosena Brown knew she was looking at a long spell in jail. In her late forties, it wasn't a pleasant prospect. After putting on a typically bright face as she poured me a coffee from a flask, she sounded forlorn as she talked about perhaps pleading guilty in the hope of getting a reduced sentence. In reality she didn't have anything to offer the prosecution. Certainly she wasn't going to tell tales about her IRA colleagues – she spoke bitterly about her belief that somebody, somewhere must have informed on her unit. When her case came to court in 1993 the judge handed down a sentence of twenty years. 'At your age,' scolded Lord Justice MacDermott, 'you should have known better than to engage in terrorist activity and I appreciate you will be elderly when you are released.' The detectives to whom Rosena Brown had given her perfunctory one-line statement appeared to have had the last laugh.

One detective of whom Rosena had a particularly low opinion was Derek Martindale. In the prison visiting room she told me about one evening when a squad of RUC officers, led by Martindale, had raided the home she shared with Davey Adams in west Belfast. The police found nothing, but Derek Martindale left a lasting impression on Rosena Brown. 'He was one cold bastard' was how she summed him up.

I met Derek Martindale a short time later to talk about his work as head of the RUC's anti-racketeering squad. Whilst to visitors like me he was pleasant and pointedly witty, I could see that some of his subordinates held him in awe. As a boss, he appeared a hard taskmaster. 'The problem is,' confided one police officer, 'he wants everything and he wants it all within thirty seconds.' The urgency and drive which Derek Martindale put into his work made him one of the RUC's best weapons against terrorist groups. According to one lawyer who defended many IRA suspects he was 'one of the zealots of the RUC'. The approach got results. In the early eighties he was credited with making serious inroads into the IRA structure in Derry. In November 1983 he was seriously injured when gunmen opened fire on his car as he left the Strand Road police station in Derry. Admitting responsibility, the IRA claimed Martindale had personally recruited two informers, Raymond Gilmour and Robert Quigley, who had testified in the notorious 'supergrass' trials. The police denied the claim.

My appointment had been to talk to Derek Martindale about how paramilitary groups on both sides made money out of pirate videos and other counterfeit goods. But I couldn't resist asking him about Rosena Brown. He reacted to her name with surprise and venom. 'You're talking to the wrong sort of person there. That is one very, very bad woman.' I hinted that she hadn't exactly taken to him. He replied that when he had been searching the house she shared with Adams, Rosena had threatened him and his family.

A few months later I took another trip on the ferry. This time I was going to see Martin McGartland, a young west Belfast man who had joined the IRA at the behest of the RUC. Over a period of three years McGartland, working under the pseudonym of 'Agent Carroll', fed back valuable information to the RUC about the activities of the Belfast IRA. Martin knew Davey Adams and Rosena Brown very well. For months he had been a member of an IRA unit led by Adams.

Besides confirming Davey Adams's status as a senior republican, Martin told me a great deal about what Rosena Brown had done for the IRA. He believed she had never actually been sworn into the organisation 'but when you're friendly with people like Davey Adams you don't have to be'. Martin described Rosena as a family woman who had got drawn into things through the people she knew, 'But don't get me wrong, Rosena Brown has done an awful lot of bad things in her time.' She was particularly good at intelligence work and could always be guaranteed to lose anyone from the security forces who might be tailing her. Sometimes she used the Gaelic version of her name 'Róisín De Brún'. With Christopher Hanna, she had called herself 'Ann Brown'.

Rosena had clearly manipulated Hanna very effectively. After he was jailed a rumour went around that he wanted former girlfriends to write to him. Rosena Brown went into her work, serving behind a bar on the Falls Road, and the regulars erupted into a chorus of 'Dear John'. The RUC believed Rosena had traded sex for secrets. But both she and Hanna denied they'd ever had a full sexual relationship.

Whatever the truth, Christopher Hanna wasn't Rosena's only source of information. According to Martin McGartland, she would hand over to an IRA intelligence officer cigarette papers on which were written the names and addresses of scores of likely targets, police officers and other security force members. Martin said the recipient of all this information had already served a life sentence for an IRA murder but on his release had been given a 'desk job' inputting the names and other details into his computer. Talking in late 1993, McGartland told me: 'The IRA has enough names of policemen it could be killing them for the next twenty-five years. It's killing policemen who are inspectors but the IRA first got their names and details when they were constables.'

On 10 February 1994 the IRA renewed its assault on a senior police officer who was clearly one of its prime targets. The RUC intercepted a van in the Belmont area of east Belfast, arresting three men fleeing the scene and a fourth man in a nearby car, and seizing two rifles, a handgun and a 'coffee jar bomb' packed with Semtex. During the operation the police tackled one of the suspects and broke his leg. At a special court inside the Ulster Hospital, Davey Adams was charged with conspiracy to murder, conspiracy to cause an explosion and possession of guns and explosives. In May 1995 he was sentenced to twenty-five years in jail. Three years later he won £30,000 in compensation from the police for the injuries he suffered during his arrest.

In the days that followed the arrests, some local Belfast papers went public with the rumours circulating around RUC HQ that the bombers' target had been Derek Martindale. Ever since its first attempt on his life in 1983, Martindale's name had remained on the IRA's hit list, his details no doubt updated in some intelligence officer's computer. His dedication and courage, evidenced by his willingness to make high-profile appearances on television programmes like my *Spotlight* report, had only exacerbated the IRA's urge to kill him. The fact that Martindale had raided Davey Adams's house also made the mission personal.

Rosena Brown never struck me as an especially ideological republican. She seemed to have got involved largely because she was brought up in the crucible of the troubles during their most pivotal early years. Whilst behind bars she wrote for the republican prisoners' magazine, the *Captive Voice*. Other IRA inmates concentrated their literary efforts on examinations of loyalist violence or the comparative history of Northern Ireland and Catalonia. But Rosena penned breezy nostalgic pieces about her first job, a pet dog who died, or cooking 'Ulster fries' for her children. At the same time her dedication could not be doubted. When I chatted with her she told me about 'odd jobs' she had performed for the IRA going back to the early seventies, including one occasion when she persuaded a British army patrol to give her clapped-out car a push-start, without the soldiers realising that the vehicle was packed with explosives and guns. She said she wanted peace, but her definition of peace wasn't the same as everyone else's: 'One more push, we've just got to get this thing over and done with.'

As the peace process of the mid-nineties developed, however, Rosena watched it closely from her prison cell. She found life in Maghaberry jail tough, but was kept going by the support of her family and her much younger jailmates. After the publication of the Downing Street Declaration in late 1993 she wrote me a Christmas card saying that we were all living in interesting times and that she trusted the republican leadership would make the right decision. That was the last I heard directly from her, but by perusing the pages of *Republican News* I noticed she had been one of those who benefited from the early release of prisoners which formed an essential part of the Good Friday Agreement. In December 1998 Rosena told *Republican News* about the difficulties of adjusting to life on the outside. She felt nervous finding her way about and unable to cope with the noise or the crowds. She found it hard to hear what people were saying because of an ear infection she had contracted inside jail. She hoped, however, to settle down in time and looked forward to getting to know her grandchildren who had been born whilst she was in Maghaberry.

Rosena Brown saw the outside world much sooner than Lord Justice Mac-Dermott had predicted when he jailed her five years previously. The RUC's attempt to end her stage career by publicising her terrorist background also came to naught. After her early release she talked about her urge to return to the stage and the particular value of community theatre. Within months she landed a new role with a Belfast-based company, this time taking the part of a Protestant mother whose loyalist gunman son had just been shot dead by the police.

For Jean Armour, the widow of prison officer Brian Armour, there has been no early release. Mrs Armour forced herself to read the post-mortem report on her husband because, despite the pain it caused her, she felt she needed to know the truth about what she calls his 'long, lingering painful death'. At the time of the referendum in 1998 on the Good Friday Agreement Mrs Armour told the newspapers she couldn't bring herself to vote yes because she could not forgive her husband's murderers and she felt people were being blackmailed into believing that only the deal could achieve peace. Still frightened to go out, Jean Armour described her life as 'not normal. I am constantly scared, and there must be many people like me in Northern Ireland ... I know that I'm not the only widow in Northern Ireland. I'm not the only one who has been through this. But there is no handbook you can follow. You have to find your own way through it.' Turning to the memory of her late husband, Mrs Armour told the *Belfast Telegraph*, 'You know, I still love him. There is no tap to switch that off. That will always be there.'

13

Tragedy in Coalisland

SPRING 1992–SPRING 1993

At *Spotlight* we frequently had young people on work experience watching what we did. Some appeared either overawed by the media or alternatively so bored that they did not communicate, watching passively what we were doing. Others seemed genuinely fascinated and would ask questions or even chip in with suggestions which showed that they could become enthusiastic journalists in time. Into this latter category I would place Enda McKernan.

Enda's sister Ann lived next door to one of the *Spotlight* producers, American Jay Jones. Jay arranged for her little brother to follow us around during a week's filming and editing. Seventeen years old, doing his A levels at a school in Dungannon, Enda was keen to see how the media worked. We were making a programme which involved interviewing Gerry Adams. As we set up our camera tripod on the side of the pavement opposite the Falls Road press office, Gerry Adams asked how everyone was doing. Finding out that Enda hailed from Coalisland, Gerry got quite chummy. Coalisland in County Tyrone is well known in Northern Ireland as strong nationalist territory, the home patch of, amongst others, the former MP Bernadette McAliskey.

It wasn't only Gerry Adams who pigeonholed Enda because of his Coalisland background. One day Jay asked him to pick up some still photographs from a developers in the city centre. Enda didn't return for an age. When he finally appeared he told us he had been 'p-checked' by an army patrol, who insisted on holding him while they confirmed his true identity. His Coalisland address ensured the soldiers held him for over an hour, even though he gave them a phone number which they could have easily rung to verify his story that he was in Belfast spending time with the BBC.

When his brief period of shadowing came to an end I said goodbye to Enda, wished him well with the dreaded examinations, and expressed the view that he had what it took to get into journalism if he should decide that's what he wanted to do. I didn't expect to see him again for a while, but that May of 1992, an especially warm one for Northern Ireland, Coalisland featured heavily in the news. There were fights in and around the town's three pubs between locals and soldiers from the 3rd Battalion of the Parachute Regiment. Enraged that one of their comrades had been wounded in an IRA attack, the soldiers took revenge on the local people by attacking them without provocation. Even the Northern Ireland Office minister Richard Needham has described the soldiers' behaviour as over the top and counterproductive. Not only that but during a later fracas between soldiers from a different regiment and local youths a soldier lost his machine gun, presumed stolen. The army cordoned off the town and conducted house-to-house searches for the weapon.

The clashes and the searches raised temperatures locally and I went to Coalisland one evening to cover what looked like being an especially lively demonstration outside the town's RUC station, which is in full view of the pubs where the fights had taken place. Before the rally got going I bumped into Enda. He had no plans to stick around for the demonstration, telling me, 'I'm having nothing to do with it.' He had come into town because his widowed mother Mary had to bring her car in to get some petrol. As the only son left at home he felt protective towards her and, in case there was any trouble in the build-up to the protest, he wouldn't let her go out on her own. 'If you get a break,' he urged me, 'come around and have a cup of tea, we're just up the hill.'

Unfortunately I didn't get a break. There was no trouble at the protest, but plenty to keep a reporter busy. The Sinn Féin councillor Francie Molloy led the protesters in a picket walking round and round in a circle beside the RUC station. Bernadette McAliskey was at her rhetorical best, denouncing the British and all their works. 'We have seen evidence,' she told the crowd, 'of the kind of dehumanising training soldiers are put through before they're allowed into the Parachute Regiment. We don't just want them out of Coalisland, we want them out of Northern Ireland, and we want them provided with some proper form of rehabilitation.' Appealing to the fighting spirit of the people of Coalisland she said, 'The British army challenged the youth of this town to a bare-knuckle fight, and the British army lost.'

The tension felt in Coalisland had not dissipated by the time of the Bank Holiday weekend at the end of May. Mary McKernan spent the evening of Sunday, 24 May, visiting a friend about fifteen miles away at Sixmilecross.

When she let herself in not long before midnight she called out for Enda but got no reply. She looked for the note he would normally have scribbled for her if he went anywhere. She did not find one. Instead in the kitchen beside the back door she discovered Enda crouched in a foetal position. He had been shot at close range in the back of the head.

I heard the news the following morning on the radio. But no names were mentioned and I assumed that loyalists had picked on some poor youth in the area opportunistically in order to raise the temperatures in Coalisland still further. By this stage I was working on a quite separate story and I have to admit the radio report of the shooting went in one ear and out the other. It was only when I bumped into a couple of friends in the centre of Belfast later that Bank Holiday Monday that I realised who the victim had been. 'Jay's taken some time off work,' one of them told me. 'Apparently he knew that young boy who was killed in Coalisland yesterday.'

My forehead and hands felt clammy. It couldn't be. A seventeen-year-old teenager, who had been such good fun, who had so much to look forward to, who had just spent a week or more shadowing me, dead with a bullet in the head.

Most commentators initially assumed that the murder must have somehow been connected with the recent tension in Coalisland. Enda's headmaster, the Dungannon priest Father Denis Faul, went on television talking about an apparent 'mistake' by loyalist paramilitaries. The IRA issued a statement saying they had nothing to do with it. The Ulster Unionist MP John Taylor, whose newspaper company employed Enda's mother, said he rarely commented on the catalogue of terrorist deaths. But this murder moved him to 'repeat yet again that those who so behave have no mandate from their communities; they will carry the burden of their evil behaviour for the rest of their lives; and will eventually have to answer to GOD for these murders'. 'What a great wee country we could make of Northern Ireland,' the MP concluded, 'if together we invested our all into its future rather than tear ourselves apart in vain and with no outcome.'

Enda's brother Brian reflected the family's sense of utter loss and confusion. 'He was gunned down and we would just like to know why,' Brian told reporters. 'He lived for his mother, his studies and the rock band in which he played drums. He has never been involved in any organisation. He was perfectly innocent.'

A couple of days later I broke off filming on the border and drove up to

Coalisland to attend Enda's wake. The streets around were full of the parked cars of the family's many visitors. Although I had known Enda I felt a bit of an interloper as I had never met his family or friends. His mother Mary stood at the door, looking drawn and distressed. I recognised that stage shortly after a death when the feeling of pure grief is to an extent overshadowed by the shock and confusion caused by suddenly being the centre of attention. Visitors call and arrangements are made for an event which just a few days before you never imagined would happen.

'Mrs McKernan,' I said, 'you don't know me but my name's Mark and I work for the BBC.'

She looked at me and gave me a big hug. 'I don't know you but I've heard everything about you – everything you did. Enda told me. He loved his time at the BBC.'

'That night I was in Coalisland,' I told her, 'I really did mean to come up for that cup of tea. I never thought I'd regret so much not being able to make it.'

The large number of sixth-formers hanging around the house, most wearing black leather jackets, provided proof of Enda's popularity at St Patrick's Academy in Dungannon. The drummer in the school band, Enda had been music-mad. One of the youths I chatted to at the house talked about how he had seen Enda on the evening of his murder. He said he'd dropped around to borrow a CD before heading off to a disco at a nearby town.

Before I left, at Mary's urging, I accompanied Enda's uncle, Father Malachy Sheehan, up the stairs to see his body. Enda lay in his best suit, covered in condolence cards. With a little make-up, the undertakers had tried to soften the coldness of death on his face.

The next morning hundreds of pupils from Enda's school lined the route to the Church of the Holy Family. A few police officers stood to attention as the cortège passed. Unusually for Coalisland at this time, they wore no body armour, indicating that they knew no paramilitary organisation would besmirch the sad occasion. Inside the church Malachy Sheehan told the congregation not to believe anyone who said Enda's death had been God's will. 'God gives human beings free will, and some of them abuse that free will. To say this is God's will is a gross calumny on the maker.' He repeated a call already made by Enda's brother Brian: that the family simply wanted to know why Enda had been murdered, why Mary's home had been violated.

Apart from the usual hymns, the service also featured a song by the surviving members of Enda's rock band, with his brother-in-law sitting in on the drums. The singer wasn't the only one in the church who wept openly as they played.

Whilst Enda's family had absolutely nothing to do with the disturbances in Coalisland involving the army, a sub-plot developed to the killing which did have a connection. During the house-to-house searches for the army's missing machine gun, the McKernans, like everyone else in the town, expected a knock on the door. Enda's brother Paul, who had spent the past eighteen months working in the Middle East, owned a shotgun which he had left in the house whilst he was away. The weapon was legal and the police had its details. The family expected any callers from the security forces to ask them to produce the weapon, but when they looked for it, it wasn't there.

As the police and army search for the missing gun continued, Enda and Mary launched their own frantic hunt. Paul, contacted in Saudi Arabia, said he felt sure the shotgun should still be in the house. But it was nowhere to be seen.

Quite what happened next is still unclear. Enda, concerned about all the worry the missing gun had caused his mother, might have started doing a bit of digging. What he did confide to Mary was that another teenager, who called around occasionally, had some kind of fixation with the weapon. Apparently he'd once asked Enda to give it to him so 'he could blow his dad's brains out'.

In fact this other teenager, Philip Lappin, had been at the McKernans' home the evening of Enda's wake. He protested his grief at the loss of his 'closest' friend. At night he slept in Enda's bedroom. On the day of the funeral he helped carry Enda's coffin. At the wake, he had been the youth talking about borrowing a CD from Enda on the night of his death.

From the outset detectives concentrated on Philip Lappin. Within a few days they announced they'd recovered the missing shotgun. Shortly after that they charged the seventeen-year-old with murder. Lappin's solicitors contended that what had taken place had been a tragic accident, two schoolfriends had indulged in a bit of horseplay with a shotgun and the prank had gone terribly wrong. Shortly before the case came to court in February 1993 the murder charge was reduced to manslaughter. Philip Lappin pleaded guilty to unlawfully killing Enda McKernan and received a four-year sentence of imprisonment in a young offenders' centre.

The judge said he was satisfied there had been no animosity between the two youths, and that the discharge of the gun had been caused by Lappin's rough play and had been unintentional. He believed Lappin had shown genuine remorse.

The peculiarities of the case meant that after an initial rush of publicity, it dropped out of the news. It never featured in any documentary illustrating some general point about the pernicious nature of sectarianism or the ease with which young people could get caught up in violence. But for the McKernan family the grief continued unabated. The family never accepted Philip Lappin's version of what had occurred, and continued to raise detailed questions about the account presented in court. For Mary McKernan, these doubts compounded the deep pain caused by Enda's death. On one occasion, she told the *Irish News*, she received a phone call from a woman warning her, 'Don't rake up your son's past. Let him rest in peace.' Exactly what happened only Philip Lappin knows. As I write this I am staring at a newspaper cutting which features a photograph of a smiling Enda McKernan, taken outside the BBC. It was one of the photos our producer Jay Jones asked him to collect from the developers as we edited our programme. He was a bright, lively teenager, who deserved much, much better.

14

From Belfast to Baidoa

AUTUMN 1992

Reporting for the local Northern Ireland news, you thought you were going on an exotic expedition if the producer sent you to Derry. With *Spotlight* you grew rather more used to regular filming trips to London and Dublin. But being spoilt a little only increased a *Spotlight* reporter's wanderlust. Journalists would regularly come up with an idea which involved a trip to the United States or Europe. Just as regularly the editor would roll his eyes and remind us of the latest parlous budgetary position.

But in the course of 1992 an international story began to attract a level of attention which it became hard for even a Belfast-based current affairs programme to ignore. After the fall of its dictator Siad Barre, the African country of Somalia plunged into civil war. Fierce fighting between rival clans combined with the effect of a drought in the Horn of Africa to create a famine which rivalled the terrible tragedy of Ethiopia in its scale and horror. At one stage two hundred children were dying a day in the Somali capital Mogadishu alone. People in Northern Ireland are well known for their charitable instincts – in fact the statistics show they give a higher proportion of their income to charities than any other area in the UK. Like the rest of the developed world they were horrified by the images they began to see on their television screens and started donating money by the bucketload. The Irish aid agency Concern had been amongst the first to deploy nurses, doctors and relief workers to the worst-affected areas. So much support had been flowing in from Northern Ireland that Concern organised a massive Russian cargo jet to take off from Belfast International Airport heading for Somalia. The departure date fell just a few days before the Irish President Mary Robinson was due to visit Mogadishu.

The trip was not the kind of junket which journalists sometimes had in mind when lobbying to go abroad. Nevertheless to trace the fortunes of the food aid and relief workers all the way from Belfast to their destination in Somalia promised to be a fascinating story. With a great deal of detailed research work from producer Jay Jones, our editor Andrew Colman was persuaded. I had been following a related story, a charitable appeal for Somalia with local Northern Ireland involvement which didn't quite seem to add up. Andrew told me to do the aid story first and foremost, but if I could find out anything about the other matter so much the better.

We lumbered out of Aldergrove airport in a giant Ilyushin 76, the biggest plane ever to take off from Belfast. It put regular air travel into perspective as we perched on top of the sacks of around £100,000 worth of food aid, mostly infant formula, paid for by the generosity of Northern Irish people. The plane had no seats, and certainly no seat belts. Take-off involved grabbing hold of the chains which anchored the cargo in place and hanging on like grim death. The toilet was a bucket at the back. That said, lying on cushions on top of bags of food is in fact rather comfier than being strapped into your economy seat overnight. I would have slept very well indeed if the cameraman and sound recordist, who made their way to the cockpit to take pictures of the flight crew at the controls, had not reported back that the Ilyushin was on autopilot and the entire crew were fast asleep.

After two nights and a day which took us on a circuitous route via Russia and Egypt, we made our final run into Mogadishu airport, which had no air traffic control, no customs and no immigration, just a band of men with guns who ran the area. Once we stepped out onto the tarmac people came at us from every direction. Everyone wanted to be our guide or our guard. A Somali musician wanted me to deliver a painstakingly compiled document to 'the United Nations' Special Committee responsible for getting solutions to the Somalis' problems, New York, USA'. And the leader of the clan which ran the airport wanted me to settle an argument which I discovered I had been responsible for starting.

Before we left Belfast I filed some news copy for Radio Ulster about the relief supplies heading for Somalia. The Ilyushin was packed with forty-six tons of aid, but for the sake of simplicity I had rounded the figure up to 'around fifty tons of relief supplies'. To my surprise the copy found its way through the BBC system from Radio Ulster to the BBC World Service, which had duly reported that a plane was on its way carrying a film crew and fifty tons of aid. The clan in control of the airport had worked out a standard cut which they demanded from all aid agencies for every ton of relief they allowed through. Concern handed over the required sum, only to have the clan leader tell them they were trying to cheat him. 'You say you've only got forty-six tons, but the BBC says there's fifty.' I had to explain that the discrepancy was down to me and that sometimes the media dealt in approximations rather than precise figures. The clan leader looked at me as if he would never believe a word he heard on the BBC again.

To make a specifically Northern Ireland-related film, as opposed to a pro-gramme about the horrors of the famine in general, it was necessary not just to follow the path the infant formula and food aid took on the ground, but more importantly to have sensitive and powerful characters from Northern Ireland through whose eyes we could see the enormity of the task facing the interna-tional community. In this regard we could not have been blessed with a better, more efficient organisation than Concern nor more down-to-earth people than Linda McClelland from Bangor and Paddy Maguinness from Newry. They not only held our film together but they kept me sane, which at times appeared to be very much in question. Jay Jones and I also had great support from Donal Hamilton, whose images of Somalia often looked more like oil paintings than television pictures, and Peter Moore, whose enthusiasm and technical prowess proved invaluable.

I saw all the horrors I had presumed I would witness. We drove along heavily rutted dirt roads into the countryside, passing impoverished people walking for days in search of food. The sun beat down on them as they made their way across the parched landscape. In the town of Baidoa, four hours' drive outside Mogadishu, the famine continued to be desperate and we watched as the trucks went around picking up the bodies of young children. No one knew their names. In an orphanage in a broken-down building I met a little girl battling hunger and carrying a bullet in her leg. Whilst I had expected to be desperately moved by the evidence of the famine before my eyes I have to confess my reaction was more muted than I had imagined. To some extent I think this was because I knew from the moment I got off the plane that these were the scenes I was likely to see. In addition I had a strong feeling that I wasn't there to dwell on my personal emotions, instead my job was to record the truth and bring it back to my audience. Above all, however, I think the stress and strain of working in a country in a state of absolute anarchy made me focus entirely on getting the job done. As we worked, drug chewing gunmen circled around us. If they were in a good mood, they laughed and joked shouting 'BBC' or swapping stories with me about all the foreign correspondents they had met. If they weren't they would train their guns on our camera making it clear that we had better stop filming. We had armed guards but they couldn't provide any guarantee of protection against the gangs roaming around on lorries equipped with light artillery pieces or heavy machine guns.

At this stage a small Pakistani peacekeeping force controlled little beyond its own compound. The ill-fated American-led military intervention remained some distance off in the future. The sense was that anything could happen. If a drug-crazed man with a rifle decided to shoot you, so what: there was no law and order. If misfortune befell a Somali then tough luck: there were virtually no networks of support. I witnessed this lottery of life on a number of occasions and I tried to sum this up for the people back in Northern Ireland in the following article, which the *Belfast Telegraph* published in October 1992.

LIVING ON THE EDGE

I never thought when I travelled to Somalia to report on the famine and war which has blighted the country that one of the things which would shock us most of all would be a traffic accident.

We were on the road to start filming at Baidoa, a town where some two hundred people are dying of hunger every day, when our jeep hit a rut. Inside the vehicle we were thrown about, one of us grazed his head. But on top of the jeep, where armed guards perched precariously on the roof, the impact had much more serious consequences.

One of the guards, Hassan, lost his grip and flew off into the air. I turned and looked back just in time to see him hit the gravel road. He rolled over two or three times before lying still.

Accidents can and do happen anywhere in the world. But this one said a lot about Somalia, a country without a government, a place where the lack of a system means that everyone is living on the edge.

Hassan had been on top of our jeep because in Somalia it is too dangerous for any westerner, or anyone with something worth selling, to travel without the company of a band of armed men. The war, in which the old dictator Siad Barre was overthrown, ended in the spring. But war has been replaced by anarchy, with the country divided between rival clans and plenty of freelance gunmen around owing allegiance to no one but themselves.

Everywhere you look a new weapon appears – Russian Kalashnikov rifles, American M16s, heavy machine guns and rocket-propelled grenade launchers. In the towns vehicles known as 'technicals', fitted with still heavier guns, roam ominously around the streets.

En route to Baidoa there was an extra need for security as we were accompanying trucks loaded with relief supplies – possibly a target for looters. We were rushing to catch up with one of these lorries when the accident occurred.

I grabbed our emergency medical kit and headed towards the injured man. Our producer Jay Jones put his first-aid experience to use.

Sound recordist Peter Moore and Linda McClelland from Bangor, who is in Somalia working for the relief agency Concern, jumped out of the vehicle too. Together we moved Hassan into the back seat of the jeep.

In Northern Ireland there would have been an ambulance to call, a fully equipped hospital only minutes away. But in Somalia all we could do was feel for a pulse. Cameraman Donal Hamilton wiped away the blood and vomit from the injured man's mouth.

We headed for Afgoi, back along the road to the Somali capital Mogadishu. When we got there we discovered that Afgoi hospital consists of one doctor equipped with nothing more than a supply of one thousand paracetamol tablets.

We drove on – the journey must have lasted an hour – to Medina hospital in Mogadishu. Here there are more doctors, but all they could really do was observe. In the jeep we had already concluded that Hassan had a serious internal head injury. At Medina hospital there's no equipment to carry out a brain scan. Even basic surgery carries a high risk of infection.

All over Somalia I saw pieces of good luck and bad luck which, like our rut in the road, had profound consequences. With no law and order and no health service to speak of, there's no safety net for anyone to fall into when bad luck strikes.

It was good luck that a little boy, Mohammed Ahmed Osman, made it to a feeding centre run by Concern after losing both his parents. It was better luck still that one of Concern's local employees decided to adopt him.

It was bad luck for a ten-year-old girl, Beshara, that on top of suffering from malnutrition, she was caught by a stray bullet in one of the meaningless shoot-outs which happen here on a daily basis. The bullet shattered her knee, and with no proper medical care a month after the shooting the entry wound is still clearly visible. Walking around since then must have been agony.

The one thing not down to luck is that fate will, wherever you are, deal more kindly with the haves than the have-nots. Even in Baidoa, where lorries ply a regular round picking up dozens of bodies, men with guns and property still wander around looking as if nothing out of the ordinary is happening, cutting deals over the corpses of the famine victims.

For our guard the luck was bad. Later on the day of the accident, Hassan passed away. He was nineteen years old. His mother said it must have been Allah's will, but this is the workings of fate in a desperately poor country. In our world he might have stood a chance.

After recording images of the famine I decided to check out the story of the suspect appeal for Somali aid which had come to our attention. One of the Belfast morning newspapers, the *Irish News,* had featured an appeal for money from a man who called himself the foreign minister of the Democratic Republic of Somalia, His Excellency Haji Mohammed Hashi Haile. This was suspect in itself as Somalia had no recognised government, but what made the story more intriguing from a Belfast perspective was that two of the foreign minister's faithful retainers were Ulster men with a colourful background.

I tried to contact the two main factions in Somalia, both of which claimed to be the rightful government, to check out Haji Mohammed Hashi Haile's credentials. One faction, which followed General Aideed, provided a piece of paper dismissing the minister as an imposter. The other faction summoned me across the notoriously dangerous Green Line, which divided Mogadishu, for an audience with the self-styled Somali President Ali Mahdi.

As we crossed the line we heard a burst of gunfire but it didn't seem to be coming in our direction. We transferred vehicles and made our way to Ali Mahdi's headquarters. There a lengthy interview produced results. Provided with a copy of the *Irish News,* the President burst into laughter.

'I am very sorry. Every person who is not honest can call himself what he wants. He has never been in our government, he is not in the cabinet, he is not a foreign minister, he has never been a politician.'

Another minister chipped in that His Excellency was a conman. The

President continued, explaining that the 'foreign minister' was a cinema owner who had last been seen leaving a hotel by a bedroom window. If this wasn't good enough another member of the 'government' chipped in that he knew Haji Mohammed Hashi Haile very well because he had murdered his sister.

Flabbergasted I sat back, realising that one way or another, because of the Northern Ireland connections with the apparent scandal, *Spotlight* had material for two quite separate films on Somalia. Then all of a sudden the surreal scene became rather sinister. As a film crew we had arrived at Ali Mahdi's headquarters more or less under the wing of Concern, who as an aid agency heavily involved on the ground could usually be counted on to command a degree of respect. But when I innocently asked the President a question about the sterling work Northern Ireland's nurses and doctors were doing he erupted into a tirade. Why, he wanted to know, was Concern in the other faction's territory but not in his? The factions didn't care about whether the starving got relief. For Ali Mahdi any aid agency brave enough to operate in his extremely unstable patch of the city would be a source of welcome revenue. I swiftly changed the subject and our conversation moved on. But unbeknownst to me a 'government minister' sidled up to Linda McClelland, as the Concern representative, and berated her about her organisation's 'bias'.

'I am sorry, sister,' he told an aghast Linda, 'but I am the minister in charge of executions. I am the man in this government who arranges the ambushes. I am sorry, sister, but if this does not change immediately I shall have no alternative but to have you killed.'

The camera crew were keen to avail of the President's kind offer to take a few more pictures. They could not understand why I insisted that we had more than enough already. They did not have Linda next to them whispering 'Get me out of here.'

As we went back across the Green Line I thought we had experienced quite enough misadventure for one trip. But Somalia still had one trick up its sleeve. On our last day before we were due to hitch a lift out of the airport I decided we should film a sequence at Medina hospital in Mogadishu where most shooting victims were treated. We already had plenty of images of famine but we needed more pictures which illustrated the civil war. All seemed to go smoothly. The French doctors from Médecins sans Frontières warned me that filming could be dangerous as some Muslims objected to having their picture taken, so I should check very carefully before switching the camera on.

In the wards I went around every patient and every family meticulously finding out if they were happy for us to go ahead. Having got a universal thumbs up we proceeded to film. It was only as we prepared to depart that a man arrived on the scene asking to see our certificates of permission. I produced paperwork which we had acquired from all the relevant clan leaders, but he told me this wasn't good enough. I had to see the 'hospital management'.

Back in Belfast an appointment with the 'hospital management' is not something likely to strike fear into any reporter's heart. But as I ambled into the relevant office I realised that Medina hospital's management amounted to something completely different. An officious man sat behind a desk and gestured brusquely for me to take a seat. Behind him stood half a dozen men brandishing rifles. He stared at me then launched straight in.

'I am very very angry with the BBC. You have broken all the rules. You have flouted all the regulations. You did not seek our permission. This situation is intolerable. You white men think you can come in here and do anything you want to do. You cannot. You shall not leave this hospital.'

Somebody had told me before I set off for Somalia to smile, hug people if possible and never ever show fear. Smiling proved difficult. Both the desk and the tirade made hugging appear out of the question. So I stayed calm and started to explain and apologise without appearing ruffled. Unfortunately beads of sweat appeared unbidden on my forehead which had nothing to do with the heat. I explained that I had checked with the French doctors.

'Pah, who are they, they think they run this hospital, they are not the management, we are, they are only doctors . . .'

At this point my driver, who had made his way into the room with me, valiantly jumped to my defence. In rapid Somali he appeared to be saying 'Give the boy a break.' In equally rapid and vehement Somali my interrogator seemed to be telling him this was out of the question. Everyone started talking at once. The six armed men appeared to be debating amongst themselves whether it would be best to shoot me against an inside wall or an outside wall. Amidst a multitude of Somali phrases I caught the English words 'letter of apology'. Frantically I started to mime the action of writing on a piece of paper. I remembered that business cards and letterheads carried clout in Somalia. Stupidly I had no cards, but I dug around in my bag and pulled out a letterhead which I had snipped off a letter accompanying our BBC-issue medical kit. Holding the letterhead in one hand and making further writing motions with the other I finally commanded attention.

'If a formal letter of apology would help, sir, then I would be happy to provide one. But I am afraid I must beg one small favour — does the management by any chance have a spare piece of paper to which I could attach this official BBC letterhead?'

Impressed, the manager signalled for a piece of paper and a paper clip to be provided.

Clearly and laboriously I began, 'Dear Sirs, We, the BBC, profusely apologise for our ignorant and offensive error in ignoring the regulations and procedures laid down by the Medina hospital management.' I continued in the same vein for several more sentences and without a thesaurus to hand did a fairly good job in utilising just about every grovelling adjective known to the English language.

My interrogator perused the document for some time before curtly informing me, 'This is in order. You may go.'

15

Rogues and Doorsteps

SPRING 1990–SUMMER 1993

When we got back from Somalia, it became a little easier to put the troubles of Northern Ireland into some kind of perspective. The film about Concern's work achieved a lot of advance publicity, but not especially high viewing figures. The editor put it down to 'compassion fatigue'. My disappointment about the quantity of viewers was allayed, however, when Concern told me that the *Spotlight* audience had provided just the 'quality' they were looking for. The transmission provoked a series of calls from doctors and nurses and other trained staff keen to help in any way they could. Perhaps the most important part of the programme, though, was its four-word title strap: 'From Belfast to Baidoa'. Concern took the title and made it the slogan for their renewed Somalia campaign. Current affairs journalists have to be careful about their relations with outside organisations and maintain an independent stance, even if they are charitable agencies. For that reason, in our film we had involved other groups like the Save the Children Fund as well as talking to the UN peacekeepers, the Somali Red Cross and several local clan leaders. But I was profoundly impressed by what I saw of Concern's operations on the ground and proud to see their posters bearing our programme name.

The Somali scandal story also grew in the telling. A new reporter to *Spotlight*, Wendy Robbins, took it over. She had, via a circuitous route, wheedled her way into the little circle surrounding our fake foreign minister. Wendy, who had been an assistant producer on *Panorama*, is quite simply one of the most gifted investigators I have ever seen in action. I worked alongside her as a producer and although we never felt we really got to the bottom of His Excellency Haji Mohammed Hashi Haile the twists and turns we unearthed, from Mafia connections to illegal oil deals to accusations of murder, were quite enough to provide an engaging half-hour. The film, called 'Haji at the Hilton' after the London hotel the benefactor most liked to frequent, won a

European prize for best regional investigative documentary. Whatever he was, Haji was a fascinating rogue. As I sat in the editing suite, making final changes to the programme on the day of transmission, members of the public rang me to tell startling stories about Frank Fitzpatrick. Frank was a lawyer who ran into problems with the taxman in the Irish Republic. He headed to Spain and got involved in a timeshare development which went belly up losing a lot of Irish investors' money. After telling their tales of Frank, which weren't especially flattering, my callers would, however, invariably end the conversation with 'but he's such a nice man'. Having met Frank, I heartily agreed.

During our film Wendy successfully confronted both Frank Fitzpatrick and his sidekick 'Lord' David Hamill on camera. Frank stood and answered a series of questions, whilst 'his Lordship' turned and fled. In the era of *The Cook Report* it became de rigueur for more or less any investigative television film to feature the 'doorstep' – the sequence in which the reporter pursues the reluctant rogue down the street, finally bringing him to book for his misdeeds. Most viewers prefer these films if the reporter at least gets slapped around a bit.

Whilst many of my colleagues in Northern Ireland, such as Wendy Robbins, Stephen Walker or Jeremy Adams, seem to flourish in these situations, I have always been terrible at them. The BBC has strict rules about such confrontations: a reporter should have already approached a potential target for a conventional interview and there should be strong evidence that anyone to be filmed or recorded in this way is guilty of either illegal or highly questionable behaviour. Producer Bruce Batten spent a great deal of time investigating a company which appeared to be offering Northern Ireland people an extremely shoddy service with their double glazing. But when I slunk around the firm's head office looking suspicious I managed to miss every possible executive coming and going, so the allegations went largely unanswered.

In another case, producer Jay Jones and myself made what I think we would both admit wasn't an especially strong programme about the Kincora scandal, in which figures linked to a shadowy loyalist group called 'Tara' were convicted of involvement in the sexual abuse of the boys in a children's home in east Belfast. We gathered interviews with former Kincora residents and with those, such as the former army press officer Colin Wallace, who alleged the scandal had been suppressed by British military intelligence. But the challenge remained to get William McGrath, the main culprit in the scandal, and by now a very elderly man, to speak about the truth of the conspiracy theories. Mr McGrath, who had been convicted of abuse, had consistently refused to talk to journalists and failed to reply to my letters asking him for a meeting.

We drove down to McGrath's home village of Ballyhalbert on the Strangford peninsula and surveyed his retirement bungalow. The house looked out to sea and there was no way one could hang about unobtrusively without being noticed. So we parked a fair distance away and tried to keep an eye on the property through a pair of binoculars. If anyone thinks a spy or an undercover cop's life is exciting they should try sitting in a car for a few hours keeping somewhere under surveillance. It is mind-numbingly tedious. Eventually we saw a sign of movement – a man on a bicycle. We were so far away it was hard to make out exactly what was going on. Had the cyclist just come out of McGrath's house or not? We decided to drive past him and check.

As we were pursuing the cyclist we drove past William McGrath's bungalow. There before my eyes was the man the tabloids had dubbed 'the Beast of Kincora' standing on a box, his back to us, cleaning his windows. I vowed to get a new pair of binoculars.

'Right,' I told the crew, 'we're going to have to turn, park, jump out, you're going to have stay behind me, keep the camera running and I'll see if he will answer any questions.'

We aborted the chase after the cyclist and turned the car.

'Okay, ready to go?' I said to the cameraman.

'Yes,' came the reply, and with that I leapt out of the car and sprinted towards William McGrath.

We had the element of surprise on our side and I was right beside McGrath and his box when I introduced myself. 'Mr McGrath, Mark Devenport from the BBC's *Spotlight* programme, you didn't reply to my letters so I want to give you the opportunity to answer some of the many questions people still have about the Kincora scandal . . .'

As I mouthed these words William McGrath looked at me, understandably aghast, and jumped off his box. He really was very sprightly for a man in his eighties. I backed towards his front door in an attempt to slow him down without impeding his access to his own house, but he sprinted around me in a little circle.

'Mr McGrath, was there a cover-up? Why won't you speak about Kincora?'

I got out two more questions before 'the Beast' dived through his door and slammed it shut.

When we got back to the edit suite we put the tape into the player. I had detected from the cameraman's mood that he wasn't very happy about how things had gone. When we pushed 'play' the first image on the screen was a closing door, you couldn't make out who was behind it. The first sound on the tape were my words 'Did you get that?' and the cameraman's reply 'I think so.' However William McGrath had transgressed, someone had certainly been looking down on him that day in Ballyhalbert.

Not every 'doorstep' I had to do turned out so drastically. In May 1993 I made a film about video and audio tape piracy, which the RUC claimed to be a significant source of cash for the paramilitaries on both sides. The police co-operated with our filming and during a trip to the Sunday market at Nutts Corner in County Antrim we found it easy to covertly film a selection of pirate videos on sale. But getting any 'pirates' to talk to us proved more difficult. Eventually I talked to one convicted 'pirate' who operated around the border region and carried his words in a reconstruction of our conversation. But I continued to search for another case study which I hoped might make an interview. That's what put me onto Richard Morrow, a video dealer who operated in Bangor who had a previous conviction for piracy. I should make it clear that there is no evidence and no suggestion that Richard Morrow's activities had any connection with paramilitaries. But he did have a history of handling 'blue movies' which were so explicit that they could not get a certificate in the UK.

When I spoke to him on the phone, Richard Morrow gave me the brush-off. I thought I would abandon this line of enquiry but then I got word that he was up in court on a further video piracy charge a few days before my pro-gramme was due to be broadcast. Unfortunately I had already scheduled a couple of interviews for the same day in London, so I had to ask my colleague Jeremy Adams to keep an eye on the proceedings. Jeremy wasn't able to iden-tify Richard Morrow on his way into Bangor Magistrates' Court, so made his way inside and sat through the case in which Morrow pleaded guilty to having pirate tapes, forging video covers and offering for sale what was referred to in court as 'hardcore porn'. Two of the films in question were videos called *Bums for Hire* and *Body Cocktail*. The prosecuting lawyer made it clear there was 'nothing to suggest paramilitary involvement'. Nevertheless it was a second offence. First time around Morrow had been fined £500. This time the magistrate doubled that to £1,000, even though under the Video Recordings Act he could have faced a much more severe financial penalty.

At the end of the hearing Jeremy nipped outside to tell the cameraman to get a picture of our video pirate as he left. This seemed a fairly easy task as Bangor Magistrates' Court had only one public exit. Jeremy waited and waited. Eventually an employee at the court emerged to tell him he was wasting his time. Morrow had gone. This was perplexing – how could our man have disappeared when the rear exit to the court was restricted to court officials and the police?

With a couple of days left to the programme we decided to persevere a little more. We sent a young researcher, Paul Rocks, to Richard Morrow's shop in search of illegal tapes. It didn't take much more than a wink for our man to spring into action, supplying the necessary for what Paul told him were 'a bunch of lads having a carry-out'. He told Paul all about his conviction and the fact that the *Spotlight* programme had been hassling him. Morrow added that if Paul hired any 'blues' it would have to be for five days, not one, as he needed the money to pay off his fine! Whilst Paul paid over his money he heard a bang behind him and looked a bit startled. Morrow told him not to worry as it would only be the police who he claimed were his 'best customers'. All this took place within a week of the pirate's court appearance.

I must admit I found the story of Richard Morrow more farcical than outrageous. It got more absurd as we showed the offending videos to a Trading Standards Officer who sat stern-faced, ticking off the series of sexual acts depicted which ensured the material was illegal. Amongst the boxes ticked was one entitled 'head bobbing fellatio'. On the strength of this I returned to Richard Morrow's shop and filmed a brief encounter with him asking why he was still renting out tapes with titles like *Angels of Passion* and *Nasty Girls 3* just a few days after having been up 'before the beak'. He first denied it then retreated behind a pink curtain, telling me to leave or face his lawyer. We broadcast the footage the next day and I didn't expect to hear again from Mr Morrow, who could consider himself lucky if a third prosecution did not follow. But I underestimated our plucky pirate, who also ran a karaoke and gave shows as an on-stage hypnotist.

A few months later I saw a poster for Richard Morrow's karaoke show emblazoned with the slogan 'as advertised on BBC *Spotlight*'. A few years after that I happened by accident to walk into a bar where he was doing his show. He greeted me with a cheery 'Hello, Mark, nice to see you, please take a seat.'

Whilst not respecting his track record, I do respect his sense of humour. I didn't, however, stay to see his show. I am sure Richard Morrow is a very entertaining hypnotist but I don't think I would want to be put under his spell. He might feel rather too tempted to turn the tables on his journalistic tormentor.

16

Agents and Informers

During five years of documentary making I must confess I never got excited about either proving some precooked theory or engaging in a 'mission to explain'. Both approaches too often ended up in something which appeared worthy but dull on the screen. Rather I preferred the old-fashioned technique of talking to people and, hopefully, tripping over stories which grow as you pursue them. Any journalist, like any academic, brings an array of preconceptions to their subject matter which will undoubtedly guide the areas they bother to peer into, and it is as well to constantly re-examine those preconceived ideas. But there is a big difference between deciding exactly what you are going to say from the vantage point of the editorial conference before you bother to talk to anyone and finding stories by listening to people out on the ground who know better than you. A producer in London once began a request for a story with the words 'Well, we here have the following thesis', before telling me exactly which kind of 'vox pops' I was required to gather in the street in order to prove 'the thesis'. I responded by paraphrasing a famous German quotation, replying, 'When I hear the word "thesis" I reach for my revolver.'

The upshot of this is that I enjoy covering 'human' stories most of all and what I remember is the array of colourful personalities which I came across. Some were rogues like the ones we 'doorstepped'. Others were rather more lovable, like Mary Wilson, an east Belfast pensioner whom we turned into a reporter for an investigation of the impact on the elderly of an increase in Value Added Tax on home heating fuel. Given that *Spotlight* spent much of its time delving into the underbelly of the troubles many of the characters we dealt with were a little murky and hard to fully assess. Tommy Doheny, an archetypal cheeky Cockney, who surfaced in the winter of 1993, was more a spy than a rogue, although at times I did not know quite what to make of him.

Fast-talking, handsome and equipped with a streetwise charm, Tommy married an Irish girl and tried to start a new life in Ireland but got into some financial scrapes including one over a leased car. I won't attempt to explain the convoluted details of Tommy's personal story. If anyone wants to know they are best off perusing the *Sunday Business Post* and other papers of the time. Suffice it to say, the element which *Spotlight* found most interesting was Tommy's claims that he had spent considerable time gathering information for military intelligence on republican extremists. On the one hand it sounded inherently implausible as with his very obvious Cockney tones Tommy stuck out like the proverbial sore thumb in the areas where he lived and worked. But on the other hand he had a batch of authentic-sounding tapes of his alleged conversations with his army handlers which – for a current affairs programme investigating every aspect of the troubles – shone a fascinating light on low-level intelligence gathering. Moreover he had really been to the republican haunts which he had claimed to have visited.

During the making of the programme I was never quite sure with Tommy where fact ended and exaggeration began. However, an army source told me Tommy had done some work for 'the funny farm', as he called military intelligence. In addition to the tapes he had already made, we got Tommy to phone army headquarters at Lisburn and speak to a colonel in 'the funny farm' who, despite being cautious, clearly knew who he was talking to. We did not record the colonel's voice for broadcast as identifying him would obviously have imperilled his safety and it is against BBC guidelines to covertly record people for broadcast who are not clearly implicated in criminal or illegal activity. Tommy warned the colonel that he was getting nowhere with a legal campaign resulting from his financial difficulties and that he might have no option but to go to the press with more details about his life including his involvement with the army. The colonel told him military intelligence in Northern Ireland had 'broad shoulders'.

Despite all this corroboration I remained highly sceptical about Tommy's accounts of his life as an army spy – a scepticism reflected by the title of our programme, 'Our Man in Fermanagh', echoing Graham Greene's tale of unwitting espionage, *Our Man in Havana*.

During a lengthy interview I put it to Tommy, 'Aren't you a bit of a Walter Mitty character?'

'Who the flip's Walter Mitty?' was his reply.

Although Tommy did not much like our film, he still rang me up on occasion keeping me abreast of the progress he'd made in his long-running legal battle. The year after 'Our Man in Fermanagh' was broadcast, Tommy's story received further corroboration as a result of an unconnected tragedy. A Chinook helicopter crashed on the Mull of Kintyre. I had returned to news reporting at this stage and remember rushing around trying to get either a speedboat or a helicopter to get me to the scene. As cameraman Peter Cooper and I were driving out the back gate of BBC Belfast en route to board a helicopter we were called back – the authorities had ordered an air exclusion zone over the crash site dashing our hopes of getting some early pictures. In the event it turned out that we were far better off staying in Belfast as the crash turned out to be a tragedy with a difference. The Chinook's passengers, it emerged, were an elite collection of the most senior officers of MI5, military intelligence and the RUC Special Branch, all en route to a security conference in Scotland and all, unbelievably, travelling in the same helicopter. Throughout the night I kept broadcasting as more details emerged about the scale of the disaster and the nature of the blow to the government's counter-terrorist operations. In the ensuing days the names of the dead were revealed. Amongst them was Lieutenant Colonel George Victor Williams, whose voice I had heard as he chatted to Tommy over the phone about the army's 'broad shoulders'. The colonel was identified posthumously as the number two in military intelligence in Northern Ireland. Whoever the flip Walter Mitty is, he certainly isn't Tommy Doheny.

Another man who is streetwise and full of banter is Martin McGartland, the IRA mole who told me all about Rosena Brown. For several months not a day would pass without my mobile phone ringing at all times of the day or night followed by a bellowed 'HOW YA DOING?' In his own book *50 Dead Men Walking*, Martin McGartland has already told the story of how the RUC encouraged him to join the IRA, how he fed the police high-grade intelligence, how he acted as driver during the murder of a soldier and how, when the IRA rumbled him, he escaped from its clutches by plunging through a first floor window, seriously injuring himself in the process. After his first media exposure as an agent on John Ware's *Inside Story* investigation for the BBC, Martin remained fascinated by the world of the troubles and by the media covering them. Having survived almost certain death by escaping an IRA interrogation squad, common sense should have dictated that he would settle down under a new identity and have nothing more to do with Northern Ireland. But like many other past informers, Martin is a moth drawn to a flame, who quite clearly enjoys chatting to people who know a bit about the troubles and who relishes the celebrity and recognition which comes from media exposure.

When I first met Martin he was looking for money as he didn't believe he had been compensated adequately for the injuries he suffered escaping from the IRA. But at the time *Spotlight* had neither the cash nor the inclination to pay for a follow-up to the *Inside Story* programme. Nevertheless I travelled across to Scotland to meet him and we spent a day driving around the countryside and eating fish and chips, whilst I made frantic notes of his person-by-person rundown of the Belfast IRA. Despite *Spotlight*'s failure to make a programme, Martin continued to keep in touch and in the succeeding years he did quite a few interviews with me – without the payment of any cash – on intelligence and IRA-related stories. Shortly after the IRA called its ceasefire in 1994 Martin was on the phone demanding to know if people like him – living in hiding – could now return to Northern Ireland. A couple of days later I met one of the men who Martin said had abducted him for interrogation. 'So how's your friend Marty?' he asked me. 'He wants to come back then, does he?' One look at his expression made clear that in the IRA's eyes Martin McGartland's crimes had been neither forgiven nor forgotten. Not long afterwards Martin's mother received a funeral mass card in the post dedicated to Martin and signed by 'all his old friends in Crumlin Road jail'.

The nineties saw a series of informers and agents like Martin McGartland deciding to put their heads above the parapet. But these 'touts', as they are called in Belfast slang, were very different characters. Seán O'Callaghan, a former member of the IRA's southern command, was undoubtedly the most cerebral. Previously steeped in Irish republican ideology, he experienced a 'road to Damascus'-type conversion and made a 180-degree turn to a position where he decided Sinn Féin and the IRA were nothing more than fascists. His arguments now echoed those of the most trenchant critics of republicanism, such as Conor Cruise O'Brien and Ruth Dudley Edwards. Eventually O'Callaghan started advising the Orange Order on how to win the propaganda war against the IRA. It reminded me of Robert Frost's couplet: 'I never dared be radical when young/For fear it would make me conservative when old.'

Eamon Collins, who set his boss in the customs service up for murder, had a more ambiguous relationship with republicanism. He had cracked under interrogation and named his IRA colleagues but then recanted his confession and was released from jail as a judge ruled the statement had been forced out of him. Some whom he had named, however, remained behind bars so Collins's relations with the IRA were fraught. He had to leave his home town Newry for some years, then returned and decided to write his own book, *Killing Rage*, about his IRA career. Unlike O'Callaghan, Collins had a lasting respect both for Irish republican ideals and for the leaders of Sinn Féin, especially Gerry Adams. But he had nothing but contempt for his erstwhile colleagues in the IRA around Newry whom he portrayed in his book as a bunch of thugs and drunks. They, in return, simply loathed him.

After interviewing Eamon Collins for *Newsnight* in Milltown cemetery in Belfast I gave him a lift back to Newry. All the way he regaled me about other informers and ex-IRA men, none of whom he held in especially high regard. Like some journalists who never tire of running down their colleagues, Collins was a former terrorist sensitive about his place in the pecking order of former terrorists. As I drove and listened I couldn't help contrasting Collins, with his frenetic impassioned delivery and his fascination with republican ideology, with Martin McGartland. Martin was once asked on TV who exactly Pádraig Pearse was. He paused then hazarded a guess that Pearse, the leader of the 1916 rebellion, might have sold ice cream. McGartland and Collins were two very different characters united by a shared past and a shared fear. I dropped Eamon Collins at the edge of his estate after driving past the point where he said some of his ex-comrades had tried to kill him by running him over in a car. Bearing out the notion that so many people in his predicament found it impossible to stay away from home despite the obvious danger, Collins insisted on living in the area where he had been attacked, and where his family home was later burned by arsonists. In 1999 Collins was found bludgeoned and stabbed to death on a road not far from the spot where I left him off the year before. People from the area shunned his funeral service and the family said that even the local priest had proved reluctant to call. Such was the high price exacted from Eamon Collins for publicly ridiculing the local IRA warlords.

Martin McGartland knew that trying to return to his area of west Belfast would be tantamount to signing his own death warrant. When his call for a safe passage home went unanswered he stayed on in his new home in the north-east of England. He did return to attend a court case at Lisburn Magistrates' Court in which he was suing the RUC over the level of compensation he had been given after suffering serious injuries escaping the IRA. As he stood up in the dock to testify, the whole court building shook with a loud explosion.

Understandably Martin thought the IRA was going to extra-special lengths to get its revenge. In fact the target was the army's headquarters at Lisburn and the bombing in October 1996 marked the first return to IRA violence in Northern Ireland itself after the breakdown of the organisation's 1994 ceasefire.

As I was writing this book a friend phoned me from across the Atlantic to tell me Martin had been shot several times at close range whilst in the garden of his home. Although it appeared touch-and-go for several hours, his condition stabilised and he pulled through. Martin is the proverbial cat with nine lives. I hope for his and his family's sake he holds on to at least one of them.

17

Sins of the Father

WINTER 1991–SUMMER 1994

It was one of those moments when you see your career and your reputation disappearing before your eyes. For a while it looked as though it would scupper the film we were editing for that week too. The news agencies were reporting that the authorities at Full Sutton high-security jail in Yorkshire had just foiled an attempted IRA prison escape. The would-be escapee had been jailed for thirty years for his part in the IRA's campaign in England. No name and few other details had been revealed.

Our film looked at the question of prisoners held in English or Scottish jails who wanted to be transferred back to Northern Ireland to be closer to their families. A couple of these prisoners were loyalists but the vast majority were republicans. As a case study we had followed one IRA prisoner's wife and children making the difficult trip across to Yorkshire. We knew we would have some difficulties selling anything on this subject to a sizeable section of our audience whose view would be that such prisoners deserved everything they got. However, Teresa McComb proved an excellent central character: full of life and vitality, as sympathetic as any IRA prisoner's wife was likely to be to our audience and as hassled as any mother would be with two small children in tow on an apparently endless journey. The family spent the best part of a day getting to Full Sutton jail in order to spend two hours 'quality time' with their father. Then it was a night in a bed and breakfast followed by a day returning home.

When I rifled through my comprehensive list of prisoners seeking transfer to Northern Ireland, though, there was only one republican inmate serving thirty years in Full Sutton – Teresa's husband Damien. We had accompanied Teresa across in the plane to Leeds, then overland to Full Sutton. We had been with her right up until the moment when she stepped through the prison gates. The image of little Teresa carrying an apparently huge holdall bag into the jail flashed before my eyes. What had bulged that bag out so much – a rope ladder, or a cake with a file hidden inside? I knew that no real responsibility could rest with us, as once she stepped over the threshold it was up to the prison staff to search the visitors for a high-risk inmate. Nevertheless, the tabloids could have had a field day. 'Prison staff were distracted by the presence of a BBC Northern Ireland camera crew', 'The IRA plotted its most audacious attempt at a jailbreak in years – with the BBC in tow' … the potential headlines floated through my head.

The jail referred all enquiries to the Home Office, but in arranging our filming trip the preceding week I had had extensive dealings with an official at Full Sutton. For an anxious couple of hours, I waited for him to return my repeated calls. Eventually he rang back.

'I don't want to know the name of the would-be escapee, and I don't want you to tell me anything for us to report in the news,' I explained. 'I just want to know, are we in the clear? Is it our man? We will have to pull the programme if it is.'

'Relax,' he replied, 'it's not Damien McComb.'

Then why wasn't the prisoner in question on my list of those seeking transfer to Ireland?

'Our escapee isn't looking for a transfer,' the official explained. 'He is, would you believe it, an English IRA man.'

Relieved, we returned to editing. Our reputations and our next programme remained intact. Damien McComb had been caught red-handed digging up an arms cache in December 1989. The IRA had buried the cache under a rickety signpost on a path which ran along the Pembrokeshire coast. When the post was replaced police officers discovered bomb timers and mercury tilt switches for booby traps, and in another cache a short distance away they uncovered rifles, handguns, grenades and Semtex explosive. They decided to keep the scene of the finds under surveillance and forty-two days later their patience was rewarded when Damien McComb and Liam Ó Dhuibhir came to dig the caches up. The two were arrested by armed police and put on trial at the Old Bailey. In court Damien McComb described himself as an Irish nationalist opposed to violence who had been tricked into retrieving the cache. But the judge rejected his arguments, giving him a thirty-year sentence for conspiring to cause explosions.

Knowing a film on the topic of prisoner transfers would prove unpalatable for many, I was quite tough in my questioning of Teresa McComb. How could she ask for generosity from the authorities when her husband's potential victims would have been shown no clemency by the IRA? As the wife of a bomber, who had presumably spent long periods travelling away from home, surely she had known something, surely she bore some responsibility? Teresa shook her head, insisting 'That's not true, not true, it wasn't like that.'

Although the families portrayed their case as purely about making visits easier, it was also true that paramilitary prisoners in Northern Ireland jails had a much more comfortable life. The legacy of the hunger strikes meant that republicans and loyalists virtually dictated the style of their lives within the Maze. There would obviously be a lot more support for an IRA prisoner in a block shared with his counterparts than in an English jail where many inmates would have no time for bombers. The suspicion also remained that the government, seeking to deter the IRA from mounting attacks in England, had a clear aim in mind in not seeking to improve the conditions in which those convicted of bombing Britain were held. The republicans called the prisoners 'political hostages' but maybe for a government concerned about protecting the financial heart of the City of London a tough line made sense. The Conservative MP Terry Dicks, always good for a punchy quote, told us he didn't give a damn about terrorist prisoners or their families and the keys should simply be thrown away. One caller to the BBC the next day agreed, saying those responsible for making the *Spotlight* film were IRA-lovers, who should be sacked or shot or both. But the fact that this was an isolated response showed that most viewers recognised the report had been balanced.

We interviewed prison governors and probation officers who pointed up the absurdity of keeping inmates in English jails which were filled to overflowing rather than transferring them to Northern Ireland prisons which had plenty of spare capacity. We talked to other prisoners' relatives predictably echoing Teresa McComb's plea for jail visits to be made easier. But the most unlikely advocate of reform turned out to be a man never accused of being soft on terrorism – the DUP leader Ian Paisley. Dr Paisley would have been more than happy if those convicted of IRA murders were sent to meet their maker. But in the absence of capital punishment he believed family bonds were important and prisoners' children and relatives should not be punished for their loved one's crimes. It was unfair, he argued, to deliberately put inmates in far-off prisons or move them around at short notice when relatives wanted to visit them. In biblical terms, of which Dr Paisley is especially fond, the sins of the father should not be visited upon the son. 'Every man must bear his own burden,' Dr Paisley told me, adding for good measure that he believed the Christian moral precept should be kept irrespective of whether the prisoner was a loyalist or a republican as 'a Roman Catholic mother's tears and a Protestant mother's tears for a son that has gone astray are no different'.

Ian Paisley's unexpected support and Teresa McComb's straightforward answers made the case for prison transfers compelling. But the most striking images we recorded were the faces of her two children John and Caoimhe as they wilted under the stress and strain of the long journey to see their father. Caoimhe bawled her way through much of the programme. She was too young to talk to on camera, but I did interview her eight-year-old brother. Just to check the volume of our recording I asked him what he wanted to do when he grew up. He replied that he wanted to be 'a policeman' in order to 'go out and catch bad people'. This was such an unexpected aspiration for a convicted IRA bomber's son that I kept it in the film just in order to confound viewers' preconceptions.

In the normal run of events John and Caoimhe would have had to visit their father in a succession of different English jails well into the twenty-first century. But, whilst it wasn't a well-known cause at the time *Spotlight* featured it, the campaign for prison transfers eventually succeeded. Despite the publication of internal Home Office reports recommending reform, the Conservative government proved slow to approve transfers. But within hours of the 1994 IRA ceasefire being called the notorious Brighton bomber Patrick Magee was sent to a jail in Northern Ireland. Eventually Damien McComb and dozens of other prisoners followed him. For Teresa, the *Spotlight* appearance wasn't her last performance on celluloid. Eagle-eyed cinemagoers can see her in *The Boxer*, the Jim Sheridan movie which tries to analyse some of the hardships of sustaining a relationship with someone behind bars.

18

An Accident of Birth

When you are reporting Northern Ireland to an English or foreign audience it's inevitable that you will end up concentrating on the troubles and all the turmoil they have caused. But as the broadcasters making programmes for the local audience can tell you, for the majority of people in Northern Ireland life is, just like anywhere else in Western Europe, all about going to work, raising a family, ensuring your children get a decent education and trying, in between times, to be happy. People often ask me why these aspects of life don't make it onto the news, and I normally reply that you don't often see items about what a nice day it's been in Cleethorpes either − meaning that news is, by definition, something out of the ordinary. But in the same way that Radio Cleethorpes should − if it exists − reflect the life of its own community, so those pro- grammes intended for a local Northern Irish audience must tackle more than just the old old story if they are to capture the attention of local listeners and viewers.

Not every Northern Irish family's life is dictated by the troubles, and not every problem they encounter can be put down to politics. Suffering does not only come out of the barrel of a gun. Some misfortunes may befall a family irrespective of whether they are Protestant or Catholic, rich or poor. That might be a terrible truism but it was one which I had cause to think about one day as I strolled past Belfast City Hall and came across a caravan covered with posters and people collecting for charity. This is a regular spot for 'flag day' collectors and I gave it only passing attention when a board listing a long collection of 'genetic diseases' caught my eye. The caravan belonged to the Northern Ireland branch of a small charity called 'The Research Trust for Metabolic Diseases in Children'.

The reason I paid any attention was not that I am especially charitable − I am no more and no less of a 'do-gooder' than most. But this particular cause touched a personal chord. When I was born I inherited an intolerance towards sugars. The state of research into the condition was not especially advanced in the 1960s. All I knew was that it was the same thing my eldest brother Tim had, it was very rare, it meant I had to avoid sweets and the doctors gave it a very long name, 'Genetic Carbohydrate Intolerance'. This was medical-speak for 'you got it from your parents and it means you can't have certain carbohydrates'. Tim and I both demonstrated an enviable ability to chomp through bags of chips, so the definition wasn't especially helpful. Further research at the Churchill Hospital in Oxford established that if sugar was put in a glass of milk I would spew it all over the nurse. But I could eat tomato sandwiches provided there weren't too many of them. Tim and I decided that we had either 'Sucrose Intolerance' or 'Fructose Intolerance'. Yes, our parents were to blame, if you could put it like that, but neither of them had any problems eating sweet food. Rather they were both carriers who each had one affected gene which they had passed on to us. The statistical chances of two carriers of such a condition becoming a couple are very slight, whilst the odds of them having a child with the full intolerance are one in four, which explains our relatively rare status. The doctors told my mother they could count only ten similar cases in England.

There on the side of the caravan, however, I discovered in bold letters the words 'Hereditary Fructose Intolerance', one of the two possible conditions I have. This surprised me, as I was unaware of any charity covering this esoteric subject. Frankly if you share my condition you are not in need of anyone holding out a begging bowl on your behalf. All it meant was that, as a child, my mother substituted sausage rolls for birthday cake. Otherwise it did not prove a great obstacle in life at all. Hereditary Fructose Intolerance was, however, one of a large number of conditions for which the Research Trust for Metabolic Diseases in Children provided an umbrella group. My old colleague Bruce Batten, who'd moved from *Spotlight* to making television and radio documentaries, was keen for me to make occasional offbeat programmes for Radio Ulster. So I decided to investigate what might have happened if, rather than passing on an unusual but unproblematic condition, my parents had given me a different genetic code.

That's how I found myself in the sitting room of Aidan and Terri Lagan in their home in Derry. Like my parents, the Lagans were carriers of a genetic abnormality. Like my parents, they had two children, a boy and a girl, entirely unaffected by the condition. But then Terri gave birth to her second daughter,

Catherine, and the trouble started. When she was born, in medical jargon, she 'failed to thrive'. At five months old things got dramatically worse. Catherine collapsed and experienced heart failure. She was transferred to the Royal Belfast Hospital for Sick Children, where the Lagans were very fortunate to get biochemist Ray Moore on the case. After what he described as some rather hair-raising, rapid deductions about Catherine's symptoms, Ray Moore identified an intolerance to long chain fats as a possible diagnosis. At the time there were only around twenty other children in the world who were documented as having the condition.

With the help of a strict non-fat diet Catherine Lagan developed into a lively, bouncy little girl, three years old at the time I met her. However, her condition was more problematic than my sugar intolerance. At night she had to put up with a tube inserted into her nose supplying her with a constant drip-feed of no-fat milk substitute. Because of her diet her calorie intake during the day was not as good as other children of her age. The doctors feared that if she fasted for as long as eight hours she would start breaking down her body fats to burn for energy.

Despite these fears, Catherine appeared to tackle life head-on. An avid Michael Jackson fan, she was, according to her mother, 'a very special little girl, very talkative, very lively and very bright and we have an awful lot to be thankful for. We think how black the picture was at one stage and when you see her now, it's light years away.' When I visited Northern Ireland in the summer of 1999 I checked up on her progress. Terri told me that Catherine, by then nine years old, was getting on okay. She still needed to be fed overnight and had bouts of ill health but, by and large, life had been good. Michael Jackson had, however, been abandoned in favour of Ronan Keating.

Although Catherine Lagan's condition is very rare, I found that she was by no means the only child in Northern Ireland battling a genetic condition or disease. The Research Trust brought together Protestant and Catholic families scattered throughout the North doing their best to cope with rare illnesses of varying severity. In Maghera the Reverend Norman Brown's teenage sons Stephen and Russell suffered from Fabrees disease, which silted up their circulatory systems restricting them in various ways, making them walk around like old men. In Cookstown Martina Leecock's children Laura and Stephen both had the incurable degenerative condition Batten's disease. Despite Martina's loving care Laura died just before her seventh birthday. Stephen required round-the-clock care when I visited the Leecock home.

Whilst the metabolic conditions affecting the various families I met were different, some of the problems they experienced were similar. The very rarity of the conditions meant that getting a correct diagnosis and proper treatment could take some time. Doctors would often be stumped at first by symptoms they never usually came across. Once a diagnosis was made, suitable medicines might prove expensive or might simply not exist. Pharmaceutical companies will never tire of searching for a cure for the common cold because there are so many sufferers who will pay good money for any drug shown to do the job. But when you are talking about a condition which afflicts ten or twenty children within the UK, funding and interest is harder to generate. One of the areas which the Research Trust for Metabolic Diseases in Children wanted to highlight was the subject of 'orphan drugs', medicines which an individual researcher might have stumbled across which could prove vital for treating a rare condition, but which did not have the economic potential for drug manufacturers to develop by running further trials.

Some of these difficulties have been eased by new technology. The development of the Internet means that people in rare groups can contact each other across the globe. The Northern Ireland branch of the Research Trust has now established useful links with American families whose children suffer similar conditions. Apart from providing mutual support the improved information network means diagnoses tend to be made more quickly. Progress in drug development has also meant that new treatments are being discovered – despite the economic difficulties in marketing them. The Fabrees disease which afflicted the Brown children in Maghera, for instance, is now responding well to a new drug.

Looking to the future, developments in genetic engineering might help the treatment of children like Catherine Lagan. The term has all sorts of sinister connotations of mad scientists producing clones, but for David Weir, a Northern Irish man whose daughter Deborah died of the metabolic condition Lees disease, the process holds out some prospect for hope. David doesn't want to choose whether or not his children have blond hair and blue eyes, but he told me that if it were possible to engineer such conditions out of children or use the latest technology to develop better treatments for toddlers like Deborah then he thought this could be nothing but a good thing.

Talking to families around Northern Ireland like the Lagans, the Leecocks, the Browns and the Weirs was a humbling experience. I have been dealt an unusual genetic hand, but not one which handicaps me in any way. Other children all over Northern Ireland and all over the world are struggling with a much more difficult fate. I concluded my Radio Ulster programme about them with the words of Martina Leecock, nursing a son who she knew would never grow up.

'I suppose I have made Stephen the biggest priority of my life, both my husband and I,' she told me, 'but that's our choice to do that and we want to do it, and we do it with love because Stephen means everything to us. He is everything to us and we can cope with him, even through the bad times, but I don't know how we'll cope without him, and I just hope that's a long way away.'

Since my programme was broadcast Stephen has died, and Martina is using her painful personal experience of losing two children to become a 'befriender', bringing what comfort she can to other bereaved parents.

19

The Advocate

I hadn't been in Belfast many months before I met Barra McGrory, a young solicitor who dealt with a raft of criminal cases. We hit it off immediately and remain firm friends. I once gave Barra a lift home after having a drink. I jumped in the car, checked my mirror and pulled away then made an immediate right turn. Out of the dark a policeman brandishing a sub-machine gun stepped into the road and invited me to stop and get out of my car. With a sinking feeling I realised I had turned right on a no right turn just beside a police station which the RUC officer was guarding. To compound the error I had failed to turn my lights on. In the passenger seat, my solicitor advised me to 'plead ignorance'. After several accurate forays up and down the white line in the middle of the road I persuaded the RUC officer that I was below the legal limit, guilty of stupidity but not drunkenness.

Several weeks later I met up with Barra in the Kitchen Bar in the centre of town. He was having lunch with the senior partner in his legal practice, who also happened to be his father Paddy McGrory, known as 'P. J.' to everyone in the Belfast courts. Grey-haired and suitably distinguished when up before a magistrate, P. J. had a glint in his eye which gave away his love of devilment, a good story and a better punchline. Over a bowl of Irish stew he regaled us with what had been happening in court that day.

In court or in the pub, P. J. was the kind of character you could listen to for ever without tiring. A green Irish nationalist, he had played an important role in the legal and political worlds throughout the troubles. But with his rich Belfast accent he would recount anecdotes which often harked back to an earlier age, that of the forties and fifties when 'peelers' chased the light-fingered fraternity across shadowy streets, and murders were almost unheard of. Paddy grew up on the Falls Road and developed a love for amateur drama. Fascinated by stories of his uncle, John Skeffington, a well-known lawyer and advocate in the Dungannon area, he decided the law was the career for him. Paddy's performing instincts drew him towards advocacy, standing up in court holding forth. As a young solicitor his only opportunity to do that came in Belfast Magistrates' Court where he soon earned a name for himself defending those charged in criminal cases.

Paddy represented one client, Jimmy Cullen, who prided himself on knowing the law better than his solicitor. He carried a copy of the 1916 Larceny Act wherever he went and if P.J. gave him any advice he would often whip the act out and try to contradict him. One of the charges brought against Jimmy Cullen was the theft of the criminal lawyer's bible, an 'Archbold', from a second-hand book shop. Jimmy had wanted it to advise younger burglars. Another client was a con artist known as 'the Mouse' McAllister because of his mousy looks. Falling on hard times, he once took to breaking windows just to get in from the cold. The Resident Magistrate commented, 'Mouse, you're looking very, very bad, you really ought to be inside so you can build yourself up.' He agreed, so the magistrate handed down a sentence of one month's imprisonment. The Mouse objected that this was too long, saying he could be fixed up in a fortnight. The magistrate relented, changing his sentence to 'fourteen days by consent', which was the only occasion on which P.J. had witnessed the judiciary and the prisoner reach an agreement on the length of a sentence.

Paddy told me the first murder charge he had to defend involved a man from the Shankill Road accused of killing his wife with a poker. The couple were separated but every Friday the husband would visit the wife to give her maintenance money. In typically droll fashion P.J. described how 'on this occasion they were in a friendly mood, so he went out and bought lemonade and chips. They sat on the edge of the bed and consumed the lemonade and chips which appeared to have some hitherto unknown aphrodisiac qualities, as a result of which they made love. But unfortunately at some stage she cried out a name which wasn't her husband's and infuriated by this he jumped up and seized a poker, killing her by striking her with it.'

The Lord Chief Justice Lord MacDermott summed up the scenario with the words: 'In the excess of her passion, she cried out the name of her lover thereby infuriating the defendant.' It's hard to imagine nowadays, but the jury at the time decided to find the accused guilty of manslaughter, not murder, and he received a sentence of only four years. P.J. recalled it as 'the only crime passionel I have ever dealt with in Belfast ... no more need be said about his poor wife except when I contemplated a psychiatric defence for my client, the psychiatrist opened up his report by saying the strange thing about the case was that the man hadn't murdered this lady long before ... so her reputation wasn't of the highest.' Not an observation one can imagine a psychiatrist making in this day and age when domestic violence is viewed rather more seriously in Belfast as elsewhere.

Many of Paddy's stories were redolent of a bygone era, but when the troubles broke out in the late sixties his criminal practice was in the thick of the action. On one occasion whilst out doing his job he walked into a riot and was arrested along with a crowd of suspects, and loaded into the back of a lorry. By the time the lorry reached an RUC station P. J. was representing them all. As the violence worsened he grew used to dealing with clients charged with shootings and bombings, murders and mass murders. The firm was involved in numerous notorious cases such as the La Mon hotel bombing and a number of the so-called supergrass trials. Although Paddy defended loyalists as well as republicans his Falls Road background meant he got a lot of IRA and other republican cases. He represented Gerry Adams when he was charged with IRA membership in 1978. Some in the security forces identified Paddy McGrory and a small group of criminal lawyers as the 'enemy', whilst P. J. would counter that he was merely carrying out his professional duty despite a system which he believed had been distorted by the introduction of Diplock no-jury courts.

Although he was a familiar figure in Belfast during the seventies, it wasn't until the late eighties that Paddy McGrory hit the international headlines. The case took place far away from his usual Belfast haunts in the Mediterranean colony of Gibraltar. Three IRA members plotting to bomb a military band in the colony were shot dead by the SAS. The families of the IRA members approached Paddy McGrory to represent them at the inquest. Suspicious that the SAS might have opened fire first and asked questions later, P. J. agreed to represent them without a fee. If legal titles mean anything, Paddy, as a solicitor rather than a barrister, should have been punching beyond his weight. But in fact he put up such a fight against the best advocates the British government could afford that even the Senior Treasury Counsel Sir John Laws paid tribute to him as 'a man of great charm, of great talent as an advocate. He has an excellent way with the facts and with the jury. I think he was an advocate who could teach a lot of barristers a few lessons.'

Despite his skill in scoring points with the jury, P. J. failed to persuade three of the eleven jurors to find that the SAS killings were not lawful, an outcome which would have rendered the proceedings invalid. Instead, with only two jurors dissenting, the inquest returned a verdict of lawful killing, much to Mrs Thatcher's relief. But when Paddy returned to Belfast he found that not everyone was impressed by his skilful advocacy. He started receiving threatening cards and telephone calls. Then in January 1989 the Home Office Minister Douglas Hogg told a parliamentary committee that some Northern Ireland solicitors were unduly sympathetic to the IRA. The following month the loyalist Ulster Freedom Fighters, a cover name for the UDA, murdered the criminal solicitor Pat Finucane, with whom I had chatted together with Paddy McGrory inside the Belfast Magistrates' Court the year before. P.J. had brushed off the earlier threats. But now he became more worried, especially after a police officer warned him that a document had been discovered listing all his movements.

The stress of the Gibraltar inquest and the threats to his life put a further strain on Paddy McGrory's health, which had not been particularly robust. He had already undergone a coronary bypass in 1982. In 1990 he had to travel to the United States for a second complex bypass operation. At one stage the doctors told Paddy's wife Phyllis that her husband wouldn't be going home. P.J. experienced an 'out-of-body' sensation, where he saw himself lying on the operating table and heard hushed voices talking urgently about death. It suddenly dawned on him that he was in terrible danger and that he had to put up a bit of a fight if he was going to make it. Paddy McGrory was altered by the experience, which he told me 'certainly had the effect of making me more convinced of the existence of an afterlife and a supreme being, not in a personalised God sense, but in a different sense. In a way it's been a comfort because I feel now that if I die, which I suppose could happen in my condition at any time, without the benefit of the loyalists wasting powder and shot on me, there is not a nothingness, there is something to go to.'

After the operation P.J. re-evaluated his priorities, passing more of the day-to-day running of the criminal practice over to his son Barra, and spending more time at his homes in north Belfast and Donegal, alternatively picking up a *bodhrán*, which he played expertly, or swapping yet more stories over a pint. Yet his mind remained far too active for him to contemplate a complete retirement. Paddy made no secret of his Irish nationalism, indeed he described himself as broadly republican with the clarification that he did not believe in physical force, largely because it had not worked. In 1992 he told me that 'lawyers by their whole training and tradition clearly see all disputes as being possible to settle by dialogue ... I think all dialogue is useful and indeed absolutely vital. It doesn't matter how ineffectual it seems at the time or even if it fails, all dialogue is useful. This idea that certain elements should be left out because they are disliked by certain people is just such an absurdity that one wonders that intelligent human beings should indulge in such a fantasy.'

Back in the seventies it had been strongly rumoured that Paddy McGrory worked as an intermediary between the IRA and the government to negotiate a ceasefire. In 1992 he told me coyly, 'Unless this is to become an interview of the seven veils in which all is to be revealed, let's put it this way, a lawyer gets in this country a number of assignments outside of the usual and when you get them you take them on.' In fact P.J. did act as an intermediary both in the contacts that led to Gerry Adams's release from internment and the IRA's subsequent 1972 ceasefire. During the truce itself Paddy continued to play a key role. He was forever having to excuse himself from court to take messages from his wife. The magistrates and Paddy's clients could have been forgiven for believing that Phyllis McGrory had become unusually demanding. In fact she was fielding constant calls to the McGrorys' home telephone from both the IRA and the army complaining that the other side had breached the ceasefire. By not taking calls at his office, Paddy ensured his role as a reference point for both sides remained secret, but that meant Phyllis jumping into the family car and driving into town whenever there was an incident.

In the nineties P.J. saw another opportunity to get involved. He held extensive consultations with Gerry Adams on constitutional and legal matters. In a background briefing he fashioned the arguments which he believed the Sinn Féin President needed to persuade the IRA to call another ceasefire, writing:

> Only madmen make war for fun, and the republican struggle has been waged for a specific political purpose, and only because of the total failure of conventional politics to advance the Irish cause. I hold the view that armed action is unlikely to secure any significant political advance, and certainly nothing to compare in importance with the political achievements to date ... I believe that peace now will garner a rich harvest of support for the republican movement such as it has not known for decades ... I believe the tide is at the flood, and is beginning to ebb. This is the hour.

Paddy McGrory was criticised by some other lawyers for discussing his politics with me during a radio profile I made of him in 1992. But Paddy was a multifaceted man who sought to turn his undoubted gifts in a number of directions. In the autumn of his years he used his renowned skills at advocacy to advocate peace. A few months after his briefing paper was circulated Gerry Adams persuaded the IRA to call a ceasefire. Paddy lived to see the day, but died before the ceasefire was broken and then restored. At his funeral in Belfast just before Christmas 1994 the mourners included some of the most significant players in the peace process, such as Gerry Adams, Albert Reynolds and Father Alex Reid, there to pay tribute to P. J.'s contribution behind the scenes.

20

American Connections

AUTUMN 1990–AUTUMN 1994

In 1991 I received an invitation to my first awards presentation ceremony, a black tie dinner held at one of the function rooms inside Belfast's Europa hotel. The EMMA awards, organised by the *Belfast Telegraph* newspaper, were intended to reward the best in the interrelated worlds of Northern Ireland's media and entertainment. One of the *Spotlight* programmes on which I reported had been nominated in the 'best factual television programme' category, but whilst this earned me a right to a chicken dinner no one had winked at me and told me to prepare a few choice words for the presentation ceremony, which was broadcast by BBC Northern Ireland. So I adjusted my dickie bow and prepared to look suitably brave and noble as I applauded the winner.

The ethos of the whole event was all about boosting good, positive, upbeat images of Northern Ireland, so it would have been frankly a bit bizarre if my film, all about IRA gun-running, had taken a prize. When the results were announced by the compère, newsreader Martyn Lewis, a series about Irish writers and their roots took first place, and I clapped heartily both because that is the done thing and because, from the short clip shown on our screens, *Hidden Ground* looked a very worthy winner. Other winners included my friend and old housemate Marie Jones, who was named best actress, and that Belfast institution Van Morrison, deemed 'best local rock star' in a horribly uneven contest.

The film which took me to the awards dinner that night had been called 'The American Connection' − a title shamelessly plagiarised from the excellent book by former *Spotlight* producer Jack Holland. The film's central character, Richard Clark Johnson, appeared in some respects not entirely dissimilar to Van Morrison. He was stocky, thickset and uncommunicative. He was also a genius of sorts, although there the similarity ended. Johnson's sphere of excellence did not encompass the blues. Rather his colleagues viewed him as the archetypal nerd, who appeared to have no friends and no obvious interest outside work. Johnson, originally from Massachusetts, excelled as one of the most gifted electronics and radar experts in the United States. His skills won him work on high-profile projects like the Voyager space probe and the Stealth bomber. But he also put his expertise at the disposal of the IRA.

At *Spotlight* I developed a fondness for arms smuggling stories, whether they involved loyalists under arrest in Paris or IRA units under surveillance in the United States. Such tales might get reported in the headlines in their basic outline. But the news always left plenty for a current affairs programme to explore, investigating the intricacies of the plot, the breaks which had led the authorities to uncover it and the implications of the affair. In Johnson's case it all proved especially fertile territory. He had been living a double life for years, fulfilling top secret US defence contracts during the week, then toiling on the IRA's behalf at the weekends inside his own workshop at his parents' home in Harwich on Cape Cod. The radar engineer proved invaluable to the IRA in a little-reported cat-and-mouse game which the bombers were playing with the security forces, racing up the radio frequency in an effort to find wavelengths for remote control bombs which the army hadn't thought of jamming. Johnson assisted in the supply of transmitters working on a frequency used only in the United States. He also provided the IRA with microswitches for bombs, whilst his pièce de résistance consisted of a scheme to build a home-made missile capable of shooting down British helicopters over south Armagh by triggering a 'proximity fuse' whenever the rocket sensed it was close to its target.

The FBI caught up with Johnson by dint of a batch of letters discovered hidden in a gas cooker in Ireland, listening across nine hundred telephone lines in the United States, rummaging through luggage, placing a microphone inside Johnson's car and finally bugging a number of picnic tables where they believed Johnson intended to meet his IRA contact. The benefit of all this bugging, from a broadcaster's point of view, was that the FBI recorded reams of audio tapes of its suspect discussing in endless detail the technicalities of bomb making and the rightness of the IRA's cause. FBI agents Dick Watson and Brendan Cleary and US prosecutor Richard Stearns put their vast collection of tapes and photographs at our disposal. During one lengthy conversation with a Dundalk IRA man, Martin Quigley, Johnson talked with the animation of a teacher about how the IRA had to get its volunteers young and convince them that the apparently mundane business of signal intelligence – monitoring the army's communications and jamming broadcasts – wasn't as boring as it appeared, but was vital for the goal of military victory. 'The American Connection' benefited by being able to let the viewers hear the principal players incriminate themselves on air.

When we broadcast our programme Johnson had already been sentenced to ten years in jail for his part in the conspiracy to supply the IRA with arms. But he remained out on bail staying at his parents' home on Cape Cod, pending an appeal. His lawyer did not respond to my telephone requests for an interview, so we decided to call at the Johnsons' home, to do one of those 'doorsteps' I have a long and ignoble record of fluffing. This one turned out, like the FBI's bugging, to be good for sound but not for vision. As a dog barked at me through the lattice of the front door, Johnson told me through a gauze grille that, no, he did not have a lifelong burning ambition to speak to the BBC and would we leave his parents' property now. I rather pathetically asked that if there was no exclusive interview on offer, could we perhaps film his famous electronic workshop. 'There is no workshop,' he insisted.

We retreated to the pavement and took a few more pictures of the house. But at this point a police car roared up, responding to a phone call from Johnson's parents, and two officers got out, guns at the ready. Discovering we were 'aliens', they made us stand to be searched beside our van.

'But sorry, officer, what is it that we are supposed to have done?' I asked.

'Buddy,' came the reply, 'you been doing what you ain't s'posed to be doing.' Looking nervously towards our rather large driver, attired in a 'Blues Brothers'- style suit and thin black tie, my interrogator asked me, 'Who's the geek in the zoot suit?'

It looked as though we might have to spend a little time explaining ourselves at the local cop shop, but then our American producer Jay Jones dug out his passport and proved beyond question that he was no 'alien'. This appeared to bring the police back on side. Eventually we struck up a rapport with the officers, one of whom had flown helicopters in Vietnam and who didn't seem too impressed by someone using his basement to design missiles to shoot down the 'Brits'.

'Stay on the pavement, buddy, and work away. Just don't walk down his path again.'

'The American Connection' was my first working visit to the USA, but by no means my last. We also made 'The Doherty Dilemma' about the IRA man Joe Doherty in jail in New York. In January 1993 I tried to persuade my editor Andrew Colman to send me again to the States to make a film about the likely impact of the incoming President, Bill Clinton, on the White House's policy towards Northern Ireland. Andrew looked sceptically at this request for another junket, arguing that Clinton might have said one or two things about Ireland whilst he had been courting the 'Green vote' but the place was sure to slip down his list of priorities once he took over power. Fortunately for me, other reporters' projects ran into difficulties and delays, and as the start of the next series loomed we did not have a first film. Reluctantly Andrew decided to go with 'The Clinton Factor', a programme made on not much more than a single day's frantic filming in Washington at the time of the President's inauguration. Despite the hectic schedule the film looked almost respectable, featuring video of the new President talking about Ireland on New York Cable TV, the first time any comments of his on Northern Ireland had been transmitted on the other side of the Atlantic.

I also incorporated some off-the-record comments from a contact I happened to know who was an 'FOB', an old Friend of Bill's. He assured me that despite some tensions with the Major government and some election-minded statements, Clinton's instincts on Ireland would be either to avoid the subject or to take advice from the established Anglophile policymakers in the State Department. How wrong those lines of script turned out to be.

My last *Spotlight* before changing jobs also involved a trip across the Atlantic, this time pursuing an arms plot which had been played out in Arizona and Florida. Although the prosecutors weren't quite as helpful as they had been in Massachusetts, we were able to put our hands on a fair bit of striking video and audio surveillance evidence. The trial of the Tucson Six was a complex affair – the evidence against the majority of those put in the dock was too flimsy to make a case. But a couple of the accused, Seamus Moley and Kevin McKinley, who had already been convicted of trying to buy a Stinger surface to air missile in Florida, were clearly involved in a well-funded IRA arms purchasing operation.

Whilst in 'The American Connection' the narrative had been a paean of praise to the thoroughness and ingenuity of the FBI's investigation, this time our research led us to be more critical of apparent lapses in the US authorities' judgement. In Florida US agents targeted McKinley and Moley in a 'sting' operation, offering to sell them a missile. In the course of the meetings to set this deal up the IRA men told them they were just about to buy a batch of two and a half thousand commercial detonators. Detonators are small, relatively inoffensive-looking items, not unlike large electrical fuses. But in the wrong hands they can be lethal. Perhaps because the sale of a surface to air missile seemed more high-profile and more glamorous or perhaps because that was simply the way the 'sting' had been arranged, the US agents appeared to take no action to stop the purchase of the detonators and their eventual transportation across the Atlantic. There the new batch of reliable commercial detonators was put to use by the IRA immediately. The detonators were found on massive bombs defused in north London, the Docklands and south Belfast in the early nineties. The best guess is that they were used in most if not all of the IRA's so-called 'spectaculars' around this time.

The Tucson trial represented an elaborate attempt by the US authorities to close the stable door after the horse had bolted. One defence lawyer whom I interviewed, Bates Butler, went to town on this point, telling me that 'there is credible evidence that detonators were purchased and the US government let that happen and didn't try to stop it. They clearly had the resources to do it, and if in fact the detonators were used then and there was damage that damage would not have occurred had the government been vigilant and had the government taken some action to stop events that could have been stopped if they had cared. I just think they didn't give a damn at that point.'

Whilst supporters of the Tucson Six would have applauded Bates Butler's full-frontal assault on the US authorities, they were not best pleased by my eventual film, which concentrated on a bit by bit reconstruction of Kevin McKinley's and Seamus Moley's activities and a bit of Moley family history for good measure. Seamus, an outwardly affable character who appeared to be flourishing in the Arizona sunshine, had a brother called Brendan who blew himself up whilst constructing a bomb in south Armagh in the late eighties. Seamus professed to be in favour of the continuing peace process, but – on his lawyer's instructions – did not grant me an interview. However, the audio tapes at my disposal left me in little doubt about his underlying commitment to the IRA.

I sent a tape off to the defence lawyers and did not expect to hear from the Tucson Six again. A couple of years later, however, I found myself covering a triumphal visit by the Sinn Féin President Gerry Adams to an Irish American bar in New York's Bronx. After being granted a hero's welcome Adams made a rousing speech before being escorted past a seething mass of fans. I told my cameraman to stick by my shoulder whilst I 'vox-popped' the audience on what they thought of their leader. I had been at this only a few seconds when I found myself facing a handful of the Tucson Six and their supporters. Whilst Seamus Moley's and Kevin McKinley's involvement had been clear to all, the evidence against their co-accused had been circumstantial and the prosecution failed, as I had predicted in my film. Pat Moley, another of Seamus's brothers, and his friends remained less than impressed by my report. Mentioning his family's history amounted to 'guilt by association'. Concentrating on the detonators and missiles, rather than the deficiencies in the prosecution case against the co-accused, constituted proof positive of my Brit propaganda mouthpiece status.

I replied that I had to call the story as I had seen it. Somebody had shipped the IRECO commercial detonators from Arizona which had been used to blow sizeable slabs of Northern Ireland and England to smithereens. Seamus Moley and Kevin McKinley had been convicted by their own words. I had met them all at a time when they were protesting their innocence in a court case, but I suspected that in other circumstances Seamus and Kevin might have told me of their belief in the justness of the IRA's war.

I looked around at the massed ranks of Sinn Féin-sympathising drinkers. Now was not the time for a Brit journalist to engage in a strenuous exchange of views with a group of Irish American republican heroes. Fortunately, after having made their points, the Tucson Six did not want to prolong the conversation either. Strangely, they declined my invitation to record a quick reaction to Gerry Adams's speech.

21

Network News

Around the end of 1993 my friend Gary Duffy, then one of two BBC Ireland Correspondents, signalled to the BBC network news management that he wanted a change. As correspondent it had been Gary's task to meet the non-stop demands of BBC London's news and current affairs programmes, especially on the radio. Denis Murray, formerly BBC Northern Ireland's political correspondent, took the lead role on the television. For both correspondents the job was high-profile, but incredibly demanding. Gary appeared to be forever getting dragged from his sleep to charge off to some far-flung part of Northern Ireland covering overnight bombings and shootings. He was on call twenty-four hours a day with no time off for good behaviour.

I had considered going for the Correspondent's job when Gary got it, but never applied. It wasn't the fear of hard work which put me off, but stage fright. I had grown up in a family which listened to Radio 4. Programmes like *Today* with Brian Redhead and John Timpson or *The World at One* presented by Gordon Clough filled me with a sense of awe. Broadcasting to the viewers and listeners in Northern Ireland no longer held any fears, but dealing with live on-air interrogation from the likes of these legends and their successors? I did not feel convinced I could do it.

I retreated into the warm cocoon of *Spotlight,* but you can have too much of a good thing. Four years into my stay there I knew I had lost the plot – I wasn't generating the story ideas I once had, and I suffered from too long a memory. When someone else put up a suggestion I tended to say, 'Didn't we do that three years ago?' I applied around for jobs with no success. Then Gary's job was advertised. It was time to screw up my courage and convince myself, and the 'board', the BBC's term for an interviewing panel, that I could handle the responsibility. The interview, when it took place, seemed a chapter of accidents. Word of the date reached me whilst I was making my IRA arms film in Florida. My plans had been to return from the work trip, switch flights at London, then head off directly to France for a week's holiday with friends. The date of the board meant that I would have to cut the holiday short, return to London and walk straight into the interview. Fate, I decided, was against me. However, when I arrived at the interview room everybody seemed extraordinarily pleased to see me. The panel had got a message that I had not been contacted in time to attend. Reluctantly, they had agreed to reconvene on a later date to see me. Just by turning up I had gained points, as they could get the whole business over with there and then.

Whilst I had a lot of Northern Ireland experience under my belt my work was entirely unknown in London. Some people therefore took a lot of persuading that I should be given a chance. But my old boss from the Belfast newsroom, Keith Baker, weighed in heavily on my side and the former Belfast correspondent Clive Ferguson also seemed willing to be convinced. They offered me a three-month attachment to see if I was up to the job. Clive and Keith later told me they both got calls from the overall boss of BBC News at this stage, the famously brusque Chris Cramer. Cramer barked down the phone, 'How dare you appoint to one of our most high-profile correspondencies somebody I have never even heard of?' Clive and Keith kept their fingers crossed that this wasn't a decision they would live to regret.

I spent a fortnight in London in 1994 trying to get the hang of national news and, on my first shift at television centre since my days as a trainee, I found myself leading the *Six O'Clock News*. The lead story was the bloody tribal genocide in Rwanda, but the satellite picture feeds from Africa were proving extremely unreliable. For that reason a correspondent had to compile a standby genocide story. The challenge consisted of finding pictures suitable for broadcast on British early evening screens. The BBC had strict guidelines about the use of dead bodies with gaping wounds – the international picture feeds offered by the news agencies were full of this kind of horrendous material. I especially remember one image of a little baby boy, who looked as perfect as a doll, except that just above his ears and eyes his head had been taken cleanly off with a machete. My reports consisted of lots of pictures of refugees and a few very distant pictures of bodies, with a script which tried to convey something of the horror of the scenes we were not showing.

Whilst the spell in the TV newsroom helped me get the hang once again of short reports compiled against tight deadlines, I retained the instincts of a long-form current affairs journalist. I returned to Belfast by way of Dublin where I gathered material for a feature which I sold to the *Today* programme on the increasing threat posed by loyalists to targets in the Irish Republic. Back in the Belfast newsroom I pored over hours of cassette tape dubbing off only the very best bits. I had honed it down to about half an hour of vital material when my new researcher, Cathy Grieve, offered to lend me a hand. 'Half an hour?' she blurted. 'The *Today* programme won't take any more than three and a half minutes absolute max. Here, let me at it . . .' I stared in terror as Cathy tore into my lovingly collected interviews with her razor blade, chopping off great lengths of tape at a time. 'Now that's more like it,' she pronounced. Even with her inestimable help it remained beyond midnight before we got out of there.

My promotion to national news correspondent coincided with two developments, one in the BBC, the other in Northern Ireland politics. Both trends served me well. So far as the BBC was concerned this was the time of its first venture into continuous news, the advent of the 'news and sport' medium wave network Radio Five. Meanwhile the political scene in Northern Ireland, which had so long seemed to be permanently frozen, showed signs of a possible thaw.

As a beast which lived off breaking news, Radio Five's hunger could never be fully satisfied. But this suited me fine as it gave me plenty of experience of live broadcasting. In its early days it really sounded like a newsroom on air with a team of young producers who seemed only too ready to throw out their preprepared schedule and go with the flow of any breaking story. Sometimes I would jump on the line without taking any time to tell them what was up and go straight through to the on-air studio. The listeners would learn the latest at exactly the same time as the presenter, who would say, 'We're joined now by our Ireland Correspondent, Mark Devenport, who has got a story . . . what's happening, Mark?'

This rough-and-ready approach gave the audience the impression that they were at the cutting edge, but it also had its pitfalls. As reports came in of an explosion near a public house in Downpatrick I resisted going on air because we still hadn't been able to establish exactly what had occurred. Eventually the pressure to go with something, even if I had to insert a lot of caveats, became too much. Initially it seemed unlikely the IRA would be behind the attack because a high-profile group of Irish Americans were in town talking peace and mounting an operation during their trip might embarrass them. When it emerged that the pub was Catholic-owned the possibility of loyalists having further developed their explosives capability appeared to loom larger. I went on air, making it clear that the full circumstances were not yet known, but talking at great length about the fact that the loyalists seemed to be improving their bomb making expertise. Nine-tenths of the way down this speculative path, the producer Cathy Grieve crept into the studio and held a piece of paper in front of me. It read 'IRA mortar attack on nearby RUC station'. On air I heard myself saying, 'However, the theory about the loyalists is only speculation and another strong probability that is now gaining ground at the scene is that this may well have been the work of republicans . . .' I could sense the presenter's brow furrow down the radio line.

If Radio Five was often 'seat of the pants' broadcasting, it gave correspondents like myself the chance to learn to chat informally on air. In the early days we would joke that, because it broadcast only on medium wave, no one was listening. Perhaps that actually made it easier to relax and communicate in an easy manner, something which took longer to achieve on the more august Radio Four. It was only when I travelled across to London and started chatting to people (almost invariably cabbies or policemen) that I realised the informal mix of sports and news was netting a sizeable audience.

Just as much as in my first days in Belfast it seemed a case of 'learning on the job'. But for my intensive education I could be in no better company. The production team of Cathy Grieve, Darragh MacIntyre and Derek Crawshaw provided constant back-up and encouragement and cameraman Peter Cooper, with whom I had worked many times before, made every job seem far simpler than it was. Moreover, in a profession sometimes noted for its backbiting and petty rivalries, my 'oppo' Denis Murray is without doubt the most decent, generous and intuitive professional you could wish to meet. Denis shared his years of experience with me and I responded by constantly pulling his leg. He took it as nobly as anyone could.

The developments which Denis and I were telling the BBC's listeners and viewers about consisted in large part of bombings, mortar attacks and shootings. To this extent my job picked up exactly where Gary Duffy's had left off. But alongside this depressing list of violent incidents came a series of heavily nuanced statements from political leaders which signalled that change might be in the air. In April 1993 the Sinn Féin President Gerry Adams had been spotted leaving the Derry home of the SDLP leader John Hume. The two were working on Hume's theory that, in a modern Europe where borders meant less and less, it must be possible to find some new governmental institutions and some new forms of words which would blunt the divide between nation-alists and unionists, Irish and British. John Hume was strongly criticised for sitting down with the leader of a movement which remained philosophically and practically committed to the use of violence to achieve its goal of a united Ireland. But Hume weathered the verbal attacks and through the course of 1993 his dialogue with Adams set the tone and tempo for political develop-ments. Despite the IRA's Shankill Road bombing which killed ten people in Belfast in October 1993 and the loyalist shooting of seven people at Greysteel near Derry in the same month, the British and Irish governments did their best to respond to the Hume/Adams dialogue. When John Major and Albert Reynolds announced the Downing Street Declaration in December 1993 they presented it as a quite separate initiative from Hume/Adams. In fact it was closely related, integrating the thinking of the two nationalist leaders with input from unionists and loyalists.

By the time I became network news correspondent in the spring of 1994 the politicians had digested the Downing Street Declaration, but we were still awaiting, especially in Sinn Féin's case, a 'definitive response'. It had also emerged that the government which had banned us in the media from broad-casting the words of republicans had in fact been talking to them, in secret, for years. Used to chasing ambulances, the Northern Ireland media now had to make sense of a complex multidimensional chess game, where not all the pieces were in full view. During one of my last *Spotlight* films, which looked at the republican reaction to the Downing Street Declaration, I attended a debate held in the Irish language on the Falls Road. The producer Paul Larkin Coyle did his best to translate the gist of the arguments. I could follow quite clearly Bernadette McAliskey's drift when she held up a copy of the Downing Street Declaration and threw it in the bin. But it wasn't until I got a word for word translation that I realised the significance of the comments from the Sinn Féin councillor Maírtín Ó Muilleoir who said that it had always been foolish to talk about peace by Christmas 1993 but it wouldn't be so silly to talk about peace by Christmas 1994.

The declaration of a three-day ceasefire by the IRA at Easter 1994 was widely derided as insufficient. But it remained clear that something big was afoot. In the meantime, however, the violence continued unabated. In my first feature for *Today* on loyalist attacks in the South one of my interviewees had been Ray Smallwoods, spokesman for the Ulster Democratic Party. I was under no illu-sion about Ray Smallwoods's background. Whilst he presented himself as a purely 'political' loyalist spokesman, and for a while went under the pseudo-nym of 'Ray Simpson', it had in fact been a *Spotlight* film I made together with Paul Larkin Coyle which first identified Ray Smallwoods as one of the gang which had tried to murder Bernadette McAliskey and her husband in January 1981. Relations with him had been a little fraught at the time of that pro-gramme, but eventually we got back on good terms. Ray often took uncom-promising loyalist positions. But he explained them in a logical manner with a quiet, unassuming voice which appeared to take the sting out of the words. After recording the interview for my *Today* feature I remember chasing around Ray's front garden in hot pursuit of his young son who seemed intent on running out into the road. Ray appeared very much the doting father. Just a few weeks later, on 11 July 1994, a report came in of a shooting on Lisburn's Old Warren estate. Without thinking I rang the only person I knew on the estate in order to see if he knew what was going on. But Ray Smallwoods did not answer his phone – he lay outside his house – shot dead by the IRA.

The first few months of 1994 were filled with uncertainty and violence as we waited to see how the peace process might develop. About three weeks before Ray Smallwoods's killing I had been at Paddy McGrory's home watch-ing Ireland play Italy in the World Cup. The Irish team had enjoyed a tremen-dous run throughout the tournament and we stared at the television screen with mounting excitement as they continued their giant-slaying act. As the final whistle blew and we all cheered Ireland's victory, my bleeper went off. The message told me to ring the newsroom immediately. I made my way through to the McGrorys' kitchen and learned over the phone that there had been a shooting at a bar in County Down. It looked as though there were multiple casualties. I made my excuses and left. It was already eleven o'clock at night and the BBC would want as comprehensive a report as possible for mid-night. Getting to the scene and filing wasn't an option. I headed to the news-room to see what I could do from there.

Driving from north Belfast to the city centre I passed scores of soccer fans celebrating Ireland's victory in the streets. It seemed unreal. They didn't know about the carnage which had occurred only half an hour's drive down the road. However, they must have been aware of the widespread fears that loy-alists might attack Irish soccer fans in reprisal for an INLA shooting of three loyalists on the Shankill Road a couple of days previously, but they didn't seem to care. Once I got to the BBC newsroom in the centre of the city, I found two other journalists inundated by calls and striving with not much luck to establish any facts. We rang and rang the RUC press office but it seemed every other journalist in the world was doing the same and we couldn't get through. One of my colleagues got the ambulance service on the line and they gave him their first impression of the scale of the casualties. We still didn't have enough. I tried ringing shops and bars in Loughinisland, the village where the attack had taken place. We also rang local councillors but they all seemed to be out.

At last in desperation we remembered that certain surnames were especially common in the area. We started flicking through the phone book ringing any likely-looking name and address. Eventually I got a local woman on the line.

'I am terribly sorry to bother you, but I am phoning from the BBC, do you know anything about a shooting at the Heights Bar?'

'My husband's just gone down there,' she said. 'Phone us again in a few minutes, I am expecting him back.'

Five minutes later I was on the phone to an eyewitness who did not want his name used but told me the whole story, how the regulars had been watching the match with their backs turned to the door, how the gunmen had burst in and opened fire indiscriminately, how more could have died if the pub owner and a number of his clientele had not been away on a charity trip to help Romanian orphans. His first words to me were 'We have lost an awful lot of good people from the parish tonight . . .'

Loughinisland is a quiet country hamlet where people don't readily speak to outsiders about politics. In the days that followed the murder of six men by the loyalist UVF waves of journalists came over from London but few had much luck in persuading the locals to talk. After that first panicked night I did not get sent to the scene of the killings for a while, as the BBC preferred that I concentrate on the possible political fallout. But a few days later I went down to cover the funeral of the oldest victim of the Loughinisland shooting, indeed the oldest ever victim of the troubles, 87-year-old Barney Green. The logistics of getting the sermon recorded and making my way back to the radio car in time to broadcast a piece kept me rushing around without too much thought for what I was covering. But I pulled up with a jolt when the funeral procession made its way out of the church and headed towards the graveyard. A group of the mourners turned and waved at me. They were Mr Green's cousins, neighbours of my girlfriend's parents whom I knew well. As a jour-nalist coming from outside it is very easy to report on the most atrocious incidents with a degree of detachment. But Northern Ireland is a very small place and you cannot live there very long without getting to know people who have lost neighbours or cousins, people who do not necessarily classify themselves as 'victims' but who have had to live with the shadow of the troubles nevertheless.

22

'First and Live'

SUMMER 1994

August 1994 had been in the diary of most news organisations for some time as a month to be covered. This was because it marked the twenty-fifth anniversary of the arrival of British soldiers in Northern Ireland. Anniversaries often send a shudder up the spine of a journalist, because you know your bosses will want you to report on them, yet it is always a real struggle coming up with anything vaguely original to say. My colleague on the TV, Denis Murray, took what seemed the wisest option and booked his holidays. This left the TV producer Darragh MacIntyre and myself to face the demands of the various news programmes for 'special reports'. We ended up with a series of features with related themes. One film looked at life on Belfast's peace line. Another concentrated on the soldiers themselves. A third – I don't know whose brainchild this was – endeavoured to look at why young people continued to be attracted to 'terrorist' organisations.

I found this last piece especially difficult to put together. Who did you talk to? 'Respectable' groups of youngsters might be offended if you implied in your questioning that they were all on the verge of signing up to the IRA or the UVF. Teenagers living on estates where the paramilitaries ruled the roost were normally too worldly-wise to say anything for or against them. You could talk about drugs or joyriding, for sure, but not the 'organisations'. And with the ban still in place it was hard to go to the paramilitaries themselves.

Hard but not impossible. At this stage one 'youth' organisation operated on the borderline of legality. It called itself the UYM or 'Ulster Young Militants' and was in effect the youth wing of the Ulster Freedom Fighters. Despite its obvious connections the UYM had not yet been declared illegal or brought under the aegis of the broadcasting ban. With the assistance of some loyalists in north Belfast I met a group of Ulster Young Militants to arrange to

134

take some pictures of them painting murals and interview them about why they wanted to get involved in such a group. We discussed possible questions over a drink in a loyalist bar not far from the Rathcoole estate.

On the first pint the UYM members were emphasising their moderation and reasonableness. One told me he had plenty of friends who were Catholics, it was just the IRA he couldn't stand and anyone who wanted to sell Ulster out. After two pints the moderation appeared to be waning – the RUC were a 'bunch of bastards' who deserved to be shot dead for the way they went around harassing loyalists. After a third pint they asked me whether I wanted to film them in their 'working clothes', at which point one of them pulled out a balaclava for good measure. After the fourth pint I was treated to a full recital of the Ulster Freedom Fighters' oath, a recital which made clear that any differentiation between the UFF and the UYM was a piece of fiction. By this time I had also had four pints and I have to admit that I cannot remember the wording of the oath.

The next day I returned to film the mural being painted. I breathed a sigh of relief that I had declined the invitation to film the group in their 'working clothes' as no sooner had we started rolling than an RUC patrol car appeared on the scene, and enquired what we were up to. It was probably a coincidence, but I did wonder for a moment whether anyone at our table in the pub the night before had been rather closer to the RUC than he had let on and might have passed our filming plans on to the authorities.

The army provided a series of carefully orchestrated picture sequences and facilities for our anniversary pieces. I remember going to Derry for one radio facility during which every soldier repeated that there may once have been friction, but now relations with the local community were very good. I tried to probe further to get more illustration of this but time and again all I heard was the same mantra, which sounded suspiciously like the 'line' agreed with the army press office. Eventually when one young soldier gave me this line I told him I couldn't quite believe it because I knew all the estates around his post were strongly republican.

'Well, they still come out at night and throw rocks and bottles at us,' he told me, 'and we pick the rocks up and throw them back at them. But they enjoy it and we enjoy it and relations really are quite good . . .'

As it turned out the main newsline from any of the anniversary pieces was provided by an interview which the RUC Chief Constable Sir Hugh Annesley gave me for a piece broadcast on *Breakfast News*. In the course of an interview in which he paid tribute to the role the army had played in supporting the police during the previous quarter of a century, Sir Hugh indicated that the level of army patrolling could be scaled down in the future if the IRA did indeed call a ceasefire. Looking back this seems a fairly innocuous remark which simply stated fairly obvious security practicalities. But at the time, with the IRA yet to declare a ceasefire, it was seized upon as part of the elaborate game of semaphore then being conducted between republicans and the authorities. The Ulster Unionist Ken Maginnis accused the RUC Chief Constable of trying to offer inducements to buy an IRA ceasefire, and called for his immediate resignation. The comment was seized upon by a number of newspapers who speculated about its purpose and timing.

Sir Hugh, I presume, felt a bit taken aback by the angry reaction to an interview which he had intended primarily as a tribute to the army and I imagine he wasn't too happy about the emphasis we placed on his comment. Whilst in my script I had pointed up his tribute to the soldiers, I had chosen what seemed to be the more newsworthy clip for my film on *Breakfast News*, which also included wounded soldiers and veterans whose courage and commitment appeared self-evident. Rejecting the criticism levelled at him, Sir Hugh stood by his remarks, deeming it 'unhelpful for any commentator to jump to conclusions on the basis of isolated extracts'. Whilst my *Breakfast News* film only had room, unfortunately, for an isolated extract, I tried to ensure that as many outlets as possible played the Chief Constable's interview at length in order to provide the context which, with a degree of justification, Sir Hugh thought had been lacking.

Within days, however, the fuss about Sir Hugh's interview would be entirely forgotten as the IRA ceasefire which he had talked about as a future possibility became instead an imminent reality. How things would develop had not seemed so certain when we all went to Letterkenny at the end of July for a special Sinn Féin conference in which the party was to announce its 'definitive response' to the Downing Street Declaration. The event appeared something of a damp squib as the response read like a qualified rejection of the Declaration. My colleague Shane Harrison, who has always had a better grasp of republican thinking than I, ran around the car park outside the hotel where the conference took place telling anyone who would listen not to write off the chances of an IRA ceasefire, but to read between the lines of the Letterkenny statement. Taking on board both Shane's views and the lines of 'spin' being touted by Sinn Féin press officers Rita O'Hare and Richard McAuley, I made it clear to listeners that the game was not yet up. However, by this stage we had been talking about the possibility of an IRA ceasefire for many months and I must admit that my growing sense that it was time for the republicans to put up or shut up was beginning to infect my analysis. A few days later I found myself down in Newry reporting on another IRA mortar attack on an RUC station and I delivered a piece-to-camera which concentrated on the yawning gap between republican words and deeds.

After the anticlimax of Letterkenny, however, events began to move more swiftly. I knew Gerry Adams and his associates were engaging in detailed background work preparing for future political negotiations with other parties and that could mean only one thing. A team of Irish Americans led by former congressman Bruce Morrison came to Dublin and Belfast at Sinn Féin's invitation. After some arm-twisting of the US authorities by the Irish prime minister Albert Reynolds, the veteran IRA man Joe Cahill got a visa to head across the Atlantic to brief American sympathisers. It looked unmistakably like window dressing for the big announcement.

I had interviewed Bruce Morrison on a number of occasions during the year and a half since his friend President Clinton had come to power. He is always unfailingly polite and helpful. But this time under the pressure of the attention of the media in general and the BBC in particular, he had a bone to pick.

'What is it with you people?' he wanted to know, one morning in the Belfast newsroom. 'I came in this morning to do your breakfast news programmes. I did the radio. I did the television. I did the national programme. I did the local. I left and I got back to my hotel and the receptionist handed me the phone – it was you people looking for another interview. I got to my room and the phone was ringing, and it was another BBC programme. I got into the shower and the phone went again, and yes, you guessed it, it was the BBC. You people need management consultants.'

I apologised profusely, told him that if he got a moment he should put it in writing, and made a mental note to try, Canute-like, to stem the flow of requests. It's a problem which, with the expansion in BBC outlets, has repeated itself on many occasions. It's hard to explain to an interviewee that to compare like with like they should lump all their requests from Channel 4, ITN, CNN, Independent Radio News, Ulster TV and the local Downtown radio into one category and then weigh them against the demands of the BBC. From time to time the corporation has tried to tackle the problem of multiple bids by stipulating which programme or person should make an approach on behalf of all. But inevitably individual producers want their own programmes to be as distinctive as possible and all attempts to corral them appear doomed to failure. I don't think, once the deluge had subsided, that Bruce Morrison ever wrote his letter.

The Americans came and went and by now only the timing of an IRA announcement appeared in any doubt. Minute by minute we bothered our Sinn Féin contacts with the same questions – when and how will it be announced, how long will it last? Programme presenters asked me on air hour by hour exactly when this ceasefire was going to happen. In the end I got so tired of saying 'We don't exactly know' in various ways that I adopted a silly joke passed on to me by a republican.

'One republican has told me,' I confided to the *Today* programme, 'that it will be called on a day that starts with a "T". Now that could be Tuesday, or it could be Thursday. Or it could be Tomorrow as it always seems to be Tomorrow rather than Today.'

The presenter appreciated the sense of world-weariness which had prompted me to resort to this, but not everyone did. I had no sooner come off the air than my phone was ringing with an urgent call from a television producer.

'We want you on the air immediately,' he told me.

'What's the rush?' I responded. 'I thought I was doing your programme in half an hour.'

'We just heard you on the radio announcing the ceasefire would be on Tuesday and we want to lead on it . . .'

I clarified my comments and vowed not to be fatuous again about something so important.

Amidst the endless serious news analysis Denis Murray and I were called upon to provide, there came a bit of light relief when the *Independent*'s television critic Allison Pearson produced a programme for Channel 4 criticising the format of television news. My series of reports on the twenty-fifth anniversary of the troops had just aired, and I felt glad that she had noticed. Glad, that is, until I realised she was showing my piece-to-camera from the report (and some extracts of reports from my ITN colleague Tom Bradby) to illustrate her theory that the news bosses only wanted to put young male 'bimbos' on the screen – 'reporters telling you about Northern Ireland who weren't even born when the troubles began'. At this stage I had been reporting Northern Ireland for eight years, which coincidentally was about how old I was when the troubles began. Flattery, however, could get Allison Pearson anywhere. I withstood the barbs of my ever-attentive colleagues who had noticed the comparison made between me and Tom on the one hand, and Barbie's boyfriend Ken on the other.

As August came to a close it seemed ever more obvious that the announcement would come on the last day of the month. BBC Belfast's Chief Security Correspondent Brian Rowan has excellent contacts with republicans, loyalists and the security forces. Brian expected a phone call would summon him to a meeting with a contact. In Dublin my colleague Shane Harrison also had a direct line to the republicans and prepared for a similar contingency. BBC Northern Ireland's News Editor, Tom Kelly, sat in his office with two phones, waiting for either Brian or Shane to ring. The minutes ticked by to eleven o'clock in the morning, which everyone agreed seemed the likeliest time for an announcement. Journalists and camera crews from the BBC in London and from other broadcasters around the world spilled out of every corner of the Belfast newsroom. There amidst it all was Chris Cramer, the man who had wondered who the hell I was when I had been appointed Ireland Correspondent. Chris called me over at about half past ten for a little reminder.

'Mark, you do remember what the motto of Radio Five is?'

'Umm, not sure, Chris . . .'

'The motto is "first and live" and I suppose today is the ultimate test.'

With those words the boss left me pondering on the notion that, as soccer commentators say, the day could go only one of two ways. Tom Kelly looked anxiously at his telephones, with a computer screen in front of him. He planned to rattle out the script on his keyboard, hit 'save' and with that transmit the story to a newsreader waiting in a nearby studio. My plan was rather more primitive. I hovered nervously over his shoulder, waiting to scribble down the first line of any statement then to sprint to a studio in another part of Broadcasting House in Belfast, where Radio Five Live's *Magazine* programme was live on air. The phone rang. Brian Rowan had the first line of the ceasefire announcement. Within seconds Shane's phone rang too, but I didn't wait for that. With Chris Cramer's words ringing in my ears I was already off down the corridor, running full pelt, ignoring shouted questions from other journalists.

As I ran across the newsroom, down one corridor, past a lift and down another corridor it occurred to me that I had flagrantly breached the first rule of broadcasting: never run when you are about to go on air as you will get out of breath. A sin, but clearly in Chris Cramer's view letting ITN or Independent Radio News beat us to the punch would have been a bigger sin. I kept running. The presenter, an old colleague of mine Diana Madill, had just started reading the cue to a piece about the withdrawal of the last Russian troops from Berlin, when I burst through the door, ignoring the red light and thereby again breaking another cardinal rule of broadcasting. Diana broke off and handed over to me, and I blurted out that I had just heard the news that as of midnight all IRA units had been instructed to observe 'a complete cessation of military operations'. Predictably, I then ran out of breath.

Afterwards a radio critic wrote that the announcement had been made by a young, rather overexcited BBC correspondent. 'Overexcited,' I bridled, vowing that if I ever met the critic I would make her dash the three hundred metres I had covered before allowing her to expand on her analysis. Once I apologised and recovered my breath, Diana asked me to comment on the one line of the IRA statement we had ready to hand. Aware of the importance of precise terminology in these matters, I seized on the word 'complete', and predicted there would be a great deal of debate about whether the IRA intended complete to mean 'total', in the sense that all its units were instructed to obey the order, or 'permanent', meaning that its violent campaign had come to a complete and final halt. I can therefore claim a little bit of credit for starting one of the first political wrangling matches to break out after the ceasefire.

After the exchange between Diana and myself *The Magazine* began to pull live guests on to the air. The Ulster Unionist MP Willie Ross talked about the need for the IRA to disarm, foreshadowing what would turn out to be another long-term bugbear of the peace process. Other guests expressed joy and emotion at the events of the day. *The Magazine* later won one of the UK premier radio prizes, a Sony award, for its IRA ceasefire edition. My breathless conversation with Diana Madill may have struck some listeners as amateurish. But more expressed the view that it conveyed the importance of the announcement and the urgency of the news. The BBC later chose the sound of the crunch of the studio door and my out of breath words to feature on a special CD illustrating seventy-five years of the corporation.

The rest of the day is a bit of a blur. Whilst Gerry Adams addressed a rally in west Belfast and a motorcade headed down the Falls Road I didn't get to attend these events as I had to commentate live on air from a studio over the pictures. I recall being pulled through to lead the *World at One* on Radio Four. The presenter said a few words then handed over to me, without asking a question. Aghast, I realised the programme wanted me to paint a picture of the day rather than simply to ad lib answers to questions. No one had passed me the message, so I had no prepared script. Instead I had little choice but to dive in and busk for thirty seconds.

Outside the BBC building, the announcement stirred deep emotions. On the unionist side of the fence, many harboured deep suspicions, believing the IRA and the government must have concluded a secret deal. For those who had lost loved ones, the announcement came too late, and served only to bring back the pain which they had tried to cope with as best they could. But for most there was joy and relief, and the hope that this would be the start of something new and better.

23

A Kick in the Ribs

SUMMER 1994–AUTUMN 1994

The loyalists did not turn the tap off their own violence immediately, instead testing the IRA's resolve by continuing to kill Catholics and attempting to demonstrate their relatively new-found expertise with explosives. I remember getting off a plane at Belfast City Airport to be greeted by the unmistakable thump of a bomb. A car packed with explosives had detonated near the Sinn Féin Press Centre on the Falls Road. So this is peace? I wondered.

But behind the scenes the process of assuring the loyalist paramilitaries that there had been no secret deal and they had nothing to fear went on apace, with intermediaries like the Church of Ireland primate Archbishop Robin Eames performing vital work. The loyalists had evolved a tier of leaders like former UVF prisoners David Ervine and Billy Hutchinson who had developed a sophisticated political analysis and were ready to be persuaded that the time had come for a change. Others, however, simply viewed violence and rack-eteering as a way of life, and took some convincing. During the troubles, if you were a nationalist in Northern Ireland and you wanted to fight for your 'cause' you had little option but to join the IRA. If you were a unionist and you wanted to do likewise you were much more likely if you were smart to join the RUC or enlist as a part-time soldier in the Ulster Defence Regiment. Only the boys in the back row of the classroom tended to get drawn into the ranks of the loyalist paramilitaries.

I remembered visiting the UDA's office on the Shankill Road back in March 1992 a few months before the organisation was banned and about a year and a half before the building we sat in was destroyed by the IRA bomb attack on Friz-ell's fish shop on the ground floor. It seemed fair to say that the calibre of the UDA inner council members whom I met together with BBC World Service producer Margaret McKee wasn't of the highest order. Aware that they were in the presence of a 'lady' the loyalist leaders tried to moderate their language, but kept forgetting or failing in their attempts. Their explanation of their political approach therefore came peppered with half-swallowed 'fucks' and occasional apologies. We clutched our cracked mugs of tea, whilst one senior UDA figure telephoned the nearby Tennant Street RUC station to complain about rough treatment he claimed he'd just been given in the street. Shouting down the phone, he treated the desk sergeant to a tirade strewn liberally with swear words.

I am no prude but in strict PR terms the UDA men's presentation left something to be desired and didn't serve to convince us of their respectable character or the rightness of their argument when they insisted that attempts to link them with racketeering and drugs was RUC 'black propaganda'. The inner council spokesman described himself as 'a loyal Ulster man. "Loyal to the crown?" Well that depends on the British government's position. We are loyal to the people of Ulster. We know ourselves that the British government don't want to be here. We know that for a fact.' He insisted that 'none of the loyalist groups are involved in terrorism – maybe in counter-terrorism. 'We retain the right to defend ourselves and the communities we come from and if people want to call that terrorism that's their problem not ours.' All the while Johnny Adair, at this stage probably one of the most feared characters in west Belfast, sat smiling at me, saying nothing.

Recalling this I had no difficulty in believing a colleague who told me that when the UDA came to vote on whether to match the IRA's ceasefire, one leading figure voted against. When asked why, all he could say was 'Just because'. It was no mean achievement on the part of leaders like David Ervine, Billy Hutchinson, Gusty Spence, Gary McMichael and David Adams that they managed to contain that kind of knee-jerk reaction and convince their grassroots supporters of the wisdom of following the IRA's example. The DUP leader Ian Paisley played on working-class loyalists' fears of a secret deal between the government and the IRA. But Ervine, in particular, countered this by labelling Paisley the 'Grand Old Duke of York', a leader who had proved in the past all too ready to march others up to the top of the hill then to dissociate himself from their actions once they engaged in violence.

Because of the twenty-fifth anniversary of the arrival of British troops and the run-up to the IRA ceasefire I hadn't taken a holiday during the summer of 1994. As we waited for the loyalists to respond to the IRA initiative I decided I could not delay any more and booked a trip to South Africa. As the date of my departure loomed closer, however, I began to worry that I would miss what had to be one of the biggest stories on my patch.

My flight left Belfast at lunchtime on 13 October. Somebody must have told the Combined Loyalist Military Command, which promptly decided to call its ceasefire on the same day. Once again, BBC Northern Ireland's Chief Security Correspondent Brian Rowan was ahead of the pack, revealing news of an 'extraordinary news conference' to be held in a loyalist estate on the outskirts of west Belfast. In contrast to the IRA, which had passed its statement to a few selected journalists, the loyalists wanted to announce theirs live on air to the world. The timing – in mid-morning – allowed me to cover the announcement then head immediately to the airport.

We managed to get an outside broadcast vehicle up to Fernhill House to transmit the ceasefire announcement. But attempts to get a separate microphone so I could talk in and out of the loyalist statement failed. So listeners to Radio Five heard me talking to Diana Madill on the telephone, but heard the loyalists in decent quality. Not to worry, I thought, at least I won't be out of breath like the last time. But as I chatted away on the phone a number of loyalist heavies dotted around the room failed to realise I was addressing the nation, instead they assumed that I was an impolite hack who couldn't be bothered concentrating on the moment in history about to be made. As Gusty Spence led a delegation of UVF and UDA members into the room I told Radio Five listeners who he was, how he had been jailed in the 1960s for the murder of a Catholic barman and was regarded by the UVF as the most venerable of their leaders. But my words were interrupted by admonitions to 'pipe down', 'show some respect' and finally 'shut the fuck up'. Lowering my voice I hunkered down, crouching close to the floor and whispering to Diana that the loyalist leaders had now taken their seats and were surely at any moment about to speak. But even whispering wasn't good enough and as I told listeners that Gusty was going to read the statement one of the loyalist heavies nearby again told me to shut up and this time, for added emphasis, kicked me in the ribs. It wasn't an especially hard kick but it did the job. Two ceasefire announcements and both times I found myself out of breath. Knowing that *The Magazine* would ask me to analyse the content of the statement as soon as Gusty Spence stopped talking, I fled the room, making it to the corridor outside just in time to answer Diana Madill's first question, without getting kicked again.

24

A False Dawn

The ink on the loyalist and IRA ceasefire statements barely seemed to have dried before people started telling Denis Murray and me that we would soon be out of a job. The theory went that, as the vultures living off the corpse of the troubles, journalists would have nothing left to do once the killing had come to a halt. The headlines would dry up and the BBC's London-based news operation would sharply scale back its investment.

As part of its future planning the BBC in Belfast started to examine how it might change the tone of its early evening news. For years the Northern Ireland newsroom had been expert at reacting to sudden events. Now it seemed it would have to ape the local magazine programmes produced in the English regions, with their emphasis on lovingly preshot features, 'lifestyle' items and chatty encounters with guests on comfy-looking sofas. The 'dinosaurs' of the troubles were out. Stories about pets and shopping were in.

The contingency plans were incorporated into a new-look local news. However, the years after the 1994 IRA ceasefire did not quite match everyone's expectations. In fact less than a month after the loyalists called their ceasefire and just a fortnight or so after John Major announced his 'working assumption' that the IRA had stopped violence for good, IRA members shot dead a postal worker, Frank Kerr, during a robbery at a sorting office in Newry. The Irish government, which had been on the brink of letting nine republicans out of jail early, swiftly halted the releases. The IRA admitted its members had been involved, but claimed the operation had not been authorised by the organisation's army council. The governments drew a deep breath and decided to continue with the peace process, but the murder of Mr Kerr turned out to be just one of a number of many setbacks along the way.

Within days I found myself in Dublin reporting on the downfall of one of the essential figures in the peace process, the Irish Prime Minister Albert

Reynolds. Although I felt confident handling any question which a presenter might throw at me regarding the Northern Irish politicians whom I knew so well, this confidence did not, at this stage, extend to the complexities of southern Irish politics. I found myself inside Jury's hotel in Dublin covering a meeting of the Irish Labour Party which was debating whether to withdraw from its coalition with Albert Reynolds's Fianna Fáil. I had questioned the Labour Party leader and Irish Foreign Minister Dick Spring on a number of occasions, but I wasn't entirely sure who all his luminaries were. At one point someone told me that government minister Brendan Howlin was about to come out of the meeting and might provide an update. I hovered near the most likely door – it swung open and five men walked out. I hadn't a clue what Brendan Howlin looked like, and suddenly realised that far from being part of a large waiting press pack I was on my own. With as loud a voice as I could muster I shouted 'Minister, what's the latest?' at all five men and waited to see who turned towards me. Fortunately Brendan Howlin identified himself and gave me a few useful comments.

A weekend Radio Five programme wanted to interview me about the meeting and I decided it was best to level with them. 'This is a horrendously complicated affair,' I told the producer, 'and I am still getting up to speed. I can give you the top line and fill in with a bit of colour, but don't push me too hard on air.' On air, however, it didn't quite work that way. The presenter, Nick Witchell, listened to me explain what the Irish Labour Party members had said, but then he wanted my analysis of what would happen next. I waffled my way through a couple of general-purpose answers where I gave a complete range of options – the coalition could survive, the government could fall and there could be a general election or Labour could find new partners in government forming a 'rainbow coalition' with a number of the opposition parties.

Nick bore with me through this, but then sought to pin me down. 'But what's your hunch, Mark?'

I drew a deep breath. I was the BBC's Ireland Correspondent after all. Instead of doing what I should have, which would be to say, 'I'm sorry, Nick, there's some interference on the line . . . I think I'm losing you . . .' I decided to plunge in with my best guess. 'Well, Nick, looking at the opinion polls I don't think Labour would really want to go for an election at this stage, so my guess is that there might well be a rainbow coalition formed with Fine Gael.'

On the other end of the line I heard Nick tell his listeners, 'Well, Mark thinks there will be a rainbow coalition. We're also joined now by Donal

Kelly, who is the political editor of the Irish state broadcaster, RTÉ. Donal, would you agree?' Donal Kelly is a recognised expert who knows more than I ever will about the machinations of Dublin politics. When he speaks it is rarely opinion, more usually the received wisdom which some senior minister has just imparted in his ear. My heart sank as I heard Donal say, 'Well, it's a possibility but I think more people here are backing the prospect of a general election for the following reasons . . .'

The next week was one of the most invigorating and quite the most insane experiences I have ever had in political journalism. The scandal at the centre of it all concerned Albert Reynolds's appointment as President of the Irish High Court his Attorney-General, who many thought had not acted swiftly enough in ordering the extradition of Father Brendan Smyth, a priest facing child abuse charges in Northern Ireland. But the essential questions which Dick Spring wanted answered about the appointment soon became buried in layer after layer of intrigue. The Dáil lurched from bad to worse with rumour and counter-rumour about stories of the Catholic church and child abuse which would 'shake the state to its core'. Senior party leaders whispered revelations into your ears which they firmly believed themselves but which turned out to be utterly inaccurate. At one point there were reports of an unprecedented joint statement by the IRA and the UVF leaping to Albert Reynolds's defence – reports no sooner broadcast than they were denied. At another stage the Democratic Left parliamentarian Pat Rabbitte made a speech which sent us all scattering in different directions and which enabled my colleague at the *Guardian*, David Sharrock, to coin the line that this was the first time 'a Rabbitte had pulled a red herring out of a top hat'. Throughout all the twists and turns, I stuck to the mantra which I had taught myself that first day – do not invent your own analysis, instead parrot what everyone else is saying. 'It's unlikely there will be a rainbow coalition, an election seems much more probable,' I told successive programmes. The next month a rainbow coalition was formed.

With his fate already sealed, Albert Reynolds arrived at Dublin Castle for a meeting and was surrounded by the local press pack. The Dublin press corps are a civilised bunch but at this stage numbers were inflated by the size of the story and for some reason the Gardaí on duty hadn't corralled us back as they should. We ended up virtually mobbing the Irish prime minister at the side of his car and he looked a bit shaken. Just a few weeks earlier I had watched Albert Reynolds clasp hands with Gerry Adams and John Hume in a symbolic underscoring of the IRA ceasefire. Now I felt rather sorry for him as the victim of such a swift and largely inexplicable political demise.

Although Sinn Féin undoubtedly missed Albert Reynolds's presence the peace process rolled on. For us reporters that meant many hours hanging around in freezing December outside the exposed Stormont parliament building whilst the republicans led by Martin McGuinness held exploratory talks with Northern Ireland Office civil servants. The grumbling exactly mirrored the reading on the thermometer. Veterans assured newcomers that the Brooke/Mayhew talks had been even more uncomfortable, but it seemed hard to imagine.

The fact that political negotiations were in existence and that, in contrast to previous discussions, they involved in some shape or form everyone – unionists, nationalists, republicans and loyalists – had to be good news for Northern Ireland. But it wasn't such great news for broadcasters because it marked the start of the 'men in suits' phase of Northern Ireland current affairs.

'Yes, I can tell you that some men in suits have just disappeared into the building behind me and they are expected to leave again in about three hours making on their way an ambiguous and opaque statement which will leave both you and me none the wiser about what is really going on . . .'

It did not make for exciting television, and the radio wasn't much better. On the other hand it encouraged reporters to use their imagination about illustrating stories. A few days after the loyalist ceasefire was called, the government announced the reopening of those border roads which had been closed and cratered for security reasons. We jumped up into the cab of a bulldozer starting the work and captured a picture symbolising political progress pushing all before it. I scanned the trees and hedges around us trying to work out whether this was the same stretch of 'unapproved road' on which I had come to a sticky end years before. The cows did look familiar.

If the ice-cold meetings at Stormont did nothing to warm a reporter's heart the tendency of Northern Ireland's political leaders, especially Gerry Adams, to head across the Atlantic at a moment's notice provided a welcome change. In March 1995 the Sinn Féin President was due to have his first face-to-face encounter with President Clinton and the BBC decided its Ireland Correspondents should be there. For the first time in my life I travelled first-class on Aer Lingus so as to be close to the man of the moment. As the gangly Gerry relaxed, his stockinged feet touched the partition in front of him. With my shorter legs I contemplated letting out the space between my feet and the chair in front to half a dozen economy passengers. Gerry agreed to record an interview before he got some shut-eye, thus justifying my hideously expensive air fare. At this point I discovered that my microphone had taken a knock in transit and a vital connection had snapped. Eventually I managed to record something on tape with all my attention fixed not on the content of my questions but on holding two bits of metal together to ensure the mike worked.

The expectation had been that the story would pick up as the encounter with President Clinton got closer, so I flew out on my own with Denis Murray and senior producer Clive Ferguson a couple of days behind. In fact Gerry was the lead story from the time he touched down. He and John Major engaged in a slanging match which was no mean feat as one of them was in New York whilst the other was in Jerusalem. By the time my reinforcements arrived I was already exhausted after fulfilling so many demands that I cracked and accused one London producer of indulging in a conspiracy to ensure I never recovered from the jet lag.

During the week Denis, Clive and I shuttled between New York and Washington DC. After watching Gerry Adams attend a swanky formal dinner with the likes of Donald Trump and Bianca Jagger I jumped on a subway and got a sense of traditional working-class Irish republicanism by sharing a heel of bread and a cup of black tea with the veteran gun-runner George Harrison in his flat in the Bronx. In his eighties, Harrison lives in a rudimentary apartment cluttered with memorabilia from every left-wing cause since the Second World War. He grew up in County Mayo in the days when the 'black and tans' were still marauding around persecuting Catholics and is firmly of the view that nothing has changed since. In George Harrison's view the conflict is an anti-imperialist struggle, pure and simple, and if Northern Ireland's million Protestants don't see the light by realising their Irishness and renouncing their Britishness there is no alternative but for some generation of patriots to push them out into the sea.

George Harrison holds his views firmly and honestly and watching him amble around his humble home in trousers and a string vest I couldn't but be impressed by his unassuming character, which provided a welcome contrast to the glitz and humbug which was then attaching itself to Sinn Féin's bandwagon in Manhattan. However, I knew this apparently lovable old guy had been responsible for supplying more guns to the IRA than any other individual with the exception of Libya's Colonel Gaddafi, and his idealism had therefore left its mark in other people's blood. I couldn't help wishing that someone might take him on a fact-finding tour to Ireland to acquaint him with the fact that the 'black and tans' had been disbanded and that some things had changed for the better.

A couple of days later I filed into the US Congress building in Washington together with a pack of journalists to get a view of speaker Newt Gingrich's lunch, which would provide the first opportunity for any personal interaction between Gerry Adams and President Clinton. The event was due to begin at 12.30 p.m. local time which made it 5.30 p.m. in Britain, just in time for the main Radio Four six o'clock news. I made my way through a designated entrance in order to be escorted to a press room. But the security guards wanted some extra time to check my equipment. My official guide and the rest of the print journalists disappeared. Only then did the guards let me through. There then followed a Kafkaesque nightmare as I tried desperately to find my way through the endless corridors and stairways of the congressional building. All the while the clock ticked towards the six o'clock deadline. Eventually I crunched into a room where my colleagues were staring at a monitor providing a closed-circuit television image of the meal in progress. 'Have they shaken hands? Has anyone said anything? Someone give me a fill . . . I've got to file in two minutes.' Noticing the look of sheer desperation on my face the others duly obliged.

Outside the Capitol later, Gerry Adams and his faithful friend in US politics the Republican Congressman Peter King gave us more detail about the encounter with the President. A Radio Five programme, very excited and just about to go off the air, demanded that I go live instantaneously on the phone. It's hard, however, to talk live to a programme from an impromptu news conference which has just begun without drowning out the person you are meant to be listening to, and from the looks of the rest of the US press corps I realised I should retreat to somewhere less irksome. As the presenter asked me, 'What is Gerry Adams saying?' I wanted to reply, 'I can't tell you because I have had to crouch behind this wall so as not to drown him out, and now I can't hear what he's saying.' Instead I waffled about the general themes he'd been elaborating on during his US visit.

Gerry Adams was by no means the only Northern Irish politician in Washington that St Patrick's week. Ian Paisley's son, Ian Junior, was in town too attending a US-sponsored course for young politicians. I well remember him looking askance at the green ribbons tied everywhere and the shillelagh-like Irishness of it all. These people don't realise St Patrick was a Protestant, he joked. We arranged to meet up later in the week – I still have a note the hotel reception left for me: 'Ian Paisley called. Will meet you in Dublin Bar.' For the benefit of any Free Presbyterian readers I should hasten to add that he didn't take the demon drink.

Whether it was the moment of stress in the congressional building or the cumulative impact of reporting non-stop, by the end of the week I got rather ill. I knew what the problem was and exactly which tablets I needed – indeed a doctor friend back in Belfast confirmed my diagnosis of shingles over the phone. But I still had to get an American doctor to sign a prescription and that appeared to be a problem as it was a weekend. My former colleague, reporter and presenter Maxine Mawhinney, who was now based in Washington, came to my aid. 'I've phoned my doctor. He's got a surgery tomorrow and he says he'll see you.' There was one small hitch, though. 'He's a gynaecologist, but he does men too.' When the assistant at the Washington Well Woman Clinic asked me to put on a smock I had visions of having to put my feet in stirrups. Fortunately it didn't come to that.

A couple of months later we were back in Washington for a major investment conference hosted by President Clinton. When I walked into the Sheraton hotel where the conference was being held the first thing I saw was the Ulster Unionist Reg Empey shaking hands with Gerry Adams's spin doctor Richard McAuley. I thought the process of reconciliation must have been moving more swiftly than I imagined but later I decided that Reg simply did not know who Richard was before he clutched his hand. At this stage the term 'handshake diplomacy' was very much on everyone's lips. Ken Maginnis had participated in a televised debate with Gerry Adams, but had refused to shake hands. Although the Washington conference was supposed to be about trade and investment all reporters' eyes were in fact on a distinctly political meeting due to take place in the margins between the patrician Northern Ireland Secretary Sir Patrick Mayhew and Gerry Adams. It would be the first time the two men would come face to face. Would they shake hands? If they did, what did that imply?

I put this question directly to the government minister Malcolm Moss, attending an opening reception sponsored by Belfast City Council. It was a curious event full of Irish music and imagery deemed appealing to Irish American business people, which one would not have hitherto associated with that old bastion of unionism Belfast City Council. Malcolm Moss appeared relaxed about the choreography of any encounter with Sinn Féin. He pointed out that only days earlier he had shaken hands with Sinn Féin's Mitchel McLaughlin during a tour of a shopping centre in Derry, implying that it was 'no big deal'. But when Gerry Adams's entourage swept into the reception a senior civil servant stepped forward and whispered into the minister's ear, 'Here comes trouble.' Deeming it unwise to upstage his boss, Mr Moss put himself into smart reverse gear and vanished from view, leaving us journalists to exchange pleasantries with the Sinn Féin President.

When the encounter between Sir Patrick and Gerry took place, the scenes inside the Sheraton were pretty farcical. The two politicians' spin doctors arranged to hold the meeting in Suite 6066, but the government wanted no cameras present to focus on the expected handshake. Left guessing about the precise venue, we had no alternative but to tail the participants and follow them in a ridiculous crocodile through the hotel. I glanced at the Ulster Unionist MP Jeffrey Donaldson staring on in dismay at the celebrity status being accorded Gerry Adams, but there was no chance to exchange words before I found myself jumping into a lift with Richard McAuley. 'Which floor are you going to?' he asked with a smile. 'Same one as you,' I replied. Eventually the seventy-strong press corp ended up in an undignified scrum outside the door of the hotel suite. We never got a picture of the two politicians together. Instead they held individual impromptu question and answer sessions in the corridor. We confirmed the handshake had taken place. Sir Patrick turned his nose up at the memory of it, claiming he 'did not care for that experience very much'.

Elsewhere in the hotel disparate delegates were getting involved in sing-songs, one reported punch-up and plenty of carousing – with the exception of the Sinn Féin group who had all vowed to stay off the drink. An ironic backdrop for the conference was provided by another gathering taking place simultaneously in the Sheraton which was a trade fair for 'small arms'. Representatives from US police forces and military units strolled past wearing T-shirts which promised to 'Clean Up the Streets' and clutching briefcases emblazoned with trademarks like Colt and Beretta. All my attempts to penetrate this parallel conference were repulsed by overefficient security men who no doubt presumed I was intent on picking up a souvenir or two to take back to Belfast.

As if the peace bug was catching, the 'semi-automatic' men packed up their bags as the week went on to be replaced by scores of born-again black American evangelical Christians. At one stage a Northern Ireland Office press officer persuaded me to accompany him down into the big hall where the evangelical delegates were holding their prayer meeting. The joint was jumping, with a big gospel band on stage pumping out a tune which sounded as if it had been taken off the *Blues Brothers* soundtrack. My civil servant friend dragged me by the arm from the back of the room where I was quite happily watching the proceedings to the front row where the enthusiastic evangelicals welcomed us with open arms and made space. The preacher on stage was summoning people from the audience to testify, praise the Lord and talk in whichever tongue happened to take their fancy. As the only two white faces in the packed audience we were a little obvious in the front row. The preacher made his way around the stage and pointed in our direction.

'I am calling you, brother . . .'

I looked around trying to give the impression that I couldn't possibly upstage the person much more worthy than me who had to be sitting at least three rows directly behind me.

'Yes, you brother . . .' the preacher was still imploring.

I looked at my press officer friend and told him, 'That's it, I am out of here.' The ceasefires of 1994 had convinced me that maybe miracles could happen. But here I drew the line.

25

Marching Feet and Angry Voices

SUMMER 1995

The handshakes might have been grudging, but the activity generated by the politicians seemed to give the impression of progress, albeit progress measured by millimetres. One of the unexpected side effects of the process was, however, that on the streets things began to get a little riskier for journalists. With uncertainty in the air, tensions between the communities rose. Also with the paramilitaries no longer engaged in plotting bombings and shootings they had to find something for their supporters to do, so urging them to take to the streets seemed the best option available.

Just before the Washington investment conference we had a little dress rehearsal of what was to come, when John Major tried to visit a museum in the centre of Derry. The local republicans decided to show the prime minister just who ran the city and gathered in sizeable numbers in order to make his entrance to the museum anything but smooth. As RUC officers and the prime minister's security men tried to clear a way through the crowd, tempers frayed and fist fights soon broke out. In the narrow alleys around Derry's city walls it proved difficult to find a spot where you could see what was going on but be out of swiping distance. I suddenly realised from the flailing arms and batons all around me that I had got myself into precisely the wrong place. Watching the punch-up get closer and fiercer I decided I had no choice but to use my height. I plunged down to ground level and waded through the legs of the assembled riot squad. An RUC officer, who appeared to be wondering what the strange rodent was doing clambering around his legs, hauled me up by the scruff of my neck.

'What the hell are you up to?' he asked, baton in hand.

'Press, getting the hell out of here!' I replied and he gave me a shove on my way.

Fortunately not many people were hurt, although the sight of a couple of men heaving a gas canister through the rear window of a police car and the proximity of the prime minister ensured that my report on the fracas got prime spot on the television news that night. In between editing pieces I settled down for a coffee at BBC Radio Foyle and a Sinn Féin spin doctor whom I hadn't met before came in and started talking about police brutality. Later I did a double take when I spooled through our raw film footage and saw the same man involved in a Keystone Kops-type incident where he ran up behind a young RUC officer who had got isolated in the crowd and aimed a sharp kick at the policeman's posterior before running off. The sequence featured strongly on our *Breakfast News* report the next morning.

A few weeks later the government released the paratrooper Lee Clegg from jail early. He had served four years of a life sentence after being convicted of the murder of Karen Reilly, a girl travelling in a stolen car on the outskirts of west Belfast. Republicans wanted to make the point that if Clegg could be let out all prisoners should be released, so they sanctioned a series of protest rallies, which were accompanied by riots and vehicle burning, this time more widespread and more intense than the disturbances in Derry. On the Andersonstown Road in west Belfast some overenthusiastic youths tried to take a car off Sean Reilly, who as Karen's adoptive father had rather more right to be upset than the rioters. The violence was fairly widespread, but most journalists covering it knew they had little need to worry. Provided you are not unfortunate enough to get caught in crossfire or hit by a police plastic bullet, the most that is likely to happen to you during a republican riot is that someone will hijack your car. So in this case we chose to travel using a local 'black taxi'. By contrast, when loyalists are on the rampage they often turn their anger on to the media. The rule of thumb is that if you have a situation where both Protestants and Catholics are rioting and you want both yourselves and your camera gear to stay intact, it's normally best to stand between the Catholics and the inevitable line of police or soldiers separating them from the other side.

That's exactly where we were standing one Saturday afternoon in Lurgan, behind an RUC riot squad keeping two rival groups separated from each other. The loyalists decided this was manifestly unfair so took their anger out on the police, showering them with bricks and bottles. If they spied a camera they tried to make sure the bottles went in its direction. The projectiles arced gracefully over the line of Land Rovers in front of us, sailing slowly enough through the air that we developed a kind of dance routine moving regularly from side to side to avoid the latest missile. It obviously became too monotonous because I remember remarking to cameraman Peter Cooper that you would have to be pretty stupid to get hit by anything when, on cue, a bottle of lager looped over, crashed against a nearby lamp-post and splintered into a hail of tiny fragments impossible to avoid. Both Peter and I caught the glass splinters on our foreheads and soon our faces were covered with blood. It didn't hurt, as the cuts were only superficial and I joked to Peter that it would look really good for a piece-to-camera when a helpful bystander came up and wiped most of the blood off, with some tissue paper, before I'd thought of anything sensible to say. Afterwards the local MP David Trimble said the fracas had been a minor affair blown out of all proportion by the media. I resisted the temptation to flourish the piece of tissue paper which I had in my pocket covered with my rhesus-positive.

Because I had notched up my fair share of riots I did not feel terribly guilty about missing out on another potential confrontation in the summer of 1995. The place was Portadown and the cause for concern was the traditional annual Orange Order Drumcree church parade. The parade dates back to the early nineteenth century. But in those days there was little need for argument about the Orangemen's route, not only because they were in the majority in the Portadown area, but because until well into the twentieth century the lanes which they marched along were mostly bounded by fields. Indeed until a farmer emigrated and sold the land for house construction the fields of Drumcree were well known for the roses which grew there. However, the sale led to the construction of the Garvaghy estate which provided homes for predominantly Catholic residents. Increasingly the parade of the exclusively Protestant Orange Order appeared to be an exercise in keeping the Catholic 'croppies' down. From the mid-1980s on tensions grew over a number of loyalist parades in the area. The police stopped marchers passing through one mainly Catholic street nearby and one Protestant died in the clashes which followed. But the Orange Order's church parade back along the Garvaghy Road continued. A group calling itself 'Drumcree Faith and Justice' protested by holding tea parties on the road but co-operated when the RUC carried them out of the way. However, with the development of the peace process and Sinn Féin's greater emphasis on the marching issue the Garvaghy estate formed what was one of a growing number of 'concerned residents' groups around Northern Ireland, dedicated to a more active and muscular opposition to the Drumcree parade.

On Friday, 7 July 1995 I attended an away day for BBC regional correspondents at a hotel in England. Given that I had covered the riot in Derry in May and the Clegg riots a few days before, I felt relaxed about taking a few days off to visit my parents, and leaving Drumcree to the others. After all, we had seen protests at Drumcree before. But as I listened to the radio at home I realised that I had underestimated the potential for trouble. On Sunday the police told the Orangemen leaving their service at the Drumcree church that they would not be able to go back along their return route. The Orangemen decided to stand their ground until they were allowed through. Orangemen and their supporters were involved in fierce clashes with the police in the fields around Drumcree. I spoke to our producer Cathy Grieve who told me she had never been so scared as the moment when she believed the police had been outflanked and they would all have to run for it. She had to temporarily pull the plug on our outside broadcast vehicle and relocate it to a safer area. The next day I flew back to help out. The dispute at Drumcree spread across Northern Ireland to other loyalist areas. The port of Larne was brought to a standstill with a blockade mounted by a group of loyalists which included the local Ulster Unionist MP Roy Beggs. By the time I arrived in Portadown early on the morning of 11 July, however, Brendan McAllister of the Northern Ireland Mediation Network had pulled off a coup. After hours of intense negotiations with the police, the marchers and the local residents, all sides agreed that the Portadown Orangemen could complete their march in a silent, dignified manner whilst the local residents moved to the side of the road and made their own peaceful protest.

Having prepared myself for covering more clashes I felt relieved that my reports that day reflected the victory of compromise. But there was a sting in the tail. We were putting together our package in the van which housed our mobile editing gear when a cameraman ran in and said, 'You've got to see this shot, it's a must.' The picture showed the local Ulster Unionist MP David Trimble and the DUP leader Ian Paisley holding hands aloft as they walked past the Carleton Street Orange Hall at the end of the Drumcree parade. Loyalists cheered them on their victory procession. One wag called it 'the gay wedding shot', but it was clear that the Catholic protesters on the Garvaghy Road would not see the funny side. They had agreed to let the march pass on its way provided there were no displays of triumphalism and no claims of victory. The image of the two Unionist MPs being treated like conquering heroes appeared guaranteed to rile the residents and make future negotiations about the march much more difficult.

For now, though, I was glad not to be camped out in Portadown for much longer. We whiled away the time in between reports by fending off the marauding packs of local children who regarded the march, the protest and the hordes of journalists with their hi-tech equipment as a great source of fun. The chief hazard in ensuring that reports were filed on time wasn't keeping out of the way of any rioters but checking there wasn't a small child secreted somewhere in the vehicle pulling out a plug which had taken his fancy. For light relief I allowed a few of the kids to tap scripts out on my computer then practise delivering them into the microphone. One boy seemed especially keen, and fairly knowledgeable about the media. As he delivered his pay-off 'Rory Dignan, BBC News, Portadown', I realised his surname sounded familiar. He told me his father had been one of three men shot dead by the IRA three years before. They had been killed after 'confessing' on tape to being RUC informers and to involvement in the murder of a woman called Margaret Perry who they thought might expose them. I shook my head and let Rory have another go with the microphone. Everyone on the Garvaghy estate, it seemed, had a story to tell.

26

'With Great Reluctance'

AUTUMN 1995–WINTER 1997

Two months after holding hands with Ian Paisley at Drumcree, David Trimble was elected as leader of the Ulster Unionist Party at a meeting held in Belfast's Ulster Hall. Not for the first time I demonstrated my spectacular incompetence as a forecaster, telling listeners that if they wanted to place a bet they should put their money on John Taylor. Mr Taylor, I am glad to say, looked every bit as surprised as me when the news of his defeat was announced. It taught us all to include the 'Drumcree factor' heavily in our political calculations in the future. Mr Trimble had undoubtedly been assisted by the broadcast just before the vote of pictures of him being awarded a 'Seige of Drumcree' medal by the Portadown Orangemen, and yes, the word siege was misspelled on the medal.

Irrespective of whether he was a 'hardliner' or a 'moderate' I looked forward to Mr Trimble taking over as he at least seemed conversant with modern technology, and appeared regularly on our television and radio programmes. By contrast James Molyneaux, whilst ever polite, seemed something of a Dickensian figure. Mr Molyneaux would react to developments some days after they had happened, often not giving an interview but instead issuing a Delphic written statement which reporters had to pore over to work out what on earth he was on about. The statements normally arrived by fax, but if Mr Molyneaux had been able to communicate with journalists by sticking a piece of sealed parchment into a cleft stick I suspect he would have availed himself of this route on every occasion.

One Sunday morning David Trimble came in to the BBC to record a 'down the line' live television interview with Sky News. Ahead of him in the queue for the same programme was the Labour Party's spokeswoman on Northern Ireland, Mo Mowlam. I showed the two of them down to the studio and tried to make contact with Sky. The Ulster Unionist leader appeared concerned about the time which was passing by as he had to get to his church service. Mo did her best to hurry things up, hollering down the line, 'Skyee . . . Oh, Skyee . . . can you get your act together and get us on, because I've got Twimble Wimble here in the corner and he's worried about getting to church.' I glanced at the rather proper Upper Bann MP whose face looked a picture, and wondered whether these two would hit it off in the future. The omens weren't very promising.

Whilst there were plenty of words being spoken on air and off, there appeared little real progress on the back of the two paramilitary ceasefires. The discussions between Sinn Féin and the government remained bogged down on the subject of paramilitary disarmament. At a special delegate conference in Dublin in September 1995 the mood amongst republicans appeared bleak. Gerry Adams talked about the peace process being in 'deep, deep trouble'. The one glimmer of hope on the horizon was the much-vaunted visit by the US President Bill Clinton.

For the BBC in Northern Ireland, as the lead broadcaster supplying pictures all around the world, the presidential visit constituted an incredible challenge. The corporation carried day-long live coverage of every stage of the President's itinerary. It was an enormous technical exercise which required immense preplanning, masterminded by Cathy Grieve and my old boss Andrew Colman. A mere cog in the big machine, I went to the Mackies factory on west Belfast's peace line incredibly early in the morning in order to get in through the White House's over-the-top security. From my commentary booth in the balcony I watched the President listen intently to the words of the children Catherine Hamill and David Sterrett. We all knew well that the White House's spin machine had been put into full gear to ensure no heartstring remained unpulled, and I was sure that both Catherine and David had been well drilled. But try as I might to be cynical it was hard not to be moved by the simple pro-peace messages of the children and the beautifully scripted reply of the President.

Through the day a fly on the wall crew watched me as I worked my way through a flurry of deadlines. By mid-afternoon I was definitely wilting, and they filmed as I talked about the President visiting the 'mainly Protestant Catholic road', a typo which I corrected before it made it onto air. In the evening I drew the short straw, not heading to Belfast City Hall where Van Morrison was playing and the President was cracking jokes about UFOs landing at Roswell, New Mexico, but instead getting sent to Queen's University where a series of serious political meetings had been scheduled to take place. Here I fell foul of White House security in a big way. I could go into the hall to watch the meetings, but they wouldn't let me out in time to go live onto the *Nine O'Clock News* to report what had been going on. I decided to stay outside but worried that my reporting was uninformed.

With my slot on the news looming I noticed Ian Paisley, Joe Hendron and a number of other politicians who had met the President heading out. I ran down to discover what they were saying. I scribbled furiously, garnering vital information for my live report. Then horrified, I realised that I had taken too long talking to the politicians. I rushed back to the live broadcast point but my watch told me I had left things far too late. I knew what to say, but I had missed my chance to say it. I failed to make my slot on the *Nine O'Clock News* and a high degree of chaos ensued on air. The viewers might not have known it, but I was only too aware that I was responsible for the news presenter Peter Sissons's discomfiture as he filled time, valiantly recapping the day's events rather than interviewing me about the significance of the President's visit. A swift post-mortem ensued back in London and I had no option but to fall on my sword, telling anyone who would listen that the debacle was all my fault. I wanted the ground to swallow me up. I had broken the first rule of live broadcasting, which is simply to be there. What you can or cannot say comes afterwards.

We drove down to Dublin in the middle of the night ready to cover the President's second day in Ireland. I let Patricia do the driving and spent the journey punching and pinching myself, disbelieving my own stupidity and running over the fateful minutes again and again in my head. The thirtieth of November 1995 had been a good day for Northern Ireland, but ended up being a lousy one for me. But then what matters? Something decent happening, or you doing a good job reporting it? There have been far more depressing events which I have had a far more successful time covering. Employing her usual common-sense tactics, Patricia kept her eye on the road and told me to 'wise up'. The BBC's senior managers appeared to share the same sentiment. When told about the circumstances one of them simply said, 'Well, he won't do that again, will he?'

If the Clinton visit appeared a little unreal to all who witnessed it then the splash of water in the face came about two months later with a statement from the IRA issued this time to RTÉ. Violence of various kinds had begun to raise its face in defiance of presidents and peace brokers. Under the cover name of

'Direct Action Against Drugs' the IRA had for several months been killing those it accused of drug dealing. Loyalists were threatening similar action and the extreme republican INLA descended into another bout of fratricidal feuding. But the main ceasefires still appeared to be holding. However, President Clinton's visit to Belfast only bought a little extra time and nothing more. Republicans remained opposed to any gesture on disarmament, and they were equally unimpressed by John Major's decision that they should stand in elections to qualify as negotiators on their community's behalf. The IRA statement issued to RTÉ claimed that it was 'with great reluctance that the leadership of Óglaigh na hÉireann announces that the complete cessation of military operations will end at 6 p.m. on February 9, 1996'.

The wording looked real enough but we did not want to believe it. RTÉ was having difficulties verifying it because of an unusual delay getting hold of its special correspondent Charlie Bird. Ironically the first call I received alerting me to the statement came as BBC Northern Ireland's news staff were gathered together in the Belfast newsroom for a team briefing on the new softer more peace-oriented news which was due to be launched on the following Monday. People thought I was being rude as I bellowed across the room to the Chief Security Correspondent Brian Rowan, interrupting the senior editors in mid-briefing. 'Barney, Barney, get over here, something's up . . .' A large number of the BBC's journalists were wearing, or about to change into, dinner jackets and bow ties as that Friday was the night for an annual local journalism awards dinner. I had a ticket too. I reread the words someone had dictated over to me down the line – could it all be a cruel hoax designed by some joker to ruin the Belfast journalists' big night?

We started ringing around republican contacts trying to establish what was going on. Was the IRA as a whole going back to violence or had the organisation split? One republican who had travelled south said darkly that he would not want to be at home in Belfast overnight – could we be about to witness a feud? When I spoke to Sinn Féin's Dublin spokeswoman Rita O'Hare within seconds of the IRA statement being issued she seemed genuinely surprised. Either that or she was a better actress than I had previously given her credit for.

At the same time as the statement went to RTÉ, the Belfast *Irish News* got another call warning about a bomb left at the South Quay British Rail station in London's Docklands. It's an eerie feeling knowing you are privy to information which could save someone's life, but might not get to those who need to know in time. As the clock ticked towards seven o'clock that evening I sat and waited with the rest of the newsroom to see what would happen. If the newsagents John Jeffries and Inan Ul-Haq Bashir had known what we knew then they might have reacted more quickly when a police constable shouted a warning to them. They might be alive today. But information takes time to get from Belfast to London, and the newsagents were only told to leave their shop three minutes before the massive bomb exploded, killing them both. Now we all knew for certain that the IRA ceasefire was over.

I never got to the IPR Belfast journalism awards dinner. According to those who did, it was a weird occasion, full of empty tables. Many of the journalists who sat down for their starters were gone before their main courses arrived. Contrary to our image as vultures, no one was popping champagne corks in celebration of the return of violence. The RUC, which had abandoned its flak jackets in line with the new-found peace, started donning body armour again more or less immediately. But the bombing and shooting did not return to Northern Ireland. Instead we had a few months of a 'phoney war' when the only devices going off were in England or, on one occasion, at a British army base in Germany. On the face of it this was the IRA's ideal kind of campaign. Instead of being drawn into the mire of sectarian conflict back home in Northern Ireland its volunteers would take on the imperialist enemy direct. However, the strategy always teetered on the edge. Concentrating on audacious attacks in England and on the Continent was good PR but it stretched the IRA's lines of communication and left its units open to interception by the security forces. Back in Northern Ireland meanwhile, any widespread loss of life in England would inevitably put pressure on the loyalist ceasefire.

Three months after the end of the IRA ceasefire the mid-Ulster UVF claimed to have left three bombs at Dublin airport. Nothing was found but the alert disrupted activity at the airport. The incident was interesting for two reasons: one, the notion of targeting the Irish Republic in reprisal for attacks on England was gaining ground amongst some loyalists; two, the fact that the mid-Ulster wing of the UVF had openly admitted its involvement in the hoaxes showed the regional divisions which were opening up within loyalism as the Protestant paramilitaries saw their counterparts in the IRA returning to what they knew best.

Shortly after the Dublin alerts I got a call from Radio Four's *World Tonight* asking me to put together a piece on the pressures on the loyalist ceasefire. To cut to the real story meant only one thing – the mid-Ulster UVF – and only one man – Billy Wright from Portadown, known to the papers as 'King Rat'. Billy Wright had a fearsome reputation and was widely believed to be a leading 'trigger man' for the UVF in mid-Ulster. At this stage, however, the police did not have any warrant out for his arrest, nor was I privy to any information about his participation in particular attacks. I decided that rather than interview journalists who had talked to Wright paraphrasing his views it was time to talk to the man himself.

I met Billy Wright in a hotel in Portadown. We then jumped into his high-powered black car and drove over to his home in a local loyalist estate. As Wright chatted to his partner and played with his child it all seemed strangely reminiscent of my interview with Ray Smallwoods in Lisburn a couple of years previously. Wright held similarly firm views about 'the decent loyalist people of Ulster' and how much they were misunderstood. That said, there was a more Messianic tone to his message, which was littered with overtly Christian evangelical phrases, and a more menacing glint in his eyes. On the one hand the loyalist was saying 'God bless you, Mark' and talking of the unionist people's love for 'her majesty, the Queen'. On the other he was praising the professionalism of the bomb alert at Dublin airport and warning of more to come. And how could I come to terms with Billy Wright's Christian message whilst bearing in mind not only everything I had read about 'King Rat', but the words of a convicted drug dealer I had met down by the border who had told me that protection had been provided for him by Wright's men? We talked for a whole afternoon, covering Christianity, the state of loyalism, the relations between the people of Northern Ireland and their counterparts in England and the strain which IRA violence was placing on the loyalist ceasefire.

Wright's message, boiled down, was that the Irish Republic should beware. He made a thinly veiled threat to respond to IRA violence in kind, saying that 'If it's acceptable for the Dublin government to shore up a movement that's killing British citizens I would imagine that among the ground support of the UVF it would be acceptable to see members of the republican community lose their lives in a similar fashion.' But he also maintained that the UVF did not want to return to war in Northern Ireland and that he personally hoped for peace. On the subject of the Orangemen's Drumcree march in his own mid-Ulster backyard, Billy Wright warned the Northern Ireland Office and the Irish government not to take the marchers on, arguing that 'There is a great risk that if violence starts it could evolve into something greater and it could be the end of this process.'

In my report I described Billy Wright as a former loyalist prisoner, but also said that in mid-Ulster his words carried a lot of sway with the UVF. Most people in Northern Ireland knew what kind of sway that meant. When I played a tape of Wright's comments to the Irish government minister Proinsias De Rossa he was so furious that he spat out a denunciation of the loyalist without any hesitation – unusual, because normally Mr De Rossa's comments carry a trademark stutter, which appeared to have been suppressed by the anger he felt.

As Ireland Correspondent I had always been given a lot of leeway by the management about what I could broadcast, but after the interview made some headlines in the local papers some Belfast-based editors expressed concern that I had allowed Billy Wright on air. Wright had been frequently interviewed by my colleagues in newspapers but this had been the first time in quite a while that he had been on either the radio or the television. A few days later I got a letter from twenty-seven people who identified themselves as members of families who had 'lost loved ones at the hands of Mr Wright and his cohorts'. Stating that Billy Wright had been involved in 'up to forty murders over the past ten years', they said my interview had caused them 'great pain and anguish' and asked if the BBC 'could see your way to keep Mr Wright off the airwaves for the time being at any rate'.

It's a point of view which no journalist can ignore, but what is the answer? Billy Wright's comments in the *World Tonight* interview foreshadowed the split in the ranks of the UVF which was then taking shape. Soon the mid-Ulster UVF reconstituted itself under the name of the Loyalist Volunteer Force and returned to violence. The main UVF accused Billy Wright of treachery and sentenced him to death or exile, a statement which immediately projected him into the headlines and ensured he was frequently interviewed on every television and radio news programme concerning Northern Ireland. The DUP MP Willie McCrea went so far as to share a platform with the loyalist, a gesture which almost certainly cost him his parliamentary seat at the next election. I don't feel at all responsible for Billy Wright's subsequent media exposure as the division within the UVF was an important story which would have been covered by my colleagues in any case. But what about the 'great pain and anguish' of my twenty-seven correspondents?

The BBC has tended by and large to interview paramilitaries only after they have served their time or after they have become spokespeople for 'bona fide' political parties. But who tests those 'bona fides'? The loyalists David Ervine and Billy Hutchinson were both regular interviewees on our airwaves long before they became elected councillors. One has a conviction for transporting a bomb, the other is a convicted murderer. We talked to them not just because of the potential votes they might be able to garner but because of their insight into the UVF. We talk to John White as a loyalist politician who has been inside Downing Street to put his case. But we know that the relatives of the couple whom he stabbed to death in the 1970s will not enjoy seeing him on the television. Gerry Adams is an elected MP, but he's well known to have been a senior figure in the IRA at the time of the Bloody Friday bombings in Belfast in July 1972. No doubt the victims of those bombings feel pain and anguish when they see him on the screen. But can we stop interviewing him because of that?

What is difficult is, as with Billy Wright, when the 'dogs in the street' − to use Irish slang − tell you that something is the case, but the police have not yet issued an arrest warrant and there is nothing official on paper. Should the journalist introduce his own category of censorship because of an individual's notoriety? In fact I did this once in the case of two republicans who gave us an interview for *Spotlight* about collusion between the police and loyalists and made allegations regarding the murder by loyalists of the Belfast lawyer Pat Finucane. At least one of my two interviewees was a man with an exceedingly bad reputation around Belfast, widely suspected to have been a close-quarter assassin on a number of recent IRA killings. We interviewed the two republicans in silhouette because of the obvious risk to their personal safety. But afterwards I argued that the contributions by unidentified men of questionable character actually damaged the main thrust of our report, which included an extremely compelling interview with Pat Finucane's widow, Geraldine, the first she had given to the media. Looking back I think I got this wrong, and should have included the two unidentified men, thus allowing our audience to make up their minds on the basis of the whole picture we had uncovered 'warts and all'. Missing the men out on the basis of their supposed notoriety was tantamount to introducing my own version of the government's broadcasting ban − creating a category of people who are deemed fit by the authorities to walk the streets, but not fit to appear on television.

It is of course a question of degree. No journalist working in the UK today would put some assassin on the television bragging about his crime not long after carrying it out. Nor would our radio stations carry the sort of exhortations to violence which were a hallmark of broadcasting in places like Rwanda when the 1994 genocide took place. On the other hand we run the rather more subtle risk of putting a premium on hypocrisy – allowing onto the airwaves only the 'terrorists' who have learned to be mealy-mouthed and deliberately ambiguous about what they are saying, the men who will praise the Lord live on air and pass the ammunition off it. For that reason, I believe we have a responsibility, when we know a 'non-violent' community activist is in fact putting out statements on behalf of paramilitary organisations, not to let them onto the air without some clear indication in our script that this is someone who 'wields great influence with LVF members' or some other legal yet suitable form of words. In addition, when the government introduced an early release scheme for paramilitary prisoners the BBC went to considerable lengths to contact the relatives of any victims before putting on air the prisoners who had caused them so much grief.

To be fair, my twenty-seven correspondents recognised the dilemmas, writing that they appreciated 'that journalists have a job to do, particularly now that the censorship laws have been relaxed'. After reading their letter I vowed to think even more carefully in the future about who I interviewed and on what terms. But I think given the choice I would have recorded my interview with Billy Wright again. My letter-writers said they had been involved in discussions with the RUC about the possibility of Wright being arrested and charged for his 'terrorist activities'. In the event the police did not convict him of any of the murders his name had been linked with. Instead he was arrested for threatening a woman on the estate where he lived. The charge was enough to get Billy Wright put inside the Maze jail, where he was shot dead by an INLA inmate on 27 December 1997. The LVF gave him a huge paramilitary funeral.

27

Groundhog Day

SUMMER 1996

It was to have been a single day's work in London, but the day had stretched out into almost a week. The reason – protracted discussions between the British and Irish governments about the precise role which should be played by the former US senator George Mitchell, the governments' choice for chairman of the Northern Ireland peace talks. Despite the end of the IRA ceasefire the government had pressed ahead with elections to choose negotiators at the talks, presenting broadcasters with the job of trying to explain on air the D'Hondt system of proportionality, something which with my non-mathematical brain I found completely impossible. Challenged by one presenter to do it I took out a piece of paper and made various squiggles and said, 'Look, there, it's simple.' It helped that I was on a radio programme at the time.

In London the sun blazed down on us as the Anglo-Irish talks went on. I finished off my report at the BBC's Westminster office then hurried over to Horse Guards Parade to go live onto the *Six O'Clock News*. In order to improve the background the cameraman had me standing on a box so I teetered nervously waiting for my turn to go on air. We had absolutely no one around us and the only other BBC staff members nearby were in the broadcast vehicle hundreds of yards away. As the studio gallery told me I had thirty seconds to go I caught sight of half a dozen teenagers with baseball caps turned backwards on their heads coming around the corner of the parade ground a couple of hundred yards away. More importantly they caught sight of me. As the presenter asked his first question, I noticed the teenagers hopping over the barrier around the perimeter of Horse Guards Parade and heading full tilt in our direction. The cameraman, staring into his eyepiece, did not see a thing. I realised the question had come to an end and started to talk in a somewhat hesitant manner about the likely role which George Mitchell would play at the talks. By now the posse were just a few yards off – did they intend to jump in front of the camera and make silly faces on national TV or were they determined to knock me off my precarious position on the box? The presenter hit me with a follow-up question, which I tried even more hesitantly to answer. My real emotion was a mixture of suppressed amusement and relief. The teenagers had decided to pretend to be a Second World War fighter squadron. They swooped in perfect formation behind the cameraman's back, simultaneously opening up 'ack-ack' fire on me for a couple of passes before fleeing to the other end of the parade ground. All the viewers on the *Six O'Clock News* saw was a rather stumbling correspondent. I wondered whether the baseball cap gang knew how close they had come to national stardom.

George Mitchell's appointment did not go down too well with some of the parties. Ian Paisley took the view that being a Maronite Christian was the next worst thing to being a Catholic so objected on those grounds alone. But eventually they all settled down. We journalists got used to taking up residence in a village of Portakabins which sprang up in the car park outside the distinctly non-televisual Castle Buildings office block where the talks took place. The main drama at the opening session of the negotiations on 10 June 1996 was provided by Gerry Adams and his Sinn Féin delegation demanding to be let in. The party had been barred because of the IRA's return to violence. The republicans spent a considerable amount of time seeking out locked gates and fences to be photographed against in order to provide a suitable image of their exclusion. At one point it looked as if having got in to the press village-cum-car park they would never get out as the horde of journalists and photographers from around the world besieged them inside a small Portakabin.

With the IRA ceasefire still off and Sinn Féin excluded from the talks the prospects for the summer marching season of 1996 did not look good. As anyone who had watched the Trimble–Paisley double act the previous year could have predicted, there was no mood for compromise in Portadown. The Drumcree stand-off handed David Trimble the Ulster Unionist leadership, but it also saddled him and indeed the rest of us in Northern Ireland with our very own 'groundhog day' – that depressingly familiar series of circumstances which looks doomed to keep repeating itself, no matter what anyone does.

Twelve months on we all found ourselves in the same cul-de-sac, saying 'hello' to the same local people and preparing for the same stand-off. The BBC sent over Kate Adie which gave one loyalist with a sense of humour the opportunity to erect a banner on the front line declaring that 'it must be war,

Kate Adie's here'. With the Garvaghy Road Residents' Coalition now adamantly opposed to any march, the RUC once again blocked the Orangemen's path. The stand-off began, with even more loyalist supporters gathering in the field beside Drumcree parish church than had been there the previous year. The disruption swiftly spread across Northern Ireland with loyalists mounting roadblocks in many areas.

The clashes on the front line at Drumcree were only part of the story. A Catholic taxi driver Michael McGoldrick was found shot dead beside his car in nearby Lurgan. My mind flashed back to my conversation with Billy Wright and his warning that there would be 'very serious trouble' if the Orangemen's parade was blocked. Much later another loyalist contact told me that he had been in the field at Drumcree the evening before McGoldrick was killed and some Portadown loyalists had told him to watch the television in the morning to 'see we mean business'. Neither side to the dispute heeded Michael McGoldrick's father's passionate plea at the funeral that they should 'bury your pride as I bury my son'. Towns like Coleraine and Cookstown were cut off by makeshift barricades. The Orange Order appeared to be trying to tell the government who was the boss. I made my way through the front line early one morning to record an interview with the Orange official George Patton and get a few 'vox pops', brief interviews with the ageing Orangemen who had camped out overnight. It was okay to do this early in the day, but venturing on the other side of the lines became less advisable for a BBC reporter from the late afternoon or early evening onwards, as the heavy mob arrived.

George Patton told me he was going to do another BBC programme on the phone. I said that if he hurried up I could record his answers in decent quality and send them down the line from our broadcast vehicle. I couldn't hang around, though, I warned him, as I had lots to do 'on the other side'. George replied that he could, if he wanted, arrange it so that I couldn't leave. He was joking, but only just. During that week, in that place, it certainly wasn't the RUC's writ which ran.

The atmosphere on the front line became ever more poisonous. RUC officers were taunted about how vulnerable their families were at home – in many instances police families living in loyalist areas came under attack. At one point a helicopter swooped low over the loyalist crowd. It turned out to be a deliberate distraction as the RUC riot squads pushed forward, pushing the loyalists back into the Drumcree graveyard. The manoeuvre bought the security forces a little time and space in order to install a concrete barrier which cut out the need for officers and rioters to come face to face.

With the disruption so widespread I divided my time between Portadown and Belfast, hammering up and down the roads at breakneck speed in order to deter anyone intent on hijacking my car. As the Ireland Correspondent on duty I was particularly called upon to give the early morning analysis on programmes like Radio Four's *Today* and BBC *Breakfast News*. I decided it would be inadequate for me to get into the office and go on air just on the basis of reports on paper about the violence which had taken place the night before. So I got up in the early hours and drove around likely trouble spots so I could see the level of damage for myself. Once in north Belfast I was surprised to see the rioters still awake and active despite the fact that the night was over.

'I wouldn't hang around here too long,' said one police officer, 'it's still a bit busy.'

I asked him what he'd been up to and he pointed to the burned-out apartment building behind him.

'We rescued a Catholic family from the first floor there, had to get them out the window because the ground floor was well alight. Whilst we were doing that somebody on the other side of that barricade over there opened up on us with automatic fire.'

The police officer had been on riot duty for three nights in a row. He looked unshaven and completely worn out. I headed back to Broadcasting House to be told by the *Breakfast News* presenter that some people in the Ministry of Defence were briefing that there wasn't really any need for extra troops to be sent over there and then, only for certain units to be put on standby. I replied that if what I had seen was anything to go by the soldiers were needed yesterday.

Getting up early and talking to politicians late into the night in order to assess whether there might be any movement in the stand-off was wearing me out. At one point I declared myself off duty for a couple of hours so I could go home and get a takeaway Indian meal with Patricia. On the way to pick up the carry-out I had to do a U-turn when a group of youths dashed out into the road and tried to hijack the bus just in front of me. The next night I resolutely refused to do any reports for half an hour whilst together with my researcher Declan Carlin I drank a beer and watched *Men Behaving Badly*. It was a way of staying on the edge of sanity.

What appeared most depressing was not only the level of violence, but the sense of foreboding that the Twelfth of July was just around the corner. The

Orangemen threatened to bring one hundred thousand people to the field at Drumcree if they did not get their way, and none of us camped out in the field opposite felt at all confident that the police and army would be able to hold the line. The RUC riot officers joked with us that when the moment to retreat came they all had assigned seats in their grey Land Rovers, whilst we would be trying to jump the hedge and break the world record for four hundred metres. We had been issued with reinforced caps, shin-pads and even gas masks, although the security forces at no point used gas. One Dublin-based journalist, however, had come up with his own rather more useful form of protection should the breakthrough occur. He showed me an Orange sash he had hidden in his pocket, which he intended to slip on before melding into the crowd.

As someone who was on the television fairly constantly during the week there was no chance of me melding into the crowd. I knew the loyalists on the Drumcree front line didn't like what I was saying because they made it obvious. One of them must have had a portable TV set because when I did a live turn from the field on the *Six O'Clock News* they erupted into clearly audible catcalls, 'What do you know, Devenport? Go home, you little bastard!' It was a charming display of Protestant culture. A bit of barracking might be off-putting but this was as nothing to the experience of my colleague Maggie Swarbrick. As we sat in the field a loudspeaker in the Orange encampment relayed to us stirring loyalist marching music throughout the day. We dubbed the service 'Radio Orange'. Coming up to the hour, Maggie prepared to do a live report on her mobile phone. Somebody in the field decided at the same time to switch their PA system to BBC Radio Ulster. As Maggie went on air every word she spoke into her mobile phone came booming at high volume back across the fields where we sat. How she kept going through her report I don't know.

Constant broadcasting has its benefits and its drawbacks. For weeks afterwards people came up to me in the shops in Belfast and thanked me for the job I had done keeping them informed. But a lot of people did not like anything I had had to say. During the week I had been secretly hoping that some kind of a compromise might be found in order to avert the doomsday scenario which we all worried about for the Twelfth of July. Some of my contacts on the Protestant side thought that some kind of limited parade might eventually prove acceptable and I referred to their hopes in one early morning live contribution. When I arrived back on the Garvaghy estate a man rushed out of his house to upbraid me. 'How dare you talk about compromise! Brendan

McKenna [of the Garvaghy Road Residents' Coalition] is our leader and there'll be no compromise here.'

In the end the talk of compromise did turn out to be a false trail. Whilst the residents' representatives and Catholic and Protestant church leaders met in a local factory the security forces got the order to clear protesters off the road and let the Orangemen pass. I still have the notepad on which I scribbled my script:

> Within the past twenty minutes the army started to remove the barrier which separated the security forces from the Orangemen at Drumcree. Orange officials told their members to prepare to march down the mainly Catholic Garvaghy Road without triumphalism, but with dignity and pride. At the same time on the Garvaghy Road residents mounted a sit-down protest. A few stones were thrown at the army who moved in quickly to drag the protesters out of the way. There has, apparently, been no agreement with the residents for the march. Soldiers used great force to move the protesters from the road.

I remained in the field watching the Orangemen move off but my colleague Juliet Bremner kept me informed of the fierce clashes taking place further down the road. As the lodges began to leave, the battery on my mobile phone gave out, but I restored service to BBC listeners with the generous assistance of my colleagues from the *Guardian* and *The Times*, whose deadlines remained a few hours away. A few minutes later I scribbled another voice piece.

> Rioting is continuing now on the mainly Catholic Garvaghy estate as people express their anger at the decision to let the Orangemen go by. A van was turned over and set alight. Plastic bullets have been fired and petrol bombs thrown. The Orangemen were under orders from their leaders to march in silence, but nationalists are furious that the parade was allowed to go ahead.

As the mayhem continued the RUC Chief Constable Sir Hugh Annesley defended his decision, saying the negotiating tactics employed by both sides had not left him with any room for manoeuvre. The stand-off, he argued, could have led to further loss of life and no parade was worth that. He added that his officers were sick to the back teeth of being the meat in the sandwich between two intransigent communities.

I watched the Orangemen walk silently and rather smugly by. For the second year in a row they had got their way. In principle I felt very concerned about Sir Hugh's U-turn – would a lobby group have been allowed to triumph by sheer force of numbers anywhere else in the UK? Selfishly, though, we were all relieved that we wouldn't be sitting in the field come the Twelfth of July. The U-turn had – for us at least – shattered that sense of foreboding which my researcher Declan and I had felt especially strongly earlier that morning as we drove towards Portadown.

Letting the Orangemen pass by inevitably led to a bitter reaction in nationalist areas. But whilst rioting and blockades in loyalist areas make the practical business of getting around Northern Ireland extremely difficult, the security forces find disturbances in nationalist areas easier to contain. Nationalists are not only in a minority, but they tend to live in areas which do not straddle the transport network and other vital parts of the local infrastructure. This is part of the legacy of the years of unionist Stormont rule. So whilst I had to vary my route home from work over the next few days, the drive back wasn't half as complicated as it had been earlier in the week.

Between 7 and 10 July the police and army fired 662 plastic bullets. Over the next two days they fired 1,000 bullets in Derry alone. A man was killed after being hit by an army vehicle during rioting in the city. Nationalist politicians complained with justification that the security forces had torn into Catholic rioters with greater force than they had shown when confronting the Protestants. I am sure a few isolated police officers felt happier beating 'the enemy' rather than taking on their 'own side'. But aside from the underlying sectarian attitudes of some members of the security forces, I believe there was interesting additional psychology at play. Many of the riot squad officers who had stood day in, day out taking the taunts of the loyalists at Drumcree were the same units who forcibly cleared the residents from the Catholic Garvaghy Road and who the next morning enforced a curfew on the Catholics of the lower Ormeau Road. I had watched them getting more and more wound up as the week went on and I believe many were keen to take their frustration out on someone, anyone. If the order had come to wade in at Drumcree then it would have been Protestant skulls which got cracked. But after Sir Hugh Annesley's U-turn, the only skulls available were Catholic skulls.

On the Ormeau Road I noted what I described on air as 'the greening of nationalism'. SDLP politicians who I talked to came out with comments I would normally have associated with Sinn Féin. Sinn Féin, in turn, sounded like the INLA's political wing. I hated to think what the INLA was saying. The

11 July U-turn justified all the green nationalist arguments about Northern Ireland being an Orange state run for an Orange people. In the immediate aftermath Sinn Féin experienced some local difficulties keeping its followers in check. However, in the longer term, republicans, who had been under pressure over their failure to restore the IRA ceasefire, could now take satisfaction from the fact that the marching issue was proving their point and recruiting them new supporters.

At the end of the week I took a short break in Donegal. The lack of sleep and pressure of work had been getting to me. My brain wouldn't stop turning over and I desperately needed a change. In a bar in Donegal I bumped into Enda Cullen, a Belfast doctor whom I had last met working for Concern in the Somali capital Mogadishu. He was just the right person to chat to as Somalia had been the only place I knew which had been madder than the scenes I had witnessed across Northern Ireland that week. Slowly I began to get matters in perspective.

But the break proved only a temporary respite. The phone went, and senior producer Clive Ferguson told me that a hotel had been bombed in County Fermanagh. Patricia and I piled into the car and headed to Enniskillen. The priest who had taken the warning call said the bombers had told him they were the IRA. But with the loyalist ceasefire on the brink, I cautioned against jumping to conclusions. The Continuity IRA, which eventually admitted the blast, regarded itself after all as the 'true' IRA. The front of the Killyhevlin hotel, a place where I had frequently stopped for lunch, had been reduced to rubble by the old-fashioned but highly effective car bomb.

I got back to the Belfast newsroom after a day broadcasting from Enniskillen. It was the first time in a week that I had a few seconds spare to check my answering machine − for days I had just been diving in and out of the office. On the machine there were reams of messages, many from members of the public, some who liked my reports and others who criticised me. One caller with an American passport wanted me to contact the US Consulate in order to seek approval for the dispatch of American peacekeeping troops to protect her home. One message went on for ever. The caller began by telling me about a sectarian attack which had just been mounted by a gang of youths on the small group of houses where he lived. When I didn't reply, he called on a neighbour to describe what had happened too. She told her story then passed the phone onto another neighbour, who did the same. Eventually what sounded like a whole streetful of people appeared to be talking on the other end of the line, partly to me and partly to each other, as if leaving a message on the BBC's answering machine provided some kind of therapy. They never said exactly where they were or left a number for me to ring them back.

28

Groundhog Day Again

Nineteen ninety-six was undoubtedly the worst Drumcree I experienced. But as I have written my account of it I have consciously had to keep stopping and checking – did that event happen in 1996 or 1997 or 1998? It is in the nature of Groundhog Days that different times and different experiences meld together. Rather than filling in the gaps in strict chronological order I think it might be useful to turn to the other Drumcrees and draw what lessons if any I can from them. Like the Orangemen, having started this long march I think it might be best to complete it. But first, a little background on the Orange Order and me.

In 1988 the BBC sent me notification that I had 'no perceived religious affiliation'. This came after it checked my records in accordance with Northern Ireland's Fair Employment legislation. But a year or so later it sent me another note informing me that it had engaged in what it called 'residual monitoring'. This meant checking my primary school records from England. It now told me that I was a Catholic. I replied that it had neither my actual religious affiliation, which was 'atheist', nor my perceived affiliation in Northern Ireland, which was 'Brit'. The personnel department, however, gave no ground.

I suspect my arguments would have cut as little ice with the Orange Order as they did with BBC personnel, which made it all the more amusing when Walter Williams suggested I should join. Walter was the veteran official of the Grand Orange Lodge when I first arrived in Belfast and I had to chat to him on a few occasions about the institution's plans to mark the landing of King William at Torbay. I thought I should be extra-attentive to try to learn about this strange alien organisation, and Walter, duly impressed by my detailed enquiries about Orange history, advised me that the Order could 'use a few good young men like you'. I did not have the heart to let him know that I would have fallen at the first fence, although in later years I regretted I did not follow this approach up further. I could have been the best-selling author of the exposé *I Was a Catholic Orangeman*.

I had a number of other very civilised dealings with the Order, especially during the making of a *Spotlight* film on the importance of anniversaries and history to both traditions. I had to turn down an invitation to dinner from the St Brendan's Loyal Orange Lodge in east Belfast. I genuinely had another engagement. It was nothing to do with them being dedicated to temperance, and therefore having nothing palatable to wash down the duck à l'orange.

But all these decent experiences to one side, I must confess that I start out with an inbuilt bias against any organisation which seeks to be exclusive. This goes for Freemasons, all-male golf clubs, and night clubs with dress codes and bouncers on the door. I cannot stand any of them. In the Orange Order's case, of course, it isn't especially helpful that it seeks to exclude me in particular. But I like to think I reserve the same amount of disdain for Opus Dei or the Knights of Columbanus or any other Catholic equivalent that anyone else can name. That said, in Northern Ireland there are a lot of organisations who wouldn't have me as a member and as a correspondent you have to deal with them all. In a society which boasts the INLA or the Red Hand Defenders you have to admit the Orange Order isn't the worst. But nor is it always the respectable upright institution it often claims to be.

Back in England my friends constantly ask me, 'Why do they have to walk down streets where they aren't wanted?' and I try to explain about historical tradition, changing patterns of land ownership and settlement and so on. But it just doesn't wash. If the Morris dancers, who have a long, proud history in Oxford, found the pub they had always performed at on a Mayday morning did not want them any more, they would merely transfer their allegiances to another hostelry. They would continue to perform their traditional dances, to wear their picturesque white costumes bedecked with ribbons and bells, to doff their funny hats and to beat their staves together as they have done for centuries. If the Orangemen are only maintaining their cultural traditions they could do the same. The fact that battle lines are drawn so firmly and, on occasion, so violently shows this is about much more than keeping colourful pageantry alive.

It's true that many Orange lodges have been caught in a trap of the republican movement's making, unwilling or unable to see that the nationalist residents' groups win both ways. During the nineties the republican leadership identified Orange parades as an excellent issue to organise around. It exposes the poor treatment still meted out to some Catholic communities, highlights elements of Protestant tradition at its intransigent worst and poses constant dilemmas for the British state and British forces which republicans have long wanted to topple. The residents' groups win if they win – by standing up for local people's rights. And they win if they lose – because the RUC beats them out of the way and they are able to cry 'Orange state!' But if at times I have felt the same urge as the likes of Seán O'Callaghan or Ruth Dudley Edwards to educate the Orangemen in the fine arts of propaganda, at other times I am inclined to say, 'Hey, Catholics have basic rights too, and the fact that Sinn Féin might be using their plight for its own purposes doesn't change that bottom line.'

In 1997 Drumcree was almost over before it began when the new Chief Constable Ronnie Flanagan made a decision that he and the government weren't ready to take on the Orange Order. Wearing sinister-looking black flameproof clothing the security forces moved in early and cleared the road, despite fierce scuffles during the night. I had been spared the night shift in order to save my energies for the day ahead, so, like many other colleagues, had to scramble down to the Garvaghy Road to catch up with the action. The road was littered with stones and broken bottles. Police officers and soldiers sat slumped against walls, already exhausted, but still summoning up their strength for what was obviously going to be a tough day.

Approaching eleven o'clock in the morning local people started complaining that they weren't being allowed to cross the road to get to their church. Some of these complaints were synthetic, coming from people whose only *raison d'être* was to get out on the road again in order to renew their protest, something the police would never allow as it meant having to fight to clear them off all over again. One of these characters confronted a soldier just yards away from me and told him, 'The only mass you'll be going to will be in a box.' It did not seem an especially Christian sentiment for someone so eager to get to church.

But at the same time there were old folks in the little cul-de-sac on the Garvaghy estate who seemed bewildered and distressed that they could not stroll over to their regular Sunday mass. I thought of my own father, a devout Catholic, and wondered what he would feel if a soldier stood between him and his church. Surely it was wrong that the British government was treating the right of people to walk down a road where they did not live as more important than the right of the people who lived there to go to their regular religious service?

In the event the local priests – to mix my faiths if not my metaphors – decided to bring the mountain to Muhammad, by holding an open-air mass in the estate. It made for great pictures which played very badly across the world for both the security forces and the Orange Order.

The march went ahead, the Orangemen crunching over the debris of the battle the night before, and the security forces holding their lines just long enough to get the whole business over and done with. Then, nervously and rapidly, the soldiers and police began to retreat, well aware that they would be followed by a hail of bricks and petrol bombs. The previous year I had been stuck at a commentary point nearer Drumcree church and out of line of sight of the riot on the road. In 1997 I insisted on staying in the thick of the action, even if this meant I could only broadcast from my mobile phone. This was partly because I wanted to see it all with my own eyes, and partly because I didn't want my latest researcher, Jane MacSorley, charging around gathering material for me in circumstances I was not prepared to venture into myself.

However, every Drumcree the BBC sends over dozens of extra staff whom it expects to do the 'eyewitness' bit. It preferred to have Denis Murray and me, as the resident Ireland Correspondents, providing the analysis. This led to an interesting interview on *The World This Weekend* on Radio Four. The programme had probably taken quite enough of a blow-by-blow account of events on the Garvaghy Road by the time it got to me about half an hour in. But whilst it had been on air the riot, following the partial withdrawal of the security forces, had become much more intense. Jane MacSorley and I tried to dodge and weave to avoid the hail of rocks and other projectiles, but it was all, quite literally, hit and miss. Far from being the 'old hand' guaranteeing Jane's safety I managed to lead her directly into the firing line on more than one occasion. On the mobile phone, the presenter wanted me to move on to the longer-term implications. 'Mark, the march has now gone through relatively calmly, do you think that in the months ahead it will be possible for the opposing sides to come to some kind of a working arrangement?' On the other end of the line, I wanted to tell him that the situation was far from calm. On air this came out as 'Um, I shall be happy to analyse the long-term context in just a moment but, um, if you will excuse me for a second because there's a frying pan flying towards my head.' I ducked the non-stick missile then tried to mumble some apparently logical words of punditry.

The decision to push a 'quick and dirty' march down the road in 1997 led to a predictably violent reaction in some Catholic areas, but this was relatively short-lived. The Orange Order's decision to voluntarily reroute many of its main parades on the Twelfth of July got the height of the marching season over and done with, with a minimum of fuss. But it still left unanswered basic questions about the rights and wrongs of the matter. No one could pretend that the tactical decisions of that summer had ushered in a new era of co-operation. I went to one street corner on the working-class lower Newtownards Road in Protestant east Belfast where, in the space of a few yards, I heard a whole range of views about whether the Orange rerouting had been a wise move or a sell-out. But the voice which stayed with me was that of a six-year-old boy who dogged my footsteps wherever I went: 'I hate the Fenians, they won't let us do anything we want to do.' Needless to say, little Stephen didn't have any Catholic friends – there was still a lot of work to be done.

In 1998 we were back – the same cul-de-sac, the same kids crowding around our outside broadcast vehicles, the same amazing generosity from many of the local people. Denis Murray bumped into one woman and mentioned that we had not fixed anywhere to stay. She responded by producing a set of keys and giving us her cousin's house, left vacant as her cousin had decided to go away for the marching season. The family, who were clearly not well off, did not ask for a penny. The BBC responded by promptly losing their invaluable keys. With the assistance of our kindly benefactor, I then broke into the house through a back window. Fortunately we found the keys before the owner returned.

In contrast to 1997, this time the police and army were under orders to hold the line against the Orangemen. The barriers they had at their disposal were more formidable than two years before, but with dissident loyalist paramilitaries mingling with the Orange Order supporters in the field at Drumcree it remained a very dangerous situation both for the security forces and for the protesters. The RUC Land Rovers on the front line came under attack from a series of blast bombs, one of which shattered an RUC officer's knee. Powerful fireworks sent the press corps scattering as they looped in our direction. Enraged by the injuries they were taking, the security forces responded to the onslaught with a fusillade of plastic bullets, on one occasion blinding a young female protester in one eye. There could no longer be any question that the 'baton rounds', as the security forces preferred to call them, were reserved for Catholics.

In between shifts at the front line, having our own house to retreat to was a boon. But the beds inside were scarce. One night I managed to book into a local guesthouse. It meant the chance of a hot shower, clean sheets and a cooked breakfast. But it was already late by the time I set off and travelling the nearby roads wasn't necessarily a great idea. I negotiated for quite a while with soldiers to let me out of their barrier and they eventually waved me on their way, but I had not driven long when I saw a group of Orangemen stretched out across the lane in front of me. Perhaps in daylight I would have tried to talk my way through, but I wasn't convinced it would be wise at this time of night – what if they didn't like what I had just said on the TV? I took a sharp right into a farmyard, did a three-point turn and arrived back at the army checkpoint which I had just spent half an hour negotiating my way past. 'Oh, are they still there?' said the soldier. 'We thought they'd gone by now.' I wished he'd warned me about the possible roadblock on my way out.

Back in the estate, I realised there wasn't a bed left in our house. Then, as I pondered my options, I spied Drumcree House, a bed and breakfast which stands in a field just opposite the church. At midnight I knocked on the door and fortunately Mrs O'Neill had just had a cancellation. There was a very nice room free. When I headed up the stairs I imagined that I would sleep the sleep of the dead. But I had not bargained for my brain, which continued to whizz merrily round, nor for the fact that my room afforded a grandstand view of the scene at Drumcree. That night I wrote the following dispatch which was broadcast the next morning on BBC Radio Scotland's *Reporter's Notebook*.

DRUMCREE HOUSE

Last night I went to sleep in a comfortable bed and breakfast replete with floral wallpaper, tea and coffee making facilities, a TV in your bedroom. The sort of place, in fact, that you might check into if you were on holiday touring the Highlands and Islands. Peering out of my window, I could clearly make out the silhouette of a picturesque Protestant church with a distinctive spire, something I might expect to see if I had been motoring around the Cotswolds.

But there the parallels end, because the bed and breakfast in question is called Drumcree House and it's not in Scotland or England, but in Portadown, County Armagh. And beside the spire of the church the scene I looked out on was a bizarre mixture of the modern and the medieval. In the darkness, two contingents of foot soldiers faced each other across barbed wire and a deep trench. One, the British army and the RUC, the other, the Orangemen and their loyalist supporters.

Occasionally the night sky would be lit up by the flash of a rocket fired by the demonstrators. There were other cracking noises – the sound of plastic bullets and live gunfire, and above me the drone of the helicopter, almost, but not quite, drowning out the beating of the drums from the Orange encampment. A few yards from my double room, shower en suite, a battle straight out of the Middle Ages was being fought.

I had never intended to stay quite so close to the war zone, but the journey home had proved more difficult than I had imagined. Making my way through the army checkpoints, I headed out on an isolated country road. I had only advanced about half a mile when I came across around sixty characters wearing orange sashes, spread out across the road. Eleven o'clock at night, I decided, was not the best time to negotiate a roadblock. So I turned back and found my way to Drumcree House.

Roadblocks? Trenches? Drums? Foot soldiers? Fortifications? But this is the United Kingdom, Western Europe, almost the twenty-first century ... Maybe so, but here in Portadown half a mile of tarmac, a road which once ran through rose fields but now goes past the homes of working-class Catholics, has been invested with so much importance that some people seem prepared to sacrifice their lives and imperil those of others for the right to set foot upon it, whilst others exercise the right to be offended by those who set foot upon it.

If such a conflict wasn't so serious, it would be downright laughable. In my bag I have a recently published book of Irish political cartoons, which includes one of my favourites from the *Irish Times* last July. It's entitled 'If Ulster really was British'. It shows an Orangeman telling a Catholic resident, 'No, we couldn't possibly go down there, not if it would cause you any bother.' The Catholic replies, 'Don't worry, it will only take ten minutes. I'll just pop inside and have a cup of tea.'

If only.

The cartoonists aren't the only ones who can squeeze some fun out of this situation. Peadar, Gerard and Pól, my footballing friends in the Garvaghy estate, look on this as the best time of the year. They have reporters, cameramen, soldiers and police officers to play with. And they enjoy the rioting too. But the world looks very different when you are only ten years old.

The grown-ups know this dispute is deadly serious and the roadblock around the corner and the pitched battle down the road are no laughing matter.

There has been much talk of rights and of culture and of civil liberties. But let's face it, this stand-off is also about hatred and bigotry and mistrust, about who rules the roost and who runs the country, about those fearful of the future and those doomed to repeat the past, about whether there is any substance to the recent talk of peace, or whether it's just so many word games dressing up an irreconcilable divide.

If this was a disagreement anywhere else in the United Kingdom the argument, as the cartoonist suggests, would probably have been over before it began.

If it was merely a dispute over the right of way on a road then a traffic warden could have sorted it out.

But this is about whether Northern Ireland wants to enter a new century or remain mired in its history. The challenge ahead is immense and the need for a resolution is immediate.

Reading my report for Radio Scotland back in retrospect, I realise my assertion that the Drumcree stand-off could not have happened anywhere else in the United Kingdom looks a bit patronising. It's true that something similar couldn't take place in the Cotswolds, but that's because the region has a rather different history to that of County Armagh, not because its people have different blood running through their veins. I guess I was trying to answer the Orange Order's argument that the row was about the 'right to walk the Queen's highway', whilst it didn't seem to fit any traditionally British view of someone's inalienable rights that I knew about. Maybe a night without sleep, listening to the sound of violence, also tested my patience, tempting me into some of those easy prejudices I spent most of my career trying to avoid.

I did not spend all that week at Drumcree. The centre of gravity, as it had done in previous years, switched to and from the scene of the immediate confrontation. Earlier in the week I had been up on the roof of the BBC in Belfast peering out across the city as the Order's nightly protest parades got under way. 'Why don't they just come here?' I quipped to a colleague, 'it would save us going to look for the marches and make sure they got on the *Nine O'Clock*

News.' We headed back down to the newsroom to be told that, sure enough, a thousand Orangemen were at our front door, complaining about our coverage and demanding to see 'the boss, now'.

The boss in this case was my old editor Andrew Colman who strolled down to accept the formal complaint. The Orangemen said that we weren't making it sufficiently clear that theirs was a purely peaceful campaign of protests, and our news broadcasts were rolling together the violence caused by others with the marches organised by the Order. This was actually quite a difficult matter to be clear about in a short news dispatch. Normally the protest marches did start off peacefully and it was rarely the actual Orangemen wearing sashes who got involved in the subsequent violence. But the parades were illegal – having not been granted permission by the authorities – and as sure as night follows day, a protest often led to violence and disorder, usually carried out by loyalist sympathisers of the Order rather than the Orangemen themselves. Try boiling that down in your twenty-second script.

Andrew Colman rejected the criticism of our supposed lack of balance whilst assuring the Orange leaders that he respected their right to their views. I recorded the exchange for the radio, but limited my follow-up questioning to checking the name and title of the head protester. Having one thousand people behind you does lend weight to your argument and is to be advised if you want to avoid a rigorous grilling by a journalist. It is a trifle ironic, however, if the point you are strenuously trying to prove is how utterly peaceful and non-threatening you are.

Later in the week I travelled over to London to cover a deputation of senior Orangemen meeting the prime minister. Number Ten gave them a polite reception, in the hope of eventually winning them over, but on the ground the police and army's orders remained unchanged. This year the Orangemen would not pass without the agreement of the residents. Once again the Order was threatening to make Northern Ireland ungovernable and once again the place appeared to be heading towards a doomsday scenario on 13 July, which was the Orangemen's chosen day for marching in 1998 because the Twelfth itself fell on a Sunday.

Having already experienced this scenario two years previously I think my patience was getting ever shorter. It seemed that the possibility of somebody dying was getting closer all the time, and the Order was, Pontius Pilate-like, washing its hands of all responsibility for the violence which came in the wake of its protests. In fact Orange spokesmen, like Davey Jones in Portadown, were sounding more and more like a mirror image of the old Sinn Féin – all violence was regrettable, but inevitable, given the oppressive attitude of the police and the government.

After meeting Tony Blair the Orange delegation held a news conference in one of the rooms available for MPs' use in Whitehall. Standing behind them were a series of Unionist MPs, which the Orange leaders claimed illustrated the range of support for their cause. But by this time – the summer of 1998 – unionism was sharply divided between camps for and against the Good Friday Agreement and all those present were opponents of the Agreement. I raised the question as to whether some people were trying to use the Drumcree issue to fight the battle over the Agreement which they had lost at the polls. This touched a distinctly raw nerve, prompting Robert McCartney to shout 'Rubbish' and Jeffrey Donaldson to cry 'What's that got to do with anything?'

As the MPs filed out Jeffrey Donaldson stared me in the face and asked, 'What on earth has happened to the BBC?' Ian Paisley lectured me, 'Your questions did no good for the people of Ulster today, young man.' Martin Smyth just looked disgusted. Robert McCartney tore into my colleague Stephen Grimason, whose firm questioning he had also objected to.

Although I made a mental note not to venture over the other side of the lines at Drumcree whenever any of these gentlemen were addressing the crowd in the next few days, I wasn't much bothered by the criticism. Things were getting very serious on the streets and the time had come for reporters to take the gloves off. The question I was most glad to have asked wasn't the one about the Good Friday Agreement, but one which I directed to the Reverend William Bingham, the Orange Order chaplain in County Armagh. I had met Mr Bingham before, putting together a report on the boycott of Protestant businessmen around his home patch of Pomeroy in County Tyrone. I knew that, although he was profoundly committed to the Orange Order and to its culture and tradition, his first master was his God, faith in which gave him a firm moral sense. With the death of some poor innocent appearing ever more likely I asked Mr Bingham, 'How many lives is a road worth?' In his view, he replied, it wasn't worth any.

Afterwards in the BBC offices at Westminster William Bingham insisted that he meant what he said and that, for good measure, he wasn't in the anti-Good Friday Agreement camp. His colleague Denis Watson, by contrast, told me he kept a list of reporters who asked awkward questions and I was now on it. Not sure if he was joking, I replied that this was good, as I was already on Gerry Adams's blacklist, and it would even things up.

Three days later, back at Drumcree, I woke early to go on to the *Breakfast With Frost* show on the morning of Sunday, 12 July. The Belfast newsroom relayed to me the first reports of a horrendous arson attack at Ballymoney in County Antrim. Three young children, Richard, Mark and Jason Quinn, had been burned to death in their home. The three brothers, eleven, ten and nine years old, were the sons of a Catholic mother and a Protestant father, something which made them 'legitimate targets' in the eyes of some bigots. Details were scarce as to who the cowards were who set fire to their house in the middle of the night. But it appeared there had been a loyalist barricade in the area not long before.

In the hours and days that followed some Orangemen, like Denis Watson, blamed everybody else. The arson attack in Ballymoney had been the result of particular local circumstances. The media, the RUC and the government were conspiring to suppress all the details. The Orange Order had had nothing to do with the violence which had been taking place across Northern Ireland that week. But it had less than nothing – if that's possible – to do with this particular attack. In fact the death of the children could well have happened in any other week in the year, in any other town, in any other country.

At the subsequent trial of one of those responsible for the arson attack it became clear that a personal grudge against the Quinn family did indeed play a part in the warped logic of the brothers' killers. If you wanted to blame an organisation for their deaths the local UVF was far higher up the ladder of responsibility than the Orange Order. But to totally divorce the intimidation of Catholic families in Ballymoney that week, culminating in the attack on the Quinn family, from the licence for lawlessness generated by the Drumcree stand-off appears an act of sophistry. The Quinns were not the only mixed marriage or Catholic family told to get out of their housing estate that week.

The Reverend William Bingham took a different tack to some other Orangemen. He did not tell his faithful, gathered in the Presbyterian church in Pomeroy that Sunday, that the dispute over Drumcree had had nothing to do with creating an atmosphere in Northern Ireland in which some loyalists, armed with a whiskey bottle full of petrol, thought they could get away with setting fire to a house in which children slept. Instead he urged his flock and Orangemen everywhere to walk away from Drumcree, telling them that 'no road is worth a life'. The next day he was accused of betrayal by Joel Patton of the hardline Spirit of Drumcree group and there followed an undignified but suitably symbolic joust of black umbrellas between different sections of the Order. At Drumcree a few diehards lingered but most people voted with their feet.

Looking back on that summer it strikes me that while the people of Northern Ireland may be far from primitive, there is something almost primitive about the rhythm of events when the place is gripped by a crisis. Often both sides to a dispute edge ever closer to the precipice, taunting each other to jump. There is almost a demand for a blood sacrifice – in this case the poor Quinn children – then everyone retreats reassuring themselves that they aren't really as bad as all that, they are more civilised than people in the world's other conflict zones. If in 1996 the tension was taken out of the build-up to doomsday by Sir Hugh Annesley's U-turn, in 1998 it required the deaths of three young boys to convince people to pull back from the brink. Leaders on both sides never appear able to come to their senses before allowing things to go too far.

The year I left Belfast, 1999, Drumcree passed off with an eerie calm. Maybe support for the Order had waned since the security forces held it at bay in 1998. Maybe the Order believed it could cut a deal with the government at a later date. I have considerable criticism for both sides in the marching issue. On occasion certain individuals in the nationalist concerned residents' groups travel long distances in order to have the thrill of taking offence at marches. There is too often a simple win or lose mentality which I don't believe serves either beleaguered communities in particular or the Catholic population in general. Breandán Mac Cionnaith, now an elected councillor for the Garvaghy Road, should realise he has responsibilities to Catholics in other parts of Northern Ireland, such as the isolated families in Ballymoney or the parishioners at Harryville in Ballymena, as well as to those in his own backyard. Consent is a great concept, but in the twentieth century it should mean more than just letting every group living on every street corner dictate exactly what can or cannot happen in their area. That way anarchy lies.

At the same time the Orange Order must wise up. I don't care if the Orangemen won't let me join, but like countless other people living in Northern Ireland I wish they would just let me live my life. Don't lecture me about your God-given right to walk the Queen's highway, when you know that if I want to cross the road during one of your marathon parades I risk having the hell beaten out of me by one of your fine upstanding members (marchers won't countenance you crossing their path, unless specifically escorted by a steward, who if my memory serves me doesn't have any more legal powers than me). Don't wash your hands and pretend that you have no responsibility for disorder when you know full well it is likely to follow your organising protests in flashpoint areas. And wise up about the real march — the one your enemies are stealing on you. Every time you insist on tramping over the rights of others you are alienating the bulk of the British people to whom you claim you belong. They do not understand and frankly cannot be bothered trying to understand. Embrace a new future. Become Morris dancers.

29

Back to Business

SUMMER 1996–SUMMER 1997

In May 1996 the staff at a community centre in north Belfast invited me to chair a couple of 'Question Time' sessions involving candidates in the elections to the Northern Ireland Forum due to take place at the end of the month. Because of the deeply divided politics of the area the centre had to organise the event in two halves, one involving the unionist parties, the other including Sinn Féin. Sinn Féin's candidate in the elections was Gerry Kelly, convicted of bombing the Old Bailey court in London in the 1970s. Kelly's entourage arrived late for their session and promptly tried to lay down various ground rules for his participation. Principal amongst these was that a couple of journalists in the gathering – there largely because I had told them the event was happening – should be ordered to leave.

Whilst I was happy restricting questions to local people, I wasn't prepared to chair a 'secret' event and made it clear that if all journalists went I would go too. I got the impression that Gerry Kelly – a man who has wielded great authority within the IRA – wasn't used to having people say 'no' to him. But he gave way and went ahead with the discussion, which was as lively as could be expected in a sharply polarised area like north Belfast. It covered issues like contentious marches, job creation for the area and whether republicans should be allowed to participate in the forthcoming negotiations at Stormont in spite of the end of their ceasefire. Afterwards, however, Gerry Kelly complained to the organisers about their acceptance of a 'unionist agenda' by dividing the 'Question Time' into two halves. I hadn't organised the event but defended the community workers responsible who had done their best to promote debate against a difficult backdrop.

In the audience sat one of my favourite former IRA men, hunger striker and Belfast city councillor Pat McGeown. Despite his record of commitment to a violent cause Pat was always a softly spoken, thoughtful character. I told him I hoped he'd be at Belfast City Hall for the counting of the Forum votes as it would be good to have someone reasonable around. 'We have lots of reasonable people,' Pat grinned, 'and some' – he looked towards Gerry Kelly – 'who are learning to be reasonable.' Whilst Pat sat through the proceedings keeping his own counsel, one of the most voluble in Gerry Kelly's entourage that night was Michael Rogan, a Sinn Féin activist whom I had met on a number of protests around north Belfast.

The next time I saw Michael Rogan was later that year in Belfast Magistrates' Court, where he was pleading not guilty to a charge of conspiring to cause explosions. The police linked the charge to the no warning bomb attack on the army's headquarters at Thiepval Barracks in Lisburn in October 1996. The bombing caused considerable damage inside the military base and a soldier from Gateshead, Warrant Officer James Bradwell, died aged forty-three, four days after the blast from the injuries he received. When the bomb went off at Lisburn I was thousands of miles away covering an investment conference for Northern Ireland held at Pittsburgh in the United States. We grabbed a couple of quick reaction interviews to the bombing with local politicians, including the Mayor of Lisburn and the Northern Ireland Secretary Sir Patrick Mayhew, then I obeyed orders and headed for the next flight home. A few weeks later Michael Rogan nodded to me from the dock. I was surprised to recognise him as before walking into the courtroom I had not put his name and face together. At a subsequent High Court hearing, he was freed on bail, but he didn't show up for any further court appearances. As I write this, the charge of conspiracy to cause explosions is still outstanding against him and Michael Rogan is on the run.

The Lisburn bombing ended the IRA's 'phoney ceasefire' in Northern Ireland. The organisation blamed the government for the blast claiming John Major had squandered the 'historic opportunity' provided by the 1994 ceasefire 'in a vain attempt to defeat the IRA'. After the attack about one thousand people attended a peace rally outside Belfast City Hall. But despite the heartfelt pleas of the mothers of terrorist victims from both sides of the community, slowly but surely the paramilitaries returned to business as usual in Northern Ireland. Just before Christmas 1996 IRA gunmen ran into the Royal Belfast Hospital for Sick Children and opened fire. One of their bullets penetrated an empty incubator for babies. They claimed their intended targets were the policemen guarding the Democratic Unionist politician Nigel Dodds, who was visiting his critically ill son. Two days later I was on the streets of Ardoyne in north Belfast where a loyalist booby trap bomb injured a well-known local republican, Eddie Copeland.

Two months later in February 1997 we drove down to Bessbrook, not far from the south Armagh border, where an IRA sniper had killed another soldier, Lance-Bombardier Stephen Restorick. Generally the IRA could feel fairly certain that if it targeted the military near the border and scored a 'hit' there would be relatively little propaganda downside. Some people living in the area would have approved of the attack; others, who did not, realised it was wisest to keep their views to themselves.

But in this case the sniper hadn't bargained on the woman to whom Stephen Restorick chatted just before he died. Lorraine McElroy had been taken by Bombardier Restorick's smile and pleasant manner − then she heard the crack of a gunshot and found herself covered with the soldier's blood. Mrs McElroy hugged the dying soldier in the ambulance which took them both to hospital. The next morning we made our way to her house in a group, escorted by the army past the scene of the shooting. All I needed were a couple of clips for a package due to hit the air that lunchtime so I motioned to my colleague from BBC Northern Ireland, Mervyn Jess, to go ahead and ask the questions. As Lorraine McElroy spoke it became clear she didn't need any prompting. The shooting was etched into her mind, as was the image of Stephen's face. She talked with emotion and love about a soldier she had hardly known, and as she talked all the IRA's hopes that this would be a 'clean kill' on the border died.

I got back to the radio car with only a short time left before my report was due to hit air. Fortunately the mother of a friend lived locally and I took over her living room as I edited my package as fast as I could on the remarkable new mini-disc recorder. With a few moments to go I ran to the outside broadcast vehicle and connected with the *World at One* studio. We had no time to play the report over to them before its broadcast. Instead we would have to go 'as live'. The presenter introduced me and on cue, I pressed play on my mini-disc, praying that the notoriously power-hungry device did not run out of battery power before the next three and a half minutes was over. Technically it seemed amazing that pushing the play button on a machine the size of a Walkman could enable you to reach listeners throughout the UK with a crafted report direct from the scene of an incident. What was truly amazing, however, was the strength of Lorraine McElroy's words, which moved people who heard them wherever they were.

By the time the teatime programme, PM, went on air another brave woman had given another remarkable interview. Stephen's mother Rita spoke, obviously distraught, but at the same time summoning up all her strength to extend forgiveness to the murderers. She hoped her son's death would be the last in Northern Ireland. On PM our report became the story of two women who had not been aware of each other prior to the IRA shooting, but whose lives now seemed deeply intertwined. That December I watched Rita Restorick hand a Christmas card to Gerry Adams during a visit he made to London. She asked him to do all he could to bring peace, part of her ongoing efforts to build something positive from her son's death.

During the first half of 1997, the last months in power of John Major's government, the violence continued. In May Tony Blair won a landslide victory, which for us hacks in Belfast meant a change of Secretary of State. And what a change! I first met Mo Mowlam a few years before when she had been appointed by the Labour opposition as a junior Northern Ireland spokesperson with responsibility for education. I conducted her first television interview in Belfast, interrupting her during a visit to the University of Ulster campus at Jordanstown. I cannot remember anything about the content of the interview, but as a character Mo hits any reporter full in the face. We had to start and restart and restart again. In part it was due to noises off – planes, cars with loud exhausts, curious passers-by. But then we both got the giggles and kept wrecking our takes. Mo would muck something up and erupt into a string of expletives, not in anger but repeated scatter-gun as a sign of irritation. To be honest, she struck me as incredibly amateurish. But when I got back to the edit suite I wondered if it was me who was the amateur. By saying something unbroadcastable Mo had ensured that only her final perfect take made it onto air.

Certainly, as a Northern Ireland Secretary, Mo Mowlam was no fool. Her strength was in endearing herself to reporters, voters and political colleagues and then, buoyed up by being granted the benefit of the doubt, getting away with things no other politician could try. Her down-to-earth style contrasted sharply with that of the aristocratic Sir Patrick Mayhew. In Belfast city centre, shortly after Labour's victory in May, Mo swept all before her on a walkabout amongst shoppers. Later that month she dropped her first clanger by meeting nationalist residents' groups in various hot spots for Orange parades. It wasn't just that she hugged Breandán Mac Cionnaith, the spokesman for the Garvaghy Road residents and a former convicted IRA man. It was that she did it on

21 May 1997, the polling day in council elections, elections in which Mr Mac Cionnaith was standing as a candidate. The government also authorised senior officials to hold exploratory talks with Sinn Féin on the same day. It put the BBC and other broadcasters in an impossible situation. Normally we try to go into purdah while polling stations are open, avoiding any coverage which might unduly influence the voters. But now the government was organising two events of obvious national news significance whilst the voting was under way. We couldn't ignore the developments so had to push ahead with our coverage regardless. The Ulster Unionist MP Ken Maginnis had a point when he claimed that the Northern Ireland Secretary had handed republicans in general and Breandán Mac Cionnaith in particular a massive bonus on polling day.

I wasn't worrying too much, though, as no sooner had the local election results been declared than I found myself again on a flight to South Africa, off, as it turned out, to meet Nelson Mandela.

30

A Fresh Start

SUMMER 1997–WINTER 1997

The political gathering which took place in South Africa was in fact a bit of a sideshow. In the absence of an IRA ceasefire, it was always going to be impossible for the South Africans to bring unionists and republicans together – even though they did try by 'accidentally' showing Sinn Féin negotiators into the same room as the DUP. The challenge for me was working out how to cover discussions which were due to take place behind closed doors in an undisclosed location in the midst of a vast country.

In fact I got my reporting rather more convoluted than I needed to about the location. One of the organisers, Padraig O'Malley, told me so readily that the gathering was taking place at the Arniston conference centre, on a nature reserve a few hours' drive from Cape Town, that I thought he must be double bluffing. A unionist contact told me that Arniston was the one place where the talks were not going to happen, and in turn I was excessively mysterious on air as a result. In the event my unionist was wrong, Padraig O'Malley was transparently honest and the uncertainty about the location led me to stay in Cape Town rather than spend lots of time driving out to the centre. In the end this was a stroke of luck, because I didn't need to go to the venue. News agency cameras picked up some pictures of the visitors arriving, the main group in a coach and a smaller delegation, from Sinn Féin, in a minibus. The centre was a former testing range for weaponry, something which seemed suitably ironic given that disarmament remained a fundamental sticking point in the Northern Ireland process.

I had already gathered a fair number of interviews with the participants back in Belfast, shot against suitably neutral backgrounds. I had them making pretty general points about learning from the South African experience which I could use whatever happened at the Arniston talks. In the end, the ANC was quite good about providing interview material during the day and a half or so that we were in Cape Town. The ANC's former representative in Ireland Kader Asmal, who later became a government minister, proved very helpful and South Africa's Constitutional Affairs Minister Vali Moosa also gave a news conference.

But neither I nor my colleague from RTÉ Michael O'Kane could quite believe our luck when the staff at the reception of the hotel the BBC had booked me into, the Table Bay, told us that Nelson Mandela was coming to our hotel for a formal opening ceremony on the very day of the Northern Ireland talks. This was just too good to be true. Michael and I divided the stake-out up between us – we each took one side of the hotel entrance and agreed to pool whatever film we gathered.

A marimba band started up as Nelson Mandela's cavalcade arrived. He stepped out, smiled at the waiting knot of people then made his way in. He came just past me and I began to shout, 'President Mandela, what message do you have for the people of Northern Ireland?' The President smiled. 'I'm sorry, I can't hear you,' he said, pointing to the band and moving on. It was a bit noisy, but I must admit I thought 'ah that old trick', having witnessed Margaret Thatcher on more than one occasion being unable to 'hear' a question she didn't want to stop and answer.

We charged on after the presidential entourage, trying desperately to get ahead of him. But Mandela's very large bodyguards were having none of it. All that was on their schedule was a brief opening ceremony and a nice dinner, there was nothing on it about a question and answer session. One especially big guy barred my way, telling me, 'You can't ask questions, and you can't run around there', this last as I did my best to evade him. With a few not so gentle shoves from the minders we found ourselves well and truly pushed out of the scrum. So near and yet so far. But as we lurched disconsolately on we saw that the President had stopped by a little statue and rockery out in the hotel garden. Here he was posing for photographs with the hotel owners and the local press were obediently not interrupting.

I looked at my cameraman and said, 'We'll have to crawl.' The only way we could get ourselves into this press pack was to go down on our hands and knees and crawl in front of them – if we had blocked their view we would have, quite rightly, been treated to a bit of sharp treatment. The cameraman and I ignominiously snaked our way into a plaintive position in front of the press pack. As we did this I could see Nelson Mandela's attention had been caught by our ridiculous antics. He looked down at me and smiled. I knew it was now or never.

'President Mandela, what can the people of Northern Ireland learn from the lessons of South Africa?' I shouted.

He smiled back and said, rather loudly, 'I'm sorry I can't hear you.'

I suddenly realised that this was no Margaret Thatcher trick – Nelson Mandela was, in fact, very hard of hearing. At his age and given what he had been through this was entirely understandable. Craning forward, he clearly by now wanted to answer my questions, if only he could work out what they were.

'President Mandela,' I was by now bawling at the top of my voice at a living legend standing only a few inches away, 'what do you think you can teach the politicians from Northern Ireland, will they achieve a breakthrough as you have done in South Africa?'

Mandela computed and then came out with a slow but perfect answer.

'While it is difficult to predict what human beings and political parties are likely to do in the future, what is significant is that they are here and that alone is a sign that they are serious in searching for peace. We are reluctant to urge other countries to follow exactly the pattern that we have followed. But whatever help they want we will place it before them.'

I followed through with a couple of extra questions and he answered them logically and gracefully. True to everything I had read about him, Nelson Mandela appeared to have time for everyone, and would have probably heard me out even if I was from the *Hitchin Gazette*, which as far as he knew I probably was. I gave him a broad, beaming smile which meant to say 'thank you for just paying for my air fare'. He smiled back and went on his way. The big bodyguard shook his head in disgust.

Such is the pressure of the news that I enjoyed my scoop for the lunchtime and *Six O'Clock News* but got dropped by the time the *Nine O'Clock News* went on air. However, this was no cause for sadness as it meant we could spend the evening in Cape Town checking out the bars and restaurants. Later on I was in a club on the main drag taking in some excellent African jazz when I felt a very firm one-fingered prod on the shoulder. Towering over me and glowering, a big African guy said, 'Hey you, I've a bone to pick with you.' For a few anxious seconds I tried to work out how on earth I could have got on the wrong side of someone who anyone twice my size would have had serious second thoughts about upsetting. Then it clicked – Nelson Mandela's bodyguard.

After a mild telling-off, this former ANC freedom fighter paid tribute to our tenacity in pursuing our quarry, even if I had 'bugged him something rotten'. I explained I was in Cape Town for literally a day and a half, and, with a deadline looming, there had been no alternative. Within a few minutes we were buying each other rounds and getting on fine. The jazz band played on into the early hours. My drinking partner filled me in on his long history of 'armed struggle' which had left several 'white boys' like me dead. The next day I had a couple of hours left to head down to the Cape before catching my flight back. I thought our work was over and together with Michael O'Kane I embarked on a bit of sightseeing at the beaches where little penguins hop about amidst the tourists, sunning themselves on the boulders. In the middle of this, however, the desk rang to say that Mandela himself had gone to see the twenty-seven politicians involved in the talks to urge them forward. Could I supply a voice track for television on my mobile phone? I borrowed a piece of paper from Michael and scribbled a script out, leaning on a boulder, watching the waves crash on the rocks all around. I enjoyed delivering my pay-off: 'Mark Devenport, BBC News, Penguin Beach, South Africa'.

Back in Northern Ireland the arrival of the new Labour government clearly provided the IRA with an opportunity to turn off its violence and make a fresh start. However, it did not respond immediately. Instead the killings went on, with two RUC officers shot at close range whilst on foot patrol in Lurgan. Tony Blair felt angry and betrayed by these murders, carried out despite his overtures via officials. Mo Mowlam told me during a short chat at the BBC's Westminster offices that she worried the prime minister would get so alienated that he might cut the republicans off altogether. She still hoped they could be brought on side. The violence continued. A loyalist mob beat a policeman to death outside a pub, and loyalist dissidents murdered an eighteen-year-old Catholic woman as she lay in bed at her Protestant boyfriend's home. Despite these horrors, and the government's decision to push the Orange Order Drumcree parade swiftly down the Garvaghy Road, the behind the scenes contacts between republicans and the government were bearing fruit.

On Friday, 18 July I was at Westminster covering an Anglo-Irish meeting where Mo Mowlam and the ministers affirmed their support for a document on the key issue of paramilitary disarmament which remained vague enough to bring the IRA on board. Because I had quite a few commitments for the radio as well as television I finished my report for the *Six O'Clock News* early and messaged the editor. The reply came that being so prompt was very dangerous as something was bound to change the story. A few minutes later the phone went. It was the Belfast newsroom telling me that Gerry Adams had just put out a statement by fax saying that in the light of the continuing discussions with government officials he had informed the IRA that in his view the necessary conditions existed for the restoration of its ceasefire. Gerry would not ask the IRA to call a ceasefire without knowing in advance what the answer was going to be. I told the *Six* that they could junk my ever so prompt report. There was now only time to 'go live'. After a quick interview for the PM programme, I joined up with my old friend Shane Harrison in Dublin for a double act on the television *Six O'Clock News*.

Second time around (not counting the ceasefires of the seventies, of course) the 'cessation of military operations' didn't have quite the same drama. But, more importantly, it represented the chance for a new beginning. In September the government admitted Sinn Féin delegates to the talks, letting them through the gates where they had been previously photographed peering through the bars. The question was whether, with Sinn Féin inside, the unionists would all walk out. Ian Paisley's Democratic Unionists and Robert McCartney's UK Unionists duly obliged. But David Trimble, thought by many to have been a hardliner when he was elected UUP leader, steered his party down a careful course. He refused to go to Stormont in answer to the British and Irish governments' summons, instead discussing his options at the Ulster Unionist headquarters in Glengall Street in central Belfast. At one point the Northern Ireland Political Affairs Minister, Paul Murphy, went to Glengall Street to answer Ulster Unionists' queries. On the PM programme on Radio Four I horribly mixed my metaphors saying that, as the unionists would not go to Stormont to see ministers, the government had decided to bring 'the mountain to Methuselah'. No sooner had this hit the airwaves than my mother phoned me to ask what on earth I was thinking. I called PM to let them know about my goof. The next day they were inundated with calls from Radio Four's listeners, putting me right. Presenter Chris Lowe acknowledged my blunder before telling the nation 'Even Mark's own mother rang up to complain – and what greater ignominy can there be than that?' I shall spend the next 969 years living it down.

A couple of days after Paul Murphy's intercession, the Ulster Unionists, accompanied by the two small loyalist parties, marched in a phalanx into the talks building. They put up a case for throwing Sinn Féin out of the talks but this was rejected. Despite that, the unionists held on to their negotiating seats. The talks were up and running once again, and our residency in the car park outside Castle Buildings began once more. The thrust of the talks was obvious to most observers even if the minutiae of what had been agreed or not agreed was hard to winkle out. Nationalists would push to give any settlement as strong an Irish dimension as possible. Unionists would tug the rope back to make sure Northern Ireland remained British. The likely compromise was always going to look something like the Framework Document which the British and Irish governments unveiled in February 1995 and which was in turn largely based on the Sunningdale Agreement of the early seventies and the philosophy espoused in the intervening years by the SDLP leader John Hume. Hume invented the jargon of the 'three sets of relationships', between the two communities in Northern Ireland, between the North and the Irish Republic and between Britain and Ireland as a whole. By building institutions along all these axes, and emphasising the European context in which everyone is living, Hume reasoned that the border could be blurred if not removed. This way the edge would be taken off the bitter clash between nationalities and traditions.

So, long before the first draft of any agreement was drawn up, observers knew there would be some kind of assembly, even though that might be hard for Sinn Féin to swallow, and there would be some kind of cross-border all-Ireland institutions, even though unionists might not like them. The question of illegal guns would have to be addressed. So too would the future of para-military prisoners, and broader questions of policing and law and order. For the correspondents following the talks, however, there was plenty of scope in chasing down these various alleyways. Sometimes one participant or another would leak an interesting piece of paper. At other stages a couple of whispered comments might give you something to work on. It was tougher for BBC Northern Ireland's correspondents than for us working for the London outlets, because they needed to get into every nook and cranny. But Stephen Grimason and Mark Simpson were more than up to the job and kept me up to date from their excellent sources. Once in a blue moon I had a little something to offer them too.

But I must admit that as 1997 drew to a close I was a little distracted. David Sharrock, the *Guardian*'s Belfast correspondent, had approached me to help him with a biography of Gerry Adams. It was tough work on top of our usual schedule and involved spending most of my free time around at David's house. As all his friends will tell you, David is a grumpy old codger so this was a bit irksome. If it hadn't been for the constant companionship of his dog

Lola and his son Pablo I don't know how I would have survived.

Our initial idea was simply to update the story of the Sinn Féin President, as there wasn't any biography still in publication and none had been written covering the peace process. After we started, though, we learned that Gerry Adams was working on an autobiography covering his early life. Our work would therefore obviously be seen as a counterblast. Readers can make their own minds up, but suffice it to say when we told it about the book Sinn Féin was not best pleased, and it didn't like it when it was published either. The party's spin doctors remained civil to me, but I knew that relations on that side of the fence were likely to be difficult for some time to come. I could still function effectively – indeed some unionists now seemed excessively warm to me, something which made me a little unsettled – but a bit of time away to let bygones become bygones seemed a wise move. That was part of the reason why, when a senior manager telephoned to ask if I would be interested in filling in for Jeremy Bowen as Middle East Correspondent for a couple of months I jumped at the chance.

31

Divided Cities

I left Belfast in a flurry of activity. The loyalist LVF leader Billy Wright had just been shot dead inside the Maze jail. On the morning of the shooting I filed the first couple of reports from the Belfast newsroom, and spoke to the prison officers' spokesman Finlay Spratt, who gave us our first account of how another prisoner, from the INLA wing, had crawled across the roof of one of the jail blocks before dropping down and murdering Wright with a handgun smuggled into the Maze. I broadcast a couple of times, then handed over to my colleague Tom Coulter as I had a plane to catch.

Soon I was at Ben-Gurion Airport at Tel Aviv, feeling sleepy and reacting too slowly to stop the woman on immigration stamping my passport, rendering it useless for travel in much of the Middle East. The driver took me on a journey which must have been made by literally hundreds of journalists before, sweeping past the rocky hillsides of Israel, then taking a back road through part of the Palestinian West Bank before sweeping down into possibly the most famous city and religious centre in the world.

Jerusalem, shall we call it? Or Al Quds to give the city its Arabic name? At least here I felt on home ground, being well used to places with two names, be they Derry or Londonderry, Northern Ireland or the North, the Maze or Long Kesh. My first stopping off point was the celebrated American Colony hotel in the east of the city, in an area populated by Palestinians, but just a few hundred yards' walk from some distinctly Orthodox Jewish areas. Since the Israeli victory in the Six Day War of 1967 there has been no formal frontier between the two, but – just like Belfast's West Link – a big dual carriageway marks the dividing line.

As this was my first extended taste of foreign journalism I was keen for some action. But, predictably given my track record, Jerusalem was going through one of its quieter phases. I sat in our office on the Jaffa Road, the scene of many devastating suicide bombs, drumming my fingers. I did not, I hasten to add, want a suicide bombing to happen — I had by now seen quite enough mayhem back in Northern Ireland. But something to do would have been nice. All the while the TV in the office relayed back scenes of the LVF's reaction to the death of Billy Wright, which was swift and bloody, and Mo Mowlam's daring visit to the Maze jail. Denis Murray, Tom Coulter and the rest of them were clearly being kept very busy.

After getting over an initial sense of frustration, however, I realised that a bit of a break might be no bad thing. It would give me a chance to check out the city and the surrounding area. One night I accompanied a colleague from the BBC's Arabic Service to some political talks about the Middle East process, then badly stalled under the influence of the intransigent Israeli Prime Minister Binyamin Netanyahu. The US envoy Dennis Ross met Palestinian negotiators in the West Bank town of Ramallah, a short drive north of Jerusalem, the exact duration of which depends on how painfully slow the Israeli soldiers in charge of the checkpoint on the main road want to be. A couple of days after reporting on the rather low-key discussions at Ramallah I filed the following dispatch for BBC Radio Four's *From Our Own Correspondent* giving my initial impressions of Jerusalem and comparing it with the divided city I knew rather better.

DIVIDED CITIES

I decided I could forgive myself for feeling a sense of déjà vu. I was standing outside a nondescript building waiting for two sides involved in political talks to come out. Before the meeting began one participant had already accused his opponents of seeking to torpedo the peace process. Knowing looks from the assembled press corps revealed this wasn't the first time the politician had deployed that particular phrase.

As the hours ticked by we shifted from foot to foot, keenly aware that, inside, the negotiators were enjoying a sumptuous meal. Outside, it felt bitterly cold.

Only when a figure emerged wearing a chequered keffiyeh, the traditional Arab headdress, did the unfamiliarity of it sink in. This wasn't Stormont on the outskirts of Belfast but Ramallah on the West Bank. Mo Mowlam and Gerry Adams were nowhere to be seen. And whilst he may have been instantly recognisable from the world's TV screens, the sight of

Yasser Arafat being whisked off in a heavily protected cavalcade was new to my eyes.

Drawing parallels, my old history lecturer once warned me, can be a fatuous exercise. For every similarity, you turn up something else which proves that two different parts of the world are entirely distinct. But strolling around one divided city having just waved another goodbye, it's hard to avoid comparing and contrasting.

They may not paint the kerbstones red, white and blue around here. But the ethnic identity of the district I regularly walk through is clear because of the black hats, beards and sidelocks of the Orthodox Jewish men beside me. The minarets and run-down housing of the Muslim part of the city where I live are, on the other hand, every bit as much of a dead give-away as any Irish republican mural.

Perhaps because of Jerusalem's historic surroundings, this conflict seems at times more ancient than the one I am used to. Inside the old walled city stands the Dome of the Rock, the mosque which marks what Muslims regard as the third holiest place in the world. Its gilded dome looks splendid thanks to the renovation efforts of some Ulster building workers.

But Jews look upon it as the site of their lost temple, destroyed twice in biblical times, the only remains of which is the Western or Wailing Wall. Back in the eighties some Jewish extremists who wanted to build a new temple on the site of the Dome of the Rock went so far as plotting to blow the mosque up. Just this month another Jewish activist planned, before being arrested, to cause chaos by throwing a pig's head at the Muslim faithful when they gathered for prayers.

In Northern Ireland I am used to conflicts over territory but no single place symbolises that in such a stark way as Jerusalem's Temple Mount. Maybe Drumcree, but even that much-fought-over church and hillside does not embody the fundamental beliefs of clashing communities in the same manner.

The other Friday I decided to walk through the old city around the time of Muslim prayers. All was calm as I wandered past the entrance to the mosque and then on past the Western Wall. Only when I started to head back by another route did I realise that, in not bringing a map, I had made a big mistake. Without warning I became engulfed in a flood of men, women and children making their way home from prayer. Because it was the Muslim holy month of Ramadan, the crowd was bigger than usual, some two hundred thousand strong, each and every one of whom wanted to get away as quickly as possible through the narrow alleyways of old Jerusalem, and each and every one of whom had apparently decided that elbowing me out of the way was the most direct way to achieve their aim.

Soon I found myself deep within the Muslim quarter of the Old City swept along in a crush of bodies, quite unable to control the direction I was heading in. On the ground the young Israeli conscript soldiers looked nervous. They might have guns in their hands, but what would they do if this torrent of humanity turned against them? Above us, as we funnelled down one ancient alley, hung an Israeli Star of David flag, dangling from the balcony of a house owned by the hardline government minister Ariel Sharon. Fortunately the worshippers, with whom I was now cheek by jowl, ignored the provocation.

Eventually I battled my way to the side and watched the Muslim faithful go by from the safety of a coffee house. The mass of numbers, the traditional dress and the ancient alleyways made it all appear like a scene from biblical times. Northern Ireland's marches and commemorations, I reflected, tend to hark back to the 1680s. But here were people who looked as if they were living out the Old Testament or the Koran.

In other ways, though, the Israelis and the Palestinians are in fact at an earlier stage of their troubled history than Northern Ireland's Protestants and Catholics. The week I arrived brought news that the government had approved the building of five hundred homes at a settlement called Efrat in the West Bank. It's the latest in a series of construction projects providing new homes for Jewish settlers in the Palestinian territories. In Ireland the Plantation, when Scottish and English settlers arrived, took place in the seventeenth century, but its repercussions are still being felt today both in the lasting disagreement about the Britishness or Irishness of Northern Ireland and in the territorial disputes which underpin the summer's marching problems.

For how many more centuries, I wonder, will Palestinians point to the new Israeli homes, just as my taxi driver did the other day, and spit out the words, 'Settlement, Settlement. All built on our land.'

Drawing lines on maps in the West Bank or approving paramilitary prisoner releases in Northern Ireland would be relatively easy to accomplish provided all those involved felt confident that promises made would be kept and that threats and violence were things of the past. In both places secret contacts and open talks, assisted by American diplomacy and leaps of faith by individual leaders, have moved matters forward spectacularly. But trust and confidence remain sorely lacking and in Jerusalem, as in Belfast, the challenges ahead appear daunting and the potential for repeating past tragedies is ever present.

As I travelled around Israel and the Palestinian territories I continued to see parallels with Northern Ireland, although I thought the hatreds I encountered were more deeply felt and widely shared and the overall problem more difficult to resolve. Nationalists sometimes complain about harassment from the RUC and the British army, but I had never seen anything quite so petty as the behaviour of an Israeli soldier at the checkpoint we went through to enter the Gaza strip. My Israeli cameraman and I went through the 'VIP' entrance, but our Palestinian sound recordist had to go around to the separate entry for Palestinian workers. Fair enough, but when he had been processed, Yousseff came to join us as we were getting into a taxi with our gear to make the half-mile journey to the Palestinian Authority checkpoint up the road. 'No,' said the soldier, as he went to get into the car, 'you have to walk.' We protested that he was with us, but the soldier wouldn't be persuaded. Yousseff duly trudged down the road to the next checkpoint as we drove ahead.

Back in Belfast first the Ulster Democrats and then Sinn Féin were temporarily excluded from the talks because of renewed instances of loyalist and IRA violence. The Ulster Democrats jumped before they were pushed, Sinn Féin fought its ejection all the way. Tony Blair went to Washington to brief Bill Clinton on the latest developments in Northern Ireland, but the President could have been forgiven for not listening too hard as the Monica Lewinsky saga was reaching, shall we say, its climax. In the Middle East the United States and the UK threatened to launch air strikes against Iraq if it did not comply with UN weapons inspections. Many Arabs ascribed the President's willingness to resort to force to the pressure he was under about the Lewinsky affair. Some Arab newspapers even went so far as to allege that because Monica was Jewish the whole scandal had been some kind of Mossad plot. I went to Tel Aviv to record some 'vox pops' with people for an offbeat piece about whether Monica really was affecting US policy on the Middle East. I was having an unusually hard time finding Israelis who spoke understandable English when an old Russian immigrant, who had been begging on the pavement not far away, put his hand up.

'Excuse me, sir,' he said, 'I speak English. I might not look as if I do, but I do.'

Slightly taken aback I tentatively asked the beggar whether he had any views on Monica Lewinsky. He launched into a perfectly fluent answer.

'I think it is a tragedy that one little girl, Miss Lewinsky, has the fate of the whole world in her hands . . .'

When he stopped I realised he had provided me with my best 'sound bite' of the day. I don't normally pay for interviews, but in this instance I felt duty-bound to dig around in my pocket to find something to put in his collecting bowl. I produced ten shekels, worth about £2.

'Ten shekels!' He stared in amazement. 'For that I will give you five interviews.'

In Northern Ireland I had covered many funerals and reported on controversies over memorials and monuments for one side or another, but I had never quite come across what I encountered in the bitterly divided town of Hebron, where I had to cover a demonstration by some left-wing Israelis who wanted a man's body exhumed and reinterred elsewhere. An extraordinary measure perhaps, but those behind it argued that the move was necessary because the dead man, Jewish settler Baruch Goldstein, had murdered nearly thirty Palestinians and his grave – close to Arab homes – had been turned into a shrine offensive to his victims. In the dispatch I filed for *From Our Own Correspondent* I drew on the rich biblical history of the area where Baruch Goldstein had been laid to rest.

A GRAVE BUSINESS

It's certainly the oldest example of pushy salesmanship on record. The book of Genesis recounts how Abraham was travelling through the hills of Hebron when his wife Sarah died at the extremely ripe old age of 127. Abraham looked around for a suitable plot to lay his wife to rest and the locals – the Hittites – assured him they had just the spot, a site called the Cave of Macpelah. Abraham liked it, but the place didn't come free. Ephron, the Hittite who owned the cave, asked Abraham for 400 silver shekels, adding, barrow-boy style, but what is 400 shekels betwixt me and thee? Abraham, understandably in no mood to haggle, paid the asking price.

With Sarah buried there the cave stayed in the family. In time Abraham was also laid to rest in the Cave of Macpelah. His son, Isaac's wife Rebecca, Jacob and Jacob's wife Leah were all entombed in the cave too. Adam and Eve are also supposed to be buried thereabouts, although it has to be pointed out that Genesis makes no mention of quite how they got there.

When Abraham struck his deal with Ephron one presumes he believed the Cave would be a nice quiet place where his wife would rest in peace. But the living had different ideas. Joshua fought battles near the Cave, David was anointed King close by. Herod sealed it off, covering it with a huge stone enclosure. Christians and Muslims fought over the site, building first a church and then a mosque over the burial place. Today the Cave of Macpelah is sacred to both Jews and Muslims and over it is built a Muslim place of worship, the Ibrahimi Mosque.

For many centuries the Muslims afforded the Jews a restricted view of the shrine and relations between the two communities were reasonably harmonious. But during the 1920s an influx of Jews prompted a fierce Arab reaction – many Jews were murdered and the survivors fled. The area remained exclusively Arab until Israel captured it during the Six Day War in 1967. Under the terms of the surrender, the Muslims continued to run the Ibrahimi Mosque but Jews were granted equal access.

This apparently fair arrangement, however, didn't guarantee the peace and quiet which Abraham may have wanted. Hebron became the scene of many violent clashes between the local Arabs and Jewish settlers who moved into the area. Then, in 1994, a Jewish doctor called Baruch Goldstein walked into the Mosque and, instead of praying at the Tomb of the Patriarch, he did what he believed was his religious duty and turned his automatic rifle on the Muslims gathered inside for prayers. He fired 111 bullets, murdering 29 people and wounding 67 others, before he himself was killed by the crowd he had attacked.

Goldstein wasn't buried inside the Cave of Macpelah. But he was laid to rest not far away in the Jewish settlement of Kiryat Arba which overlooks Hebron. And in the tradition of Abraham, Baruch Goldstein's final resting place has now been turned into a shrine. The inscription on his solitary grave proclaims him a holy one who gave his life for his people. When I visited the spot, devout Jews muttered their prayers alongside me. A young mother encouraged her toddler to touch the resting place of the martyr.

Not all Jews think this way. The vast majority look on what Goldstein did as unforgivable, an act of premeditated murder. They believe that venerating his grave is an outrage. That explains why left-wingers, such as the 'Peace Now' group, have taken the extraordinary step of protesting at the grave demanding that Goldstein's body should be exhumed and moved to a more anonymous plot in a cemetery far away from Hebron.

Left-wing politicians have been drumming up support for the removal of the grave in the Israeli parliament, the Knesset. But it's hard to see the authorities acceding to this demand. The danger of a backlash from Goldstein's sympathisers is too great. Not only that, but anyone intent on destroying the site would have to face the wrath of Israel Goldstein, Baruch Goldstein's father.

When I talked to Mr Goldstein the old man had just finished praying at the grave and sat with his back against it, as if to protect his son's remains against any marauders. Obviously livid, he denounced those who wanted his son's body moved as ghouls and warned that they would have to kill him first. 'You don't mess with a grave!' he shouted, putting so much of his energy into the cry that I seriously worried he might collapse with the emotion of it all.

Perhaps because of the acute embarrassment which Goldstein caused his fellow Jews, the argument over his grave seems to be more intense on the Jewish side of the fence than amongst Arabs. One of Goldstein's Muslim victims, who was paralysed by his bullets, can clearly see the contentious plot from the windows of his home. But, speaking from his wheelchair, Muhammad Abu Halawa told me he didn't care what happened to the burial place. He was far more concerned about the way in which Jewish settlers behaved towards Palestinians on a day-to-day basis.

Quite what Abraham would have made of all of this is a matter of conjecture. Priests, rabbis and imams have prayed over his tomb. In Hebron, worship and warfare have at different times been the order of the day. Did Baruch Goldstein's gunfire disturb Abraham's rest? And does the prophet see the irony that another grave close by has now been turned into a shrine? All these questions must go unanswered. But after all that has happened above and around the Cave of Macpelah down through the centuries, Abraham could be forgiven for wishing that the living would leave the dead alone.

As my time in Jerusalem drew towards an end the stand-off between the

Iraqi leader Saddam Hussein and the US and the UK remained unresolved. Tension grew in Israel where people feared that Iraq would respond to any US strike by lobbing a Scud missile at Tel Aviv. Jerusalem was considered fairly safe because no Muslim worth their prayer mat would take the risk of knocking the gilt off the Dome of the Rock on the Temple Mount. With no one knowing what deadly materials might lurk in any Scud warheads, Israelis queued frantically to get gas masks. In fact the only casualties were people who suffocated themselves playing with their masks and a woman who fell off a balcony whilst trying to get into the window of an apartment where she had left her mask behind.

The chance of an Iraqi attack seemed quite remote, but in the event I was due to be our man on the hotel balcony in Tel Aviv. The BBC sent over a former soldier, a Gulf War veteran, to train us in donning our NBC gear – it stands for nuclear, biological and chemical warfare. I wondered how long you could work wearing one of these monkey suits. I also wondered what attitude Israeli citizens – whose gear was rather more Second World War vintage – would take to us strolling around in our science fiction outfits. Patricia, who was visiting me at the time, had to get kitted out, which was an unusual experience for a tourist. A Palestinian producer, Nadia, asked our instructor what she should do if she was at home in Ramallah with a friend, the sirens went off and she had only one NBC suit. 'Well,' he replied, 'it depends how good a friend it is.'

Thanks to a bit of whirlwind diplomacy by the UN Secretary-General Kofi Annan, the crisis receded and the air strikes were postponed by a year. I handed back my NBC suit and within a couple of weeks I came face to face with the man who during those anxious weeks for the Israelis had his finger on the trigger.

32

A Long Good Friday

SPRING 1998

The receiving line stretched for at least a hundred yards and the people at the end must have been thoroughly bored of shaking hands, and just in case you were wondering I wasn't in Baghdad queuing to see Saddam Hussein. Rather the venue was the White House, the menu included Boxty, Colcannon, Kerry Pies, Dublin Lawyer (which doesn't sound very appetising), Irish Whiskey Truffles and Strawberry Shamrock Pie, and the event was the St Patrick's Day reception hosted by President Clinton and his First Lady, Hillary, with their guests of honour the Irish prime minister Bertie Ahern and his companion Celia Larkin.

We clutched our introduction cards and filed down a corridor to shake hands with the famous foursome. Our producer Cathy Grieve had wangled us the invitations. Since helping mastermind the coverage of the President's trip to Northern Ireland in 1995, Cathy has built up better contacts with the White House than the British Foreign Office. When we worked our way to the top of the line it was hard to know what to say without appearing a complete idiot. I think I mumbled something to Bill about having covered his last trip to Belfast and looking forward to seeing him there again. It was a banal sentiment which I am sure he heard several hundred times that night. An official photograph of the occasion shows him towering over me, and my eyes firmly shut.

The formalities over, it was time to enjoy the free food and drink. We strolled around the various state rooms taking in the ambience. Gerry Adams seemed in good form. His spin doctor Richard McAuley asked me to make myself useful for a change and take a picture of them all inside the White House. I obliged, happy to promote a truce after the sharp criticism republicans had levelled at my book. David Trimble and John Taylor sat at a table in another room, as usual avoiding any social contact with the republicans. I broke off to do a live report on my mobile phone for Radio Five from one of the state rooms, which probably broke all White House regulations. Then I went in search of my colleagues Denis Murray and Cathy Grieve, who I found enjoying a drink with Mo Mowlam. Mo and her husband, John Norton, appeared on great form, having a laugh with the British ambassador Chris Meyer and his wife. We decided it would be nice to have a photograph of us all together.

Mo spied Michael Flatley, the star of the Irish dance extravaganza *Riverdance,* a few yards away. 'Ah, he'll do,' she said and marched over to him. 'Excuse me, Riverdance man, do you mind if we have a picture?' Flatley pulled himself up, clearly expecting to be snapped. He looked a bit taken aback when Mo handed him her camera, strolled back towards us and posed for the photograph. The dancer glanced at us, glanced at the camera, did not appear to see the funny side and hesitated. One of his companions rushed in, saying 'Allow me', and took the snap.

The St Patrick's week in Washington in 1998 was undoubtedly a hugely enjoyable junket. But it was also an extremely efficient way for me to get back into gear as Ireland Correspondent. For whilst I had been in Jerusalem events had been moving apace back in Belfast. After their temporary exclusions, both the loyalist Ulster Democrats and Sinn Féin returned to the talks. The talks chairman, George Mitchell, set 9 April as a deadline for agreement. The gaps between the parties still seemed wide. But everyone knew it was in the nature of negotiations for no one to make concessions until the last possible moment.

And so it was back to the Portakabin village in the Stormont car park, the familiar surroundings made a bit more outlandish by the erection of an extra marquee where food was served to the swelling ranks of the world's press. Belfast at Easter closely resembled Belfast at Christmas, with a biting wind and, overnight, swirling snow particles. It was a shock to my system after the warm weather of Tel Aviv and the Dead Sea. George Mitchell tabled a paper which, as expected, gave a good impression of the Framework Document made flesh, but appeared rather too green in tone for unionist digestion. John Taylor, who is always a good man for lobbing verbal hand grenades when he thinks it will serve a purpose, told reporters that he wouldn't touch the chairman's proposals with 'a forty-foot bargepole'. I have witnessed Mr Taylor in action enough times to know to take some of his comments with a pinch of salt, but a few conversations with extremely concerned members of the middle-of-the-road Alliance Party confirmed there were indeed some real problems.

Tony Blair rode to the rescue in his helicopter and the hard bargaining began. Outside Stormont was now, more than ever, Spin City. Journalists huddled around politicians and press officers in a series of little groups, trying to sift the real information from the lines being thrown to put you off the trail. Many of the Westminster-based correspondents were used to getting much of their information from the Prime Minister's spokesman Alastair Campbell. They would disappear into a news conference and come out saying, 'Alastair says it's like this.' But with the talks involving two governments and eight political parties Number Ten was by no means the only source of information. Sometimes Alastair would have something genuinely new to say, but on other occasions we would tell our colleagues, 'No, that's way out of date, the unionists have already rejected that' or 'Sinn Féin is making clear that's a non-starter.'

We all felt great sympathy for Bertie Ahern, having to deal with the most important negotiations of his life at the same time as coping with his mother's death. It was moving to see him return to the grindstone straight from his mother's funeral. Despite the presence of both prime ministers, the deadline of midnight on 9 April loomed closer without any sign of a deal. With an hour to go we got word that Ian Paisley had led a group of loyalists into the Stormont grounds. We charged off towards Carson's statue to see what was up. RUC officers were running around, their dogs barking into the night air, concerned that the loyalists should not be allowed to storm the talks building. In the event the DUP leader halted the loyalist protesters at the statue, telling them they had achieved their aim by mounting their protest at Carson's feet. He and his party colleagues would go on alone to address the press.

The Big Man made his way into the car park and strolled purposefully towards the main news conference hut. But there weren't only journalists waiting to meet him. A number of supporters of the two small loyalist parties, some of whom had got fairly well oiled in the bar inside the talks building, had come out to see what the fuss was all about. They greeted Paisley with shouts of 'Go home, you dinosaur', and 'The Grand Old Duke of York' and a wide selection of choice language which no doubt shocked not only Dr Paisley but the audience in Northern Ireland watching the whole affair live on their televisions at home. Some saw the heckling by Protestants as symbolising that Ian Paisley's day was over. This was a massive exaggeration, as the next few months would demonstrate, but the confrontation was undoubtedly something to witness.

With Ian Paisley gone, the night continued, the deadline came and went but still the talking went on. I kept BBC Radio Five's *Up All Night* informed with regular chats with the presenter Rod Sharpe on the hour every hour. After my 2 a.m. contribution it was pretty obvious we were going to be continuing into the following morning, so I decided that I should nip back to my flat to get a shower, shave and change of clothes. We had plenty of correspondents around so I asked if they would cover for me whilst I was away. At 3 a.m. I was under my shower listening to the radio in case any breaking news would require me to rush back. I heard Rod tell his listeners that the vital talks were still going on at Stormont but they wouldn't be going over there just now because 'some people have to get some sleep'. Wide awake and spluttering under the shower I cursed my colleagues: 'The swines have let me down.' As it turned out there had simply been a breakdown of communications between the team on the ground and the programme in London.

Back at Stormont we started preparing for a signing ceremony but there were more glitches to come. Overnight Sinn Féin appeared unhappy – Gerry Adams and Martin McGuinness paced around the freezing car park, looking pensive. Then in the early hours one of our cameramen captured an extraordinary image of Bríd Rodgers from the SDLP hugging her party colleagues, who had clearly done a deal. The SDLP spin doctors came out and tried to brief their favourite newspapers, excluding us broadcasters, but we already had the image which told the story.

An assistant to the Ulster Unionist MP Jeffrey Donaldson left the building to get a change of clothes ready for the signing ceremony. But when he came back he found his boss profoundly unhappy about aspects of the deal. The next day, Good Friday, Jeffrey rushed off without saying anything, indicating his opposition to the final text. People were still trying to guess the details of the agreement, but then BBC Northern Ireland's Political Editor Stephen Grimason went on screen and started waving it around. I have always been pleased to work with Stephen but never so pleased as when I saw him waving his copy of the Good Friday Agreement, hours before anyone in the competition had it. Previously we had been dealing with steers and partial leaks and educated speculation. Now we had hard copy. We had the political institutions. We had the proposal for prisoner releases. We had the plans to review the RUC. We had the lot. It was a world-class scoop. Stephen divulged all in an impromptu seminar inside one of the Portakabins. On his way there some competing journalists tried to get a glance at the text over his shoulder. Kevin Kelly, my former researcher and undoubtedly one of the best fixers and field producers in the business, protected Stephen from any eavesdroppers. Kevin amused us all at Stormont that week, when he told one of the nation's best-known broadcasters in no certain terms to back off as, 'You're getting too close to my man.'

There were a few more wrinkles in need of ironing out as the Ulster Unionist leader David Trimble sought letters of reassurance from Tony Blair on the questions of disarmament and prisoners. But then, seventeen hours after George Mitchell's deadline, at 5 p.m. on Friday, 10 April, the ceremony got under way. The exhausted negotiators looked, for the most part, delighted they had cut a deal, although some – most obviously David Trimble and Gerry Adams – knew they would face an uphill struggle selling aspects of the agreement to their constituencies. A referendum to seek the people's backing for the deal had always been part of the proposed package. I remember little of the speeches at the signing ceremony apart from George Mitchell's quip that he had been 'dying to leave, but hated to go', which summed it up for most of the press corps after so many hours in our radio cars, satellite vans and portable huts. What sticks in my mind more is the image of some delegates hugging each other in jubilation at what had been achieved, not a picture traditionally associated with our coverage of Northern Ireland.

33

The Vote

SPRING 1998–SUMMER 1998

From outside, the referendum campaign looked to many like a straight battle between the forces of light and the forces of darkness. After all, who apart from a bigot or a fascist could possibly want to vote against peace? In fact it was all a bit more complicated than that, as peace at the price being requested stuck in the craw of many who considered themselves just as reasonable and respectable as the next person. For many unionists the notion that the republicans who they had long regarded as unreconstructed murderers might soon be sitting in government was hard to come to terms with. At a rally in the Apprentice Boys Hall in Derry I watched the anti-Agreement Ulster Unionist Willie Ross get the hairs on his audience's necks standing by painting a picture of Gerry Adams or Martin McGuinness in charge of their children's education.

Accepting republicans in power, however, was probably less hard to swallow for the electorate than voting for the early release of prisoners convicted of horrendous crimes. This was an issue which cut, to some extent, across the sectarian divide – it was a question of justice, of victims' families on both sides who believed the Agreement had not been written with them in mind. Tom Travers, the Catholic magistrate whose daughter Mary had been killed by the IRA in 1984 after leaving St Bridget's church in south Belfast, announced that he could not bring himself to vote for the Agreement. Many Protestant families who had lost members of the security forces thought the same. The sense of injustice stirred by the early release proposals swelled enormously when we broadcast pictures of the Balcombe Street gang being given a hero's welcome after getting temporary release to attend Sinn Féin's party conference, or ard-fheis, in Dublin. Four days later the Milltown cemetery murderer Michael Stone got a similar rapturous reception at a rally in the Ulster Hall in Belfast. The fact that both sides had matched each other did not even things out, but served only to compound the alienation of the law-abiding majority who would never have signed up to either paramilitary organisation.

These genuine concerns gave the anti-Agreement forces fertile ground to till. The *Six O'Clock News* sent me off following the DUP leader Ian Paisley to see if he really was a dinosaur whose day was over. I found him in combative form tucking into a serious plate of sausage and chips in Limavady. The Protestant faithful waited outside a café in the town centre whilst the Big Man finished his Big Lunch, in between bites regaling a *New York Times* reporter with his thoughts on speculation about a possible prepoll visit by President Clinton. 'If he decides to come here,' he told the American correspondent, 'I say to the parents of Ulster, lock up your daughters.' Once lunch had been digested Dr Paisley strolled around the streets, being glad-handed by the vast majority of local unionists. However, one housewife, obviously a committed Yes voter, tore into him, asking, 'But what alternative do you have to offer?' Paisley countered by accusing her of advocating surrender. The full-blooded encounter made great television.

The DUP leader sallied around an agricultural show in Belfast the next day. I caught up with him and asked whether, in the light of the Good Friday Agreement, he felt the icy wind of extinction in his bones. Not surprisingly, he disagreed with typical vehemence, saying, 'Mr Devenport, ask me that question when the votes are counted – the people will give you your reply.'

Like most journalists who have covered Northern Ireland my experience of Ian Paisley has been one of sharp contrasts. There have been the ear-splitting tirades and tellings-off and even a once only box on the ears, but the Free Presbyterian moderator has also treated me to plenty of his gruffly humorous remarks. Dr Paisley once drew attention to my Barry Manilowesque features by remarking, 'That's a quare nose you have, Mr Devenport, for balancing spectacles on.' During a news conference, when he thought one of my questions had been outdated by the latest developments, he retorted, 'Who are you, Rip Van Winkle?' Subtlety might not be his strong point, but no one could accuse him of being a cold fish, and his rumbustious style is a gift for any film-maker. As our *Spotlight* programme on prison transfer clearly demonstrated, the DUP leader prides himself on his equal treatment of individual Catholics while at the same time deriding their church as an institution. His assiduous work as a local MP also shows him as non-sectarian in dealing with his constituents' complaints. It's all true, but does it matter?

If the road to hell is paved with good intentions, the road to confrontation in Northern Ireland appears to be surfaced with an excess of political intransigence and theological certainty. Would the troubles have lasted so long, I wonder, if Paisley hadn't played his belligerent and uncompromising role?

If the No campaign concentrated on the traditional street campaigning tactics of familiar Northern Irish faces like Ian Paisley and Robert McCartney, on the Yes side we were treated to posters and videos. It seemed more modern, but less effective. The pro-Agreement party leaders were telling their followers to vote Yes for precisely opposing reasons – Gerry Adams said the Agreement weakened the union, whilst David Trimble said it strengthened it. They all appeared to be reluctant to push themselves too far out in front of the electorate in case their arguments had an equal and opposite effect on the other side of the Yes camp. David Trimble, in particular, seemed like a man under siege, constantly heckled by vociferous anti-Agreement unionists wherever he went.

The Yes campaign hit on the notion of bringing in celebrities from elsewhere – good advertising tactics in general, but here it ran the risk of dispersing its message amongst a series of different personalities, whilst the No camp kept wheeling out the same tried and trusted leaders. There was also the danger that suspicious Northern Irish folk would not take kindly to a message being delivered to them by a bunch of 'blow-ins'. I followed Richard Branson and Mo Mowlam around Belfast city centre, Branson's contribution being to remind the people of Northern Ireland that a vote in favour would make good sense in economic terms. I reminded the Virgin boss that his most memorable appearance in Northern Ireland had been a bit of a flop, when his balloon made a crash landing on Rathlin Island. Was that a bad omen? I couldn't make out the tycoon's reply very well. Afterwards someone pointed out to me that the headphones I was wearing were a pair I had 'borrowed' off the last Virgin flight I had taken.

The government started to get very nervous about the way things were shaping up. Number Ten were on the phone complaining about the balance of our coverage. In particular on 14 May they did not like the fact that we treated Michael Stone's release as a bigger story than the Prime Minister's visit to Northern Ireland that day. Since the PM appeared to be in Belfast more or less every other day at this stage, his presence was losing its novelty value. The images of Stone were obviously more impressive, even if he had not been let out by the government specifically to appear at the Ulster Hall rally. The fundamental news values were clear and we stood our ground.

Accompanying the Prime Minister and David Trimble on a visit to Coleraine, the Labour MP Kate Hoey, normally extremely affable, seemed a little on edge. Did we have to balance every Yes voice we broadcast with a No voice, she complained. I answered that I reckoned that we had in fact given more airtime to the Yes camp on the basis that they seemed to have twice as many likely supporters as the Nos. But we were presenting an argument – of course we had to have both sides. Kate sighed, accepting my logic but clearly very anxious about the outcome of the vote. Maybe the apparent omnipresence of Ian Paisley and Robert McCartney on our screens proved the Yes campaign had dispersed its message too widely. But Mr McCartney did himself no favours when he decided to heckle the Prime Minister during a visit to his North Down constituency. The MP argued correctly that Tony Blair had not observed the usual parliamentary niceties by tipping him off about the visit. But the resulting images of Mr McCartney shouting at the PM's entourage then himself being harangued by Yes voters probably did little to impress the wavering middle-class unionist voter.

The Yes camp dallied with the notion of a US presidential visit during the campaign, but decided against on the grounds that it would have been obvious outside interference in Northern Ireland's affairs. Then, at the last minute, the SDLP pulled off a coup. U2's Bono had always been a great admirer of John Hume and he let it be known that he would be prepared to do whatever the party leader thought best to try to rally the pro-Agreement vote. A concert was organised at the Waterfront concert hall, featuring the Downpatrick band Ash and U2. The event provided the Yes camp with the images and emotions which had been sorely lacking. The rock stars strolled along the newly developed bank of the River Lagan, a symbol of Belfast's economic renewal and the high hopes for the future. They clasped hands with both John Hume and David Trimble, the leaders of the two biggest parties, one Catholic, one Protestant. On stage, in front of an invited audience of school pupils, U2 launched into a medley of 'One Love' and 'Give Peace a Chance'. Hume and Trimble walked on to the stage in shirtsleeves and raised hands with Bono. They looked a bit out of place, but what the hell.

The climax of the concert was a bit tight for the *Nine O'Clock News*, but, cutting double quick in our edit vehicle outside the Waterfront, we made it in time. Then I went in search of Patricia, who had been inside the concert hall, then bumped into a friend who does PR for Ash, who invited us to the backstage party. One of Patricia's after dinner anecdotes was about how she had met U2 'before they were famous' nearly twenty years before when they had been supporting Squeeze at Queen's University Students' Union. I'd always taken the details of how U2 smuggled her and her friends into the gig with a pinch of salt. Having just earnestly commentated on the event for the *Nine O'Clock News,* I had reservations about turning into a 'groupie', so I left her to worm her way towards the stars and engaged in an almost serious political conversation with the SDLP and Ulster Unionist spin doctors, Conal McDevitt and David Kerr. I took some slagging from the concert promoter Eamon McCann about the young concertgoer we had interviewed who told us he planned to enjoy the gig, then vote No. I felt a tap on my shoulder – it was Patricia, and she had Bono by the hand.

'Tell him,' she ordered the rock star.

'It's true,' he said. 'We did play Belfast all those years ago, our van did break down, I remember getting some girls in through a window at the back, so she isn't making it up.'

After apologising to Patricia for having never believed her anecdote before, I congratulated Bono on the concert, telling him I thought it would make a crucial difference to what had been an undeniably lacklustre Yes campaign.

'Well I hope so. We had to do whatever we could,' he replied.

In the King's Hall on 22 May 1998 an unlikely collection of DUP politicians, Sinn Féiners and loyalists queued to get coffees. There was no question which side would get more votes, what remained open to question was the size of the majority. Symbolically this was important. Although some extreme republicans might vote against, it seemed fair to assume that the bulk of the opposition would come from unionists who felt the deal had betrayed them. If David Trimble had not convinced a majority of Protestants to side with him it would make it hard to ensure the deal stuck. When the chief electoral officer Pat Bradley announced the result it was on the basis of the second highest turnout in Northern Ireland's long history of well-patronised elections. Of the 81 per cent of voters who decided to go to the polls, 71.1 per cent of those who cast valid votes supported the Agreement, whilst 28.9 per cent voted against. Ian Paisley and his entourage swept out of the hall, the loyalists who had taunted him at Stormont again weighing in with cries of 'Easy, easy.' The DUP leader insisted that a majority of Protestants had voted against the Agreement, which begged the question as to whether a Protestant vote was worth more than a Catholic vote. With no official breakdown of the poll it was open for both sides to try to claim a victory of sorts, but the size of the majority obviously made this a rather more credible exercise for the Yes camp. An analysis by Coopers & Lybrand later concluded that 55 per cent of Protestants had backed the deal, compared to 96 per cent of Catholics. Ian Paisley had persuaded a narrow majority in his own constituency of North Antrim to reject the deal, but all the other constituencies had come out in favour.

So that was it. Everything was settled. With the democratic will of the people of Ireland established (more than 94 per cent backed the deal south of the border) all sides buried their differences, and determined to walk together into a brighter, more prosperous future. Well, not quite . . . There were some bits of undeniably good news. The Loyalist Volunteer Force, for example, called a ceasefire, saying it recognised the validity of the poll. The Ulster Unionist leader David Trimble was elected as Northern Ireland's First Minister Designate and the SDLP deputy leader Seamus Mallon joined him in what would have hitherto been considered an unlikely double act. Because Catholics couldn't be considered second-class citizens Mallon got the unwieldy title of Deputy First Minister, not to be confused with Second Minister, or indeed Second-Class Minister. Ian Paisley gave us all a laugh by calling the Queen 'a parrot' of the government after speculation that she might visit the Irish Republic. ('My Husband and I, My Husband and I' would presumably be the formal cry of a royal parrot.)

But alongside these developments there came much that really could be ascribed to the forces of darkness. A two-hundred-pound republican bomb detonated in the centre of Newtownhamilton in County Armagh, fortunately killing no one but causing massive damage and some injuries. A Catholic man who had the temerity to outpunch a leading IRA man in north Belfast after an argument over a game of cards was punished by being shot in the legs and ankles by a gang of masked men. Andrew Kearney bled to death before proper medical care could be summoned. Catholic churches were burned by loyalists in the run-up to the 1998 Drumcree parade. And then when that parade was halted we saw all the predictable disorder, culminating in the appalling deaths of the three young Quinn children.

The morning I reported on the arson attack at Ballymoney I remember thinking we could not possibly sink any lower. I had to wait only one month for Northern Ireland to prove me wrong.

34

Omagh

The weekend of 15 August 1998 Patricia and I took a couple of extra days off. We were planning to visit some friends in Spain. But our travel arrangements did not work out so we settled for time off closer to home. In the summer sun, Northern Ireland was looking at its best. Who needed to travel far away, we asked each other, when the countryside at home was so beautiful. When I turned my key in the car ignition to start our day trip, I had no idea what the next few hours would bring. I tried to piece it together for the following report which I wrote some days later for the BBC's Internet news service BBC Online.

A WAKE WRIT LARGE

It was my weekend off, so I decided to have a holiday at home. I drove down to Portaferry at the tip of the Ards peninsula and watched a golden sun glint over the waters of Strangford Lough. I walked to the top of Slieve Croob, one of the smaller peaks in the mountains of Mourne, which as the Irish ballad puts it, roll majestically down to the sea.

For those who have never visited, I can assure you, Northern Ireland truly is a lovely place.

Driving home I flicked on the radio. The presenter broke into the pop songs to read out an urgent message. The Tyrone County Hospital wanted all their off-duty staff to call in immediately. Despite the peace process, bombings and shootings have remained a fact of life in Northern Ireland. But such an emergency announcement is a rarity. It had to be bad.

I went straight to the newsroom and plunged into the business of trying to ascertain the truth. Phone connections around Omagh were down so finding out facts was hard at first.

One colleague got to the hospital, where his mobile phone served not just to let us know what was going on, but more importantly to enable medical staff to liaise with their counterparts in other local hospitals.

Another BBC producer was ushered into a room by a family – it was only when she was inside that she realised they wanted her to treat their badly injured child. She wished she was a doctor not a journalist.

When I got to the hospital the entrance to Accident and Emergency was still spattered with blood.

A man asked me what the latest casualty figures were. 'Twenty-six,' I told him, 'but it looks as if it will go up to twenty-eight.'

'I am still looking for my wee girl,' he said, in an almost matter-of-fact way. The reality of his situation still did not seem to have sunk in.

In the corridor medical staff rushed past with a trolley carrying a patient covered in blood. Outside you had to brace yourself against the downdraft of helicopters taking off with seriously injured people being transferred to intensive care facilities in Belfast and Derry.

The next few hours and days are a blur of memories. The big burly policeman confessing that he had been in tears as he went about his work. The 61-year-old who told me that, after what he had seen, he would never be the same man again. My colleague, a reporter for BBC Northern Ireland, whose wife's shop was destroyed by the blast. Thankfully they were just returning from holiday, driving back towards Omagh when the bomb went off.

I covered a vigil where people stood in stunned silence. One man shook physically with rage when asked about the apologies of the perpetrators, a group which calls itself the Real IRA. 'You've heard the phrase beneath contempt,' he said, 'but this is beneath that.'

Hearses wound their way through the traffic. I have never seen so many in the same town at the same time. The undertakers, like everyone else, were clearly stretched. At one point I was surprised to step out of my hotel and see some of them using the car park to transfer a coffin from one hearse to another – it looked as if they had simply run out of anywhere more private to do it.

Death has its particular rituals in Ireland and nowhere more than in and around Omagh. Wakes – the gathering of people at the homes of the recently bereaved – are always well attended, but never more than in the past week.

The whole town of Omagh seemed like one big wake. You could not buy a newspaper or put petrol in your car without someone telling you where they had been, what they had seen, who they knew amongst the dead and injured.

Government ministers, politicians and yes us journalists too talked about the implications for the peace process, the tightening of security, the hunt for the bombers. But the politics all seemed so irrelevant. This week has been about an act of inhumanity followed by thousands of expressions of most people's fundamental humanity – expressions of love, courage and care.

As I write the people of Northern Ireland are about to hold a minute's silence, exactly a week on from the bombing. I shall observe it. And maybe I shall drive back to Portaferry and watch the sun glint, once again, on the waters of Strangford Lough.

It will be my own way of affirming that what is good and beautiful in Northern Ireland will outlast what is bad and ugly.

I don't claim to have been traumatised by Omagh. Unlike so many people I was not there, out shopping on a Saturday afternoon, when some misguided cowards parked their car bomb and walked away. I did not have to witness the appalling scenes in the centre of the town after the device exploded in the midst of people who believed they had been moved to safety. I did not lose a brother, mother or daughter. I still have the use of all my limbs. But nobody could cover anything of that scale without feeling a dark cloud pass over them.

I went to Omagh a couple of weeks before the bombing, putting together a piece on the elections for the new assembly in west Tyrone. I trudged around the streets with the candidates, indulging in a bit of banter with local SDLP councillor Pat McDonnell. I did not expect to see Pat again so soon. A few months before, I covered a bomb alert early one morning in the same street in the centre of the town. We stood behind the white tape staring up towards Omagh courthouse, just as people must have done on 15 August. Only that time it didn't turn out to be a serious alert. We shrugged it off, had a cup of coffee and got on with the rest of our lives, just as people must have imagined they would that Saturday afternoon.

Now I took up residence with scores of other journalists in the car park at the local supermarket, Dunnes Stores. I interviewed many local people, including councillors like Pat McDonnell about something far more serious and sombre than an election campaign. I talked live on air on the TV news the night of the bombing about the possible implications. Over me floated the images of a home video taken moments after the blast, which we had just been handed minutes before going on air. The pictures really required no commentary. In the days that followed we trekked back and forth across a little pedestrian bridge to get to the spot which afforded the best view of the security forces picking their way through the rubble – they removed a vast array of items for examination, including a number of children's prams. People made their way through the gaggle of press to leave flowers for the dead. Many wept openly. At the local leisure centre families gathered to await news of their loved ones. The staff kept up a constant flow of complimentary teas, coffees and, in the morning, Ulster fries. Gerry Adams came and went. The families at the centre, like the victims, represented a complete cross-section of Omagh's population. Some rolled their eyes at the Sinn Féin leader's presence, but others welcomed him warmly. Outside the centre he used the word which had stuck in his throat so long, unequivocally 'condemning' the bombing. Apart from Gerry Adams there were many other high-profile visitors – Prince Charles, the Deputy Prime Minister John Prescott and eventually Tony Blair and Bill Clinton.

I kept to my vow and marked the minute's silence at St Anne's Cathedral in Belfast. I wasn't working, but felt the need to take part. I was a 'blow-in' but, by now, I felt I owed some kind of duty to the community I had lived in for so many years. A duty to show respect, in public, together with them. On the way to the cathedral, I bumped into Eleanor Methven, one of the people I used to share a house with and one of the first people I met after landing in Belfast. We hadn't seen each other for years. Eleanor had decided to go to the service too and we filed into our seats together. After days broadcasting about the bombing, I felt like a citizen doing what a citizen ought to do rather than a journalist peering in from the outside.

A few days later, together with my mother, I drove down to Portaferry again. The sun wasn't quite so golden, but the lough still looked stunning. Its beauty, however, was neither here nor there. In the real world the beautiful and the ugly, the good and the bad coexist. I might have felt ready to move on. But back in Omagh, for many of the living as well as the dead, the clock had stopped on the afternoon of 15 August. Several months later I went back to cover a question and answer session one evening at the local College of

Further Education. People's emotions remained as raw as ever. Lawrence Rush, whose wife had been killed in the blast, appeared a good man driven to the verge of madness by grief. Michael Gallagher, whose son died, exuded wisdom and calm, but amidst it all his lasting sadness was unforgettable. When I talked to them both, the politicians at Stormont were once again at loggerheads. The victims of Omagh quite rightly felt their leaders owed it to them to get on with it.

Great good came out of Omagh, in the shape of the acts of kindness that people showed to each other. But no one in their right mind could argue that something like that was part of some master plan, and I still cannot feel anything but blind anger about the atrocity. The people who planted the bomb, the Real IRA, might be very good at the practicalities of tinkering with Semtex and detonators and murdering innocent people. But their political thinking is outdated and their moral purpose ridiculous. Seventy-one per cent of northerners and 94 per cent of southerners made their views clear. The Real IRA demanded a recount and blew up the ballot box when they did not get it, all in the name of future generations who, as yet unborn, can hold any opinion you want to ascribe to them. I do not believe the Real IRA intended to kill civilians that day, but so what? If you are callous enough to park car bombs in crowded places you deserve all the damnation which is coming your way. It was typical that the bombers should call a ceasefire whilst at the centre of a hue and cry, then slowly but surely try to insert themselves back into the terrorist scene under different labels. In time they will regroup, explain away their actions and once again try to convince the naive of the nobility of their cause. Hopefully, in Ireland and in Irish America, they won't get too many converts. The survivors of Omagh have shown remarkable bravery and compassion. But, quite simply, the blast should never have happened.

35

Victims

SUMMER 1987–SPRING 1999

Omagh will always figure in any history of Britain and Ireland in the twentieth century. But I could name twenty-nine victims of twenty-nine different incidents who will be forgotten, because they died on their own rather than en masse. The world sits up and takes notice when the total number of casualties is bigger. But bereavement is an individual tragedy. The pain does not increase according to some mathematical formula. I think of Kathleen Finlay, who I talked to for one *Spotlight* programme, sitting on her own in her home at Victoria Bridge in County Tyrone, thinking about her husband Ronnie, a part-time UDR soldier, shot dead in front of his family by the IRA. Who, outside her own tight-knit community, remembers Kathleen's sadness? I think of Rosario McCartan staring into my eyes on the identity parade, trying to work out if I was the loyalist murderer of her brother. Who gave her the justice she deserved? I think of Brian Armour, the prison officer slumped in his wrecked car, targeted, in all probability, by someone I knew.

Some relatives of victims seem to derive an inner strength from their ordeals. Others become like ghosts, whose bereavement has robbed them of all will to exist. Some mothers and wives, like Rita Restorick or Joyce McCartan, commit themselves ever afterwards to work for peace. Others vow revenge and are toughened by the experience. Sitting in her west Belfast living room, one hardline loyalist woman explained to me why the loyalist ceasefire had been so difficult for a close friend. 'You see her husband was killed by those IRA bastards not long before they called the loyalist ceasefire. So nobody was "got" in return for him.' Would it have made it any better if somebody, anybody, had been 'got'?

I never liked knocking on the door or picking up the phone to talk for the first time to the family of a terrorist victim. Unlike the doctor, the priest, the neighbour or the social worker, I felt I wasn't offering something for nothing, but looking for something in return – my twenty seconds of raw emotion which I knew would 'lift' my report. I was never very good at making such an approach, partly because I am rather timid, partly because inside me I wasn't sure I believed the journalist's argument that telling it as it was might make a difference to the outside world. Did the outside world really care?

That said, I felt genuinely surprised about how many of those forced to endure terrible loss welcomed us journalists into their lives. Many wanted to talk, either to make a point, or just to repeat in public the story which was, in any case, running over and over again in their own heads. One of the last few reports I produced before I left Northern Ireland was a big package for Radio Four's *World Tonight* examining the old stumbling block of weapons decommissioning. We wanted 'real people', not politicians, to express views on the subject, so I went along to a news conference at the Stormont hotel organised by the Ulster Unionist Jeffrey Donaldson. A number of victims' relatives were due to appear alongside the MP and I wanted to collar one of them for my report.

When Janet Hunter started talking about her brother Joseph McIlwaine, murdered by the IRA in June 1987, it made me stop and think. Joe had been a greenkeeper at the Aberdelghy golf course, gunned down as he sat in a hut during his tea break. The shooting, nearly twelve years before, had been the first murder I ever covered in Northern Ireland. It coincided with the count in that year's general election. All the other reporters were busy, so the editor had to send his 'cub'. I had been nervous and uncertain about getting my pictures and interviews in time for my deadline. I can remember recording a piece-to-camera at the golf course, then heading to an army base in Belfast where I asked Joseph's commanding officer what the murder would do for the regiment's morale. He replied that whilst it would be an obvious blow, his soldiers' morale remained strong. Both the question and the answer seemed stock responses, a case of going through the motions, which reminded me of the local MP who, when rung up about another bombing or shooting, would tell journalists to 'Put me down for the usual.' I rushed back to the BBC to edit my piece. It made the deadline. There had not been any time to ponder the consequences, nor to think of Joseph's family at home.

I talked to Janet Hunter about her views on disarmament and the Good Friday Agreement, which she opposed. Janet suffers from ME, a debilitating illness, and spends much of her time in a wheelchair. Her brother's murder almost certainly exacerbated her condition. Nevertheless she has brought up a bunch of extremely lively children. Later together with researcher Rachel Hooper I visited Janet's home in Lisburn to record some sounds of the family playing Scrabble, just to give a sense to radio listeners that here was a 'normal' family dealing with an abnormal situation. Janet handed me a piece of paper on which she had tried to sum up what her family had gone through on 12 June 1987 whilst I rushed around piecing together my report for the television news that night. This is an extract from her account.

> Three people walked into the room where Joseph was at his tea, unarmed and only twenty years old ... The murderers shot him twelve times at point-blank range in a room with only one door and no windows. They stood there shooting a helpless boy with no way of protecting himself, nor anywhere to hide. The family found out that he was dead by hearing it on the radio twenty minutes after he was murdered. We were not even given the chance to hear it quietly in our home, together as a family. It was told over the radio. The shock still rings in our ears and minds. It was five hours later before the police came to tell us Joseph was dead. By that time we were all together in our grief ... Since that day in June we have had to live with the loss. It has divided our family so much that two sisters cannot bear to live here any more. The rest of us still watch over our shoulders wherever we go. We are still solemn with grief, numb to the reality of life. We function each day, but as many families who have paid the price of these troubles it is often less than normal life. We as a family have received no help nor counselling after the death of Joseph. No support from any organisation nor any people from any support groups. All we have had has been SILENCE ... Joseph was murdered, he was buried, he is forgotten by the government. His sacrifice means nothing to anyone other than his family and his friends.

As a reporter I have grown to know Northern Ireland, to meet people like Janet Hunter and her family, to try to understand a little. But my experience, whilst marked by its lows, has also included many highs and a lot of laughter to balance the sadness. I am not sure I shall ever fully comprehend what someone like Janet has gone through.

36

The Peace Process on Ice

WINTER 1998–SPRING 1999

I̶t felt very cold and very dangerous. I am not thinking of the night in December 1998 when we stood freezing in the laneway at Drumcree watching loyalists wrestle with RUC officers and fireworks arcing over the police line towards us, rather, I am thinking of the square in Oslo where, about a week later, Peter Cooper and I tried vainly to 'vox-pop' a crowd of Norwegian primary school children on the twin subjects of peace and Ireland. 'Coop' had stood his ground brave and strong when Michael Stone opened fire in his direction. But now this battle-hardened cameraman and I teetered on the brink of disaster, slipping and sliding on the icy Oslo paving stones besieged by excited children who appeared to want to eat my microphone and whose knee-high height only increased the likelihood of them succeeding in toppling us over.

Both of us had before us the example of our producer Cathy Grieve who had already come a cropper on the Oslo streets, and who now, like an armchair general, was continuing to direct hostilities from her wheelchair. So we were doubly careful to extract ourselves from the fray intact and keep a respectful distance as the children's parade, organised to mark the anniversary of the UN's Universal Declaration of Human Rights and the award of the Nobel Peace Prize, wound its way through downtown Oslo. The children got to the 'Rathaus' or town hall and cheered and laughed their way through a bumptious and quite inexplicable display by a series of actors in period costume. Then the star turns arrived – John Hume and David Trimble. This time there was no Bono to help them carry the occasion off, but they did their best. The SDLP leader, once again proving his linguistic and Euro credentials, launched into a greeting in his best Norwegian. The Ulster Unionist did not try to match that, just in case some loyalist back home thought he'd been speaking Irish, but he did thank the assembled toddlers and told them that what he and his fellow Nobel prizewinner were embarked on would 'make a difference for the children'.

The two politicians then lit a torch of peace, before dusting themselves down, changing and making their way inside the Rathaus, for a ceremony which looked, I imagine, not entirely dissimilar to the state weddings the Communist Party used to arrange for couples in the old Soviet Union – full of ceremony, but devoid of religion. Processing up the central aisle, Messrs Hume and Trimble made an unlikely bride and bridegroom. With the Norwegian King and Queen providing the majesty and the Belfast flautist James Galway providing the music it looked a suitably august occasion, which I witnessed from a purpose-built commentary booth in the Rathaus balcony. When I got bored by the proceedings, my booth afforded me excellent views of the impressive frescos which decorate the Rathaus walls. Mr Hume, his eye just possibly on a future political career in Europe, pleased his audience with a speech which included lots of his well-known themes of burying difference within a common European union, and pleased the folks back home by dedicating the award to them, dubbing it 'our people's prize'. Mr Trimble, who can never see a party without being tempted to poop it, told the puzzled Norwegians that he wasn't going to treat them to any 'vague and visionary statements'. Instead he made us all feel a bit as though we were sitting in a university lecture hall as he developed his academic thesis, analysing the spirit of democracy and fascism. Aware that unionist leaders did not often get this kind of worldwide attention, he again pressed home his argument that the IRA needed to disarm, stressing the need for 'a beginning to the decommissioning of weapons as an earnest of the decommissioning of hearts that must follow'. I pondered quite how a decommissioned heart might tick.

The ceremony was okay, but what had come before, with the children, was more fun. Fortunately so was what came afterwards. We all ended up in an Oslo hotel quaffing Norwegian beer and listening to the politicians embarking on a sing-song. John Gorman, the 'Captain Mainwaring' of the Ulster Unionist Party, regaled us with stories of his wartime exploits and how his father had given Michael Collins the idea of calling the Irish police the 'Guards', after his British regiment of the same name. In the next room John Hume took up position beside a piano, with the famous Derry pianist Phil Coulter at the keyboard.

I have followed John Hume through the highs and lows of the peace process. At times I managed to get on his wrong side. In the spring of 1992 I made a film about the victory of his colleague Joe Hendron over Gerry Adams in West Belfast. For one sequence of the programme we followed the victorious new MP over to Westminster to take up the seat Gerry Adams had abstained from filling. We arranged to film the party's four MPs on the tube heading towards parliament, but had to persuade them to wait a few minutes at Heathrow while we got our camera gear off the plane. Three MPs managed to be patient and wait, but not the party leader. London Transport insisted we should have a police guard to escort 'the man who beat Gerry Adams' and the police ordered us to change trains at Baron's Court. When we got to Westminster I bumped into an apopleptic Mr Hume who wanted to know 'where the bloody hell' we'd been, irrespective of the fact that three-quarters of his parliamentary party had managed to stick with us. He told me he had been up and down the stairs at Hammersmith a dozen times looking for us. I explained the police's preference for Baron's Court, which Mr Hume countered with a plaintive 'The boys know we ALWAYS change at Hammersmith.'

This little misunderstanding, however, was nothing compared to the SDLP leader's anger over a *Spotlight* programme I reported on in 1993 which explored the tensions within the party caused by his overtures to Sinn Féin. The programme featured a current and former member of the SDLP raising doubts about where the *rapprochement* with Sinn Féin would end. Hume gave it to me with both barrels after the programme went on air. One leading SDLP figure commiserated with me later, 'You know your problem − you forgot that script line saying he sits at the right hand of the Lord.'

I might have felt the white heat of his temper on occasion, but at no point did I ever doubt Mr Hume's courage and tenacity in pursuing his gut feelings, come what may. The weight of the pressure on Hume's shoulders was often very clear. He knew he was running more than political risks. At times his strategy also made him and his party colleagues potential loyalist targets. His 'single transferable speech' could be frustrating for us hacks, but John Hume's basic analysis undoubtedly underpinned the whole process. I have yet to encounter a more sensible approach to dealing with an ancient quarrel within a modern Europe than seeking to blur the border at its edges. Looking on in that Oslo hotel function room in December 1998, one could not be anything but glad for the SDLP leader as he launched into his trademark rendition of 'The Town I Loved So Well'. We were also delighted for his tireless wife, Pat. The Nobel prize provided recognition of the couple's lifelong commitment to peaceful political progress.

If John Hume's prize was a reward for trying, trying and trying again, David Trimble's constituted a recognition of a politician prepared to seize the moment. No one who watched David Trimble and Ian Paisley doing their victory dance at Drumcree in July 1995 could have forecast Mr Trimble's procession up the Oslo Rathaus aisle with John Hume less than four years later. The Ulster Unionist leader remains a prickly character. Too often he treats any encounter with the press as an opportunity to win a pedant's victory over his questioner, rather than a chance to appeal to a wider public. The least criticism can raise his ire, leaving him famously red-faced. As the flat reception to his Nobel lecture demonstrated, Mr Trimble could do with some of the 'vague visionary' rhetoric he despises in order to communicate with the majority of us who are neither lawyers nor lecturers. But anyone who watched the Ulster Unionist leader being harangued on the streets during the Good Friday Agreement referendum campaign had to recognise that here was a politician prepared to stick his nose out and lead from the front. The history of Northern Ireland is littered with unionist leaders who have been cast aside after being labelled 'Lundys' or traitors by their own side. David Trimble may, as his critics argue, have been drawn to compromise by both the persuasive powers of Tony Blair and the lure of high office. However, I am sure he would not have made his difficult decisions if he had not been personally convinced that reaching agreement represented the only realistic road ahead for both communities. Again, Mr Trimble's wife Daphne is an indispensable part of the political partnership providing, in a quiet, calm manner, a constant counterbalance to her husband whenever all the attention threatens to go to his head.

Did the Nobel committee get it right? Should others have stood in the place of either John Hume or David Trimble? Clearly the committee's choice amounted to the tidiest option from an organisational point of view. If Gerry Adams had also been named as a winner it would probably have proved very hard for David Trimble to attend. The organisers would have had the embarrassment of presenting prizes to two Catholics and no Protestant. Some argue that the Nobel committee should have given its prize to some victims or to a non-politician like the Redemptorist priest Father Alex Reid who graduated from solving republican feuds to trying to solve the biggest feud of them all. But if a collection of politicians had to get their hands on the award, I think the Sinn Féin President can feel justifiably hard-done-by in missing out. Every time Gerry Adams gets a peace prize it causes understandable pain to IRA victims, given his long history of justifying 'armed struggle' and his direct responsibility for the IRA's 'long war'. But no fair observer can deny that in the 1990s Adams's contribution was vital to the existence of any peace process worthy of the name. Gerry Adams could be far more honest about his track record with the IRA and much more transparent about his motives for changing his position. Such honesty, however, will almost certainly have to await a truth commission, should Northern Ireland ever get one. No one can doubt, though, that Gerry Adams did shift his movement light years on questions such as participation in a Dublin parliament or a Belfast assembly, and acceptance of a reformed Northern Ireland within the UK, matters which are fundamental for achieving a constitutional compromise. Various kinds of violence, such as the horrendous punishment beatings, have continued apace. Peace Adams-style proved anything but perfect. Overall, though, his ceasefire strategy has, as he told a New York audience in 1999, almost certainly saved hundreds of lives. What the future will bring remains a source of uncertainty.

Other politicians who might have considered themselves in the running for a prize included Albert Reynolds, John Major, George Mitchell, Bill Clinton, Tony Blair, Mo Mowlam and Bertie Ahern. Mr Ahern deserved an award for keeping going with the Good Friday Agreement negotiations despite his mother's death, a time when any man could be forgiven for telling troublesome politicians to take a running jump. George Mitchell deserved an award for putting up with endless earache when lobbying for big business back on Capitol Hill must have seemed less trying and more financially rewarding.

But at the time of the ceremony in Oslo, the business of handing out peace prizes seemed rather premature. Despite the Good Friday Agreement violence had persisted, whilst the old bugbear of disarmament remained deeply problematic, despite a stunt when the Loyalist Volunteer Force handed over a few guns to be chopped up. The consignment included a Mauser from the *Clyde Valley* ship which ran guns to the old Ulster Volunteer Force, an antique which should have been put in a museum rather than destroyed. With the benefit of hindsight the attachment to disarmament seems a mistake, which the Conservative government might not have made if John Major had enjoyed the sort of massive parliamentary majority which Tony Blair could rely on. It is not that paramilitary disarmament is an undesirable aim, rather that verifying the terrorist arsenal is out of commission is unachievable and impractical. A specialist RUC officer who spent his life outfoxing the IRA's top weapons engineers rolled his eyes when I asked him about his view on 'decommissioning'. 'Are you serious?' my contact joked, pointing out the window. 'There's enough fertiliser in the trucks rolling past this office every day to blow us all to smithereens. It's the know-how that counts, the knowledge that's in their minds, and that you cannot decommission.'

Unionists respond that they drew up their wagons around decommissioning because some kind of gesture was important for building trust. But this meant the politicians became obsessed about a symbolic act which would in itself probably do little to forestall future violence, whilst paying less attention to violence and killing taking place in front of everyone's noses. During my last couple of months in Northern Ireland I drove up to Strabane to interview a couple of punishment beating victims. Noel Diver explained how he'd been lying on his sofa watching the TV when a gang burst in and beat him savagely in front of his partner and child. It was only after they had already broken his leg that they realised they had 'the wrong man' – they were looking for Noel's brother-in-law, Michael Brennan, who lived next door. They went next door and beat their intended target even more ferociously, taunting him to 'listen to this one crack' as they broke his bones. I am under no illusions that the victims of punishment attacks are all little cherubs. But the vicious assaults remain primitive and unacceptable, and my skin has rarely crawled quite so much as when, at one public meeting, I heard a priest, a supposed man of God, justify them. If a test of people's democratic credentials had to be set, I always thought, why not pick an end to punishment beatings and other forms of paramilitary violence? This might be hard to verify, as undoubtedly some beatings might be the work of 'freelances'. But at least it would make a difference in the real world of broken bones rather than the symbolic world of gesture politics.

However, ending punishment beatings was not the test the government and the unionists picked and for months, then years, the disarmament stumbling block kept tripping up all comers. If pressed, normally by an eager BBC reporter, Northern Irish people would proffer views on it, but generally they preferred to discuss *Brookside*, soccer or the price of a pint. In almost our last radio package together my researcher Rachel Hooper and I tracked down some of the 'wild geese' who left Northern Ireland during more depressed times, but who had been tempted back by the prospect of peace and prosperity. They were less concerned about the theoretical prospect of weapons decommissioning than the real challenges of finding decent work, or deciding which school to send their children to. A series of returnees told me of their shared conviction that Northern Ireland was the best place in the world to live, with the friendliest people and some of the most beautiful countryside. One woman returning from New Zealand insisted that even the butter was better. With every interview my face assumed a more pained expression, for just before we started compiling the report I had decided to accept the BBC's offer of a job as United Nations Correspondent in New York.

37

Passing Time with the President

SUMMER 1999

The longest of apprenticeships over, I prepared to do battle with truly international current affairs in the heart of a truly cosmopolitan metropolis. No longer Protestants and Catholics, but Serbs and Albanians, Hutus and Tutsis, Indonesians and East Timorese. From being a recognised subject specialist I now became the reporter whose dodgy pronunciation had to be constantly corrected and who couldn't tell his Nuba mountains from his Panjshir valley. The problem with the UN is that it means covering everything, and, by definition, you cannot be an expert on everything.

Despite travelling thousands of miles I knew I was unlikely to completely leave Northern Ireland behind. This was not just because of the profusion of Irish bars in New York but more because I promised my colleagues in Belfast that I would keep them updated on any developments in the Irish American world. I guessed I would have to turn my hand to the occasional report reflecting what the likes of Senator Mitchell, Congressman Peter King, millionaire Bill Flynn or other leading US players were up to. However, I wasn't prepared for the call I received late one night in June 1999 from the head of the BBC's Washington bureau, Andrew Roy. Andrew told me to prepare myself for a potential exclusive interview with President Clinton. At first, I thought he was having me on. But after he convinced me his call was for real, I prepared myself for a restless night and a possible early start. I imagined interviewing the US President would be a memorable experience but I could not have guessed quite how off the wall it would turn out to be. As a former Ireland Correspondent I felt relatively well prepared for the job, but hadn't bargained on the technical hitches which threatened to derail the interview. I wrote the following account of what happened for BBC Radio Four's *From Our Own Correspondent*.

I didn't sleep very well last Sunday night. Just before midnight I got a call from my boss in Washington to say the White House had been on the telephone to the BBC offering an exclusive interview on Northern Ireland. He suggested that either myself or two of my colleagues would do the job. The BBC in London would make a decision overnight and one of us would get a call at four in the morning.

At four my phone rang, and it was time to shake myself and get on the road. From my apartment in New York it's about an hour's drive to Westport, Connecticut, where the President wanted to do the interview. He'd fit it in before addressing a fund-raiser in the plush home of a wealthy Democrat supporter.

We drove to Westport and got some breakfast in a diner while we waited for the White House to get in touch. Soon my mobile phone rang and a woman staffer gave me directions. However, there was a hitch. The satellite broadcasting vehicle which we had brought to beam back the interview was thirteen feet tall. Every route we tried led under a low railway bridge. The White House staffer rang again – what was keeping us? Eventually we found a circuitous way to get to our destination.

So far so good. Once at the venue we set up our equipment. Now it was just a matter of sorting out my questions and keeping calm. It is, I kept telling myself, just another interview. An official White House crew arrived and set up alongside my BBC cameramen. 'When was the last time the President gave a foreign broadcaster a one-on-one interview on US soil?' I enquired. Two years ago, they replied, when he talked to Israeli TV at the time of the Wye River valley agreement.

Eventually, just after eleven o'clock in the morning, we heard the sound of helicopters and within minutes Bill Clinton was walking towards me. I heard myself greet him and point him towards his seat, then without further ado we commenced. I led off with an open-ended question to allow him to make his general point. He began to answer, and had uttered precisely five words, when the lights went out. My expression, immortalised on video, switched from rapt concentration to sheer panic. 'What happened?' asked the puzzled President. Suspecting our equipment had blown a fuse I assured him we'd have the problem solved in a moment. And then the President and I were left staring at each other wondering what to say next.

People scuttled around us in a frenzy of activity trying to fix the problem. I found myself telling the President that the air-conditioning in my apartment had done much the same thing a few days before and it had just been a question of flipping a trip switch. He expressed understanding. An agitated handyman hurtled down the corridor towards us. In midstride he realised he was about to trip over the most powerful man in the world. He came to an abrupt halt, balanced on one foot.

'I'm sorry, Mr President,' he blurted out.

'You're trying to fix the power,' said the President. 'Don't worry, just go do it.'

Everyone burst into laughter.

I joked that Ian Paisley probably had some sort of link with the electrical contractors and was trying to keep the President quiet. Bill Clinton laughed.

'If old Dr Paisley could cut me off then I'm sure he would,' he replied. 'I always like to have meetings with him when I'm tired because I never have to say anything. One time we met for thirty minutes and I bet I talked for thirty seconds.'

Still no power, and now the truth began to dawn that this was no blown fuse. The entire region had experienced a power cut. The house had no electricity. Our interview couldn't get going until we had run a power cable inside from the generator in our broadcast vehicle.

The minutes ticked by. But now it hardly seemed to matter as I was already on the verge of being what Americans call an FOB – a Friend of Bill. We chatted about the area of New York I live in, the Broadway play the President had tickets for, the Yankees baseball team, the US women's soccer squad and Hillary's potential run for the New York senate seat. 'If that's what Hillary does then I'm going there,' he said, adding that he didn't want to stick around in Washington after he was President 'getting underfoot'.

But the man who I was by now thinking of as good old Bill betrayed a fondness for California, which he told me his daughter Chelsea liked too. If it was just up to him, he said, he'd probably go there. But it was hard, if you were interested in public affairs, being so far away from the action.

In a society where getting a few seconds with the President can cost the wealthy a serious wad of cash, I was already moving into golden time. And still the wait went on. Suddenly Bill aimed a low blow. He asked what I made of the European election results. Frantically I tried to remember exactly what had happened at the elections. Was I going to be cross-questioned about the internal dynamics of the government of Belgium? 'You mean the apathy,' I finally blurted out. 'Yes, I suppose,' he countered. 'I imagine that was more significant than the rush to the right.'

Phew. We were off again, cantering by way of Tony Blair's majority – Bill envies it – via the President's problems in Congress, where he railed against the hard right Republican blocking tactics, through to his opinions on the prospective Republican presidential candidate George Bush junior, a candidate who Bill believed was getting a free ride because he seemed nicer than the mean Republicans in Congress. Bush junior, confided Mr Clinton, wanted to be anointed President without revealing his real policies.

By the time the lights came on I had made fifteen minutes of small talk with the President of the United States. We were both, apparently, having such a good time, it almost seemed a shame to break off our little chat, but there was the rather pressing matter of the imperilled Northern Ireland peace process to address. After nearly ten minutes of formal exchanges came to an end, there was more banter, and he posed for photographs and signed autographs.

The White House aides more or less had to pull their boss away to carry on with his by now much delayed schedule.

Bill Clinton has come in for some excoriating criticism during his period in office. But if you ever find yourself in a power cut, with time to kill, I can recommend him as good company.

According to my 'after dinner' version of the encounter, I spent all the time telling myself, John Cleese-like, 'Whatever you do, don't mention Monica.' In fact this is an after dinner lie. The thought of Ms Lewinsky did not strike me at the time, as there were simply too many other things to worry about. I spent much of our 'little chat' torturing myself that at any moment a presidential aide would put their hand on my shoulder and let me know, with great regret, that the delay had gone on too long and the President would have to proceed with his busy schedule. At times I was aware that Bill Clinton was still talking to me, but couldn't really concentrate on what he was saying, as I shot anxious glances at my cameramen Eric Thirer and Rob Magee, hoping they and our satellite engineer were almost finished running a cable in from our truck outside. Eventually, however, the BBC technicians, far from causing problems for the White House, actually saved its blushes. When the President went on to address his fund-raiser, the power in Westport had still not been reconnected. So the BBC powered the White House's public address system. Just don't tell that to any US Republicans.

After the Clinton interview hit the air a lot of old friends from Belfast got in touch to congratulate me on the 'coup'. But whilst I tried kidding a couple of people that I had been working hard, lobbying the White House for months, eventually I had to admit I was merely the jammy reporter who happened to be in the right place at the right time. The truth was that a White House aide rang the BBC newsroom in London out of the blue. The White House is not in the habit of offering us exclusive interviews, so the journalists on the news desk initially assumed, like me, that the whole business was a practical joke. Once it became clear it was genuine, it did not take a genius to work out what had been going on. NATO had just successfully evicted Serbian forces from Kosovo. Throughout the conflict Tony Blair had been Bill Clinton's staunchest ally. Now the bombing was over it was payback time. Downing Street had set a new deadline for agreement in Northern Ireland and needed to exert every bit of pressure possible to try to bring the recalcitrant Northern Ireland politicians to agreement. Number Ten got on the phone to the President and asked him for a favour. Hence our rendezvous in Connecticut.

When we were able to turn our lights on at long last, the President pleaded eloquently with David Trimble to take another risk for peace and to allow a government including Sinn Féin to be formed despite the failure of the IRA to start disarming. He argued that the Ulster Unionist leader could always pull the plug on the coalition at a later stage if the republicans did not deliver. In the hot summer of 1999, however, David Trimble had more on his mind than pacifying Bill Clinton. The Ulster Unionist leader calculated that taking the risk the White House suggested would be tantamount to committing political suicide. Despite the President's interview, the 30 June midnight deadline came and went.

Five months later, however, Northern Ireland's politicians faced up to the same dilemmas, this time under the patient chairmanship, once again, of George Mitchell. After eleven weeks of negotiations, and predictions from Gerry Adams and other key players that the talks probably would not succeed, Senator Mitchell coaxed the party leaders towards another finely balanced compromise. Agreement on the creation of a power-sharing government was tied to the appointment by the IRA and other paramilitaries of go-betweens to liaise on the crucial weapons decommissioning issue. This time David Trimble decided to take the risk which President Clinton had urged upon him back in the summer. On a Saturday afternoon in November 1999 the Ulster Unionist Council gave its leader a qualified go-ahead, enabling him to form a government with Sinn Féin and the other parties provided he referred back to them in February 2000. Two days later came the extraordinary sight of Martin McGuinness accepting his nomination as Minister of Education in a power-sharing government embracing both unionists and Irish republicans.

In New York I sat down with Senator Mitchell, who assured me in a BBC interview that, whilst he would return to Northern Ireland as a visitor, his role as talks mediator was over for good. The senator had done his best to finesse the disarmament logjam away through a careful sequencing of the formation of a government and the appointment of paramilitary decommissioning go-betweens. Would Northern Ireland's politicians, without the senator to lean on, be able to stand on their own feet? On this score, my hopes jostled with my doubts. The likes of David Trimble, John Hume and Gerry Adams have demonstrated great leadership skills, but elsewhere in the body politic both trust and talent are scare commodities. Northern Ireland's leaders can out-talk most elected representatives you care to mention. But some of their lesser-ranking colleagues would have difficulty getting elected onto a parish council or a board of school governors anywhere else in the UK or Ireland. It's not that Northern Ireland doesn't have more than its fair share of brilliant, able people. It's just that for years the best and the brightest have opted to emigrate or to stick to their own private business rather than choosing politics as a career option. Sometimes observers castigate Northern Ireland's middle classes for opting out in this way. But before casting any stones look at it on an individual basis. If you had just left college and you had the world at your feet, would you have really wanted to stay in the confined world of Northern Ireland's sectarian political parties? Or you had a young family and a developing career, would you have chosen a life which placed you and your loved ones at risk?

All of these fears, of course, would dissipate in an era of 'normal' politics. For nine weeks following the Mitchell compromise, Martin McGuinness and his fellow ministers appeared to be embarking on just such an era, running their departments in the new devolved government. I covered one of Minister McGuinness's more bizarre official engagements when he visited a school in the New York ghetto of Harlem telling a classroom of black pupils that they shared a history of oppression and disadvantage with their counterparts in Ireland. The pupils weren't entirely sure who their Sinn Féin visitors were, but they seemed duly impressed by the rhetoric. The Education Minister also talked about his ambition to tackle the problem of dyslexia amongst children back home. But before he could formulate his plans, another 'd' word, the old obstacle of decommissioning, caught up with him. The Ulster Unionists threatened to resign from the power sharing administration because the IRA had failed to disarm – the new Northern Ireland Secretary Peter Mandelson staved off the resignations by suspending the whole apparatus of devolution, a course of action which he judged the lesser of two evils. With the twenty-first century barely begun, the process once again plunged into crisis, leaving the world wondering whether the politicians would prove able to sort matters out.

Perhaps the present generation of leaders, who have in many cases stuck around for the entire duration of the troubles, have it in them to deliver their people from conflict and thereby to change the ground rules of politics. But will they then be able to go on to successfully run a society, rather than to argue about how, theoretically, that society should be run? Will they settle down to a future when there is no need to rush off to the White House or Number Ten to tell tales about their opponents to Principal Clinton or Headmaster Blair? Or might such a role have to await a new generation who don't have so much experience of championing their community's cause in conflict, but instead quietly take responsibility for bread-and-butter politics in their part of the world? The greatest test facing the extraordinary figures of the troubles in the future will be the challenge of adapting to normality.

38

Boats and Planes

SUMMER 1987–SUMMER 1999

Swimming is not my strong point. I learned to swim belatedly in my early twenties and can just about keep myself afloat for a couple of lengths, but could never find gainful employment as a lifeguard. In my first year as a reporter in Belfast, I had reason to ponder this when the deputy news editor Rowan Hand dispatched me to Carlingford Lough to film a feature about a group of enthusiasts who were rowing a replica Viking longboat from Dublin to Belfast. Rowan's instructions were to 'Just get a couple of snaps from the shore, get the Vikings to row over to you, do a quick interview with someone wearing a helmet with horns, then get back here sharpish.' But when cameraman Bill Brown senior and I got to the shore we found ourselves peering out into impenetrable mist. There was nothing for it but to take a little boat out, and then transfer Bill's camera and ourselves across to a trawler in the middle of an increasingly choppy lough. As the two boats smacked together in the swell of the turbulent sea we jumped from one to another, wondering about the wisdom of our actions. Eventually the men with horns on their heads rowed into view and we got the story Rowan wanted.

Twelve years later, in August 1999, I found myself with another cameraman, Robert Waseru from the Nairobi bureau of Reuters, on another unstable fishing boat, swaying wildly from side to side in the strong currents of Lake Tanganyika. We were making a film about refugees fleeing the brutal war in the Democratic Republic of Congo. The refugees packed on to old fishing boats paying ten dollars a head for a voyage to safety. We were getting some pictures to illustrate their flight. I tried, unsuccessfully, to look calm and assured when Robert recorded my piece-to-camera. All pretence went out the window, though, when we heard a loud thump, and one of the two fishermen at the stern of the boat started rummaging frantically through his toolbox. He grabbed a hammer and a wrench and sprinted along the gunwale before jumping down into the hull. As he ran I followed him and couldn't believe it when I saw what had attracted his attention – a geyser of water shooting up into our boat.

'Do you see what I see?' I asked Robert.

'Yes, and I don't like it' was the reply.

I reflected on the wisdom of the BBC's stringent safety rules which stipulate that any member of staff going out filming on a boat must wear a life jacket. When I negotiated our trip on the lake, no gear like this had been in sight. Now the shores of Lake Tanganyika seemed an awfully long way away, the waves somewhat forbidding and the likely content of the water quite unthinkable. Bilharzia, definitely. Something with teeth, in all probability.

The fisherman went into a frenzy of hammering and bolt tightening and, within a few seconds, the geyser became a trickle. The vessel stabilised, albeit with a sizeable pond in its bottom. Our crew smiled and began to carry on their way, but I didn't feel convinced. We had only been going for twenty minutes but already had all the pictures we needed. Although we had paid for an hour all I wanted now was dry land. I asked Robert, who is Kenyan and speaks Swahili, to tell them it was okay to go back. The fishermen seemed a bit downcast.

'They want to know,' Robert translated, 'is the white man scared of the big waves?'

'Tell them,' I replied, 'the white man is totally petrified.'

Robert couldn't bring himself to participate in such a loss of face so he said in Swahili, 'No, the white man isn't scared, it's just we've got all the pictures we need and we don't have much time.'

Honour preserved, we turned and headed for the shore.

A couple of days later on a brief return visit to Belfast, with my African experience still fresh in my mind, I took a bit of persuading when Patricia decided she wanted to go on a Sunday afternoon boat trip on the River Lagan. It seemed that one close encounter with the water in the space of a week had been quite enough. Eventually she cajoled me into it and I found myself beside Belfast's newish weir, hopping on board the *Joyce*, which potters up and down the Lagan providing tourists and locals with a novel view of Belfast's up-and-coming waterfront developments. First Officer Derek Boker proudly recounted the statistics – two hundred people employed in this office block here, one hundred and fifty in the one over there, plans to develop this old factory here, and a yuppie flat changing hands for so many hundred thousand pounds there. Derek himself is just the kind of entrepreneur Belfast needs, with ambitious plans to develop his sightseeing rides into a fully fledged water taxi service. Just like Venice. Well, almost . . .

We were fortunate enough to get quite a few sightings of Sammy the Seal, who is a regular commuter popping up the Lagan to get his lunch, and thereby providing doubters with living proof of how much the river has been cleaned up. We were also lucky enough not to see anything of Willy the Water Rat – I gather he and his friends are in great profusion on the banks. If I am sounding a little like a *Blue Peter* presenter at this point, I should point out that the *Joyce* was full of children who seemed to enjoy the novelty of messing about on the Lagan. The trip was short, but long enough to convince you that, however static the politics sometimes seems, things are happening in Belfast.

Back on the Lagan bank, Patricia and I set off for the city centre. When I arrived in Belfast in 1986 Sundays in the city were absolutely dead. Shops, pubs and restaurants remained shut. In some areas of Northern Ireland even the swings were tied up. Only a few licensed clubs served alcohol. You often had to be a member to get in, and in certain establishments it paid not to ask where the profit on your pint was going to. When the government passed a law allowing pubs to open on Sundays, the teetotal Reverend Ian Paisley stood outside Belfast's bars, berating the hardened drinkers who ventured inside. But the Free Presbyterian leader, like Canute, got his feet wet, this time in a sea of 'the Devil's buttermilk'. Like it or not, Belfast has changed. In the city centre, that hot August Sunday, several major stores remained open, selling clothes, records, computers and TVs. So did a few places where you could sit down and get a coffee.

We turned the corner of Belfast City Hall and saw that Café Society was open. The café is on the ground floor of one of the Victorian buildings which line the four sides of Donegall Square. The image of this particular corner of the square which sticks in my mind is one of smoke billowing out of the windows after an IRA bomb blast which I covered in the late eighties. A figure emerged from the building clutching a book. He turned out to be an employee in a religious bookstore, who had managed to save an illuminated Bible from the rubble of his shop. The Bible and the Bomb Blast – the scene said it all about Belfast in those days.

Now we heard the tinkling of an electric piano welling out of the door of Café Society. From the distinctive sound, it couldn't be anyone else but my old mate and *Spotlight* researcher Paul Rocks, who doubles up as a journalist-cum-jazz pianist. Our minds made up, we took a seat and listened as Paul rattled out a few Bruce Hornsby and Van Morrison numbers. Paul's wife and newborn son, Oliver, made up about a quarter of the small but appreciative audience. Outside the sun beat uncharacteristically down on Donegall Square. Inside I helped myself to a moderate sample of Dr Paisley's 'Devil's buttermilk'. As Paul paused between songs an Orange lodge marched along a nearby street, its banner unfurled and an accompanying pipe band playing. None of the shoppers batted an eyelid. The banner looked rather colourful in the sun. The Orangemen could quite easily have been Morris dancers. The week before, Paul told me, the annual republican internment anniversary rally had been held outside the City Hall. There had apparently been almost more tourists watching it than republicans taking part.

With the peace process uncertain and the sunshine doomed to give way to rain, it was probably an illusory moment. But it felt like one to savour. I sat back in my seat and thought about the boat on the Lagan, the plane I was due to take back across the Atlantic all too soon, and wondered why I had left Belfast and how long it would be before I returned.

Index

O'Brien, Conor Cruise, 102
O'Callaghan, Seán, 102, 103, 179
O'Connell, Daniel, 7
O'Connor, Sinéad, 71
Official IRA, 61, 64
O'Hare, Rita, 136, 162
O'Kane, Michael, 196
Omagh, County Tyrone, 49, 50
  bomb (1998), 222–6
O'Malley, Padraig, 195
Opus Dei, 178
Orange Order, 102, 177–9, 188–9, 247; see also
  Drumcree parades
Oslo, 230–1
Osman, Mohammed Ahmed, 88
'Our Man in Fermanagh' (*Spotlight*), 99–100

Paisley, Ian, junior, 150–1
Paisley, Reverend Ian, 13, 64, 68, 150, 161, 186,
    239, 246
  on broadcasting ban, 54
  Devenport on, 217–18
  Drumcree, 157, 159, 233
  Good Friday Agreement, 213–14, 219, 220–1
  interviews, 63, 70
  loyalist criticism of, 143
  Mitchell talks, 169, 199
  on prisoners, 107–8
Panorama, 59, 93
Patrick, St, 150–1
Patton, George, 170
Patton, Joel, 188
Paul (Traveller), 13–14
Paxman, Jeremy, 58
Payne, Mickey, 4
peace process, 160–2, 193–4
  Arniston talks, South Africa, 195–8
  ceasefire (1997), 199–200
  Docklands bomb (1996), 162–3
  and Drumcree, 174–5
  Good Friday Agreement, 212–15
  marching seasons, 154–8
  Mitchell talks, 168–9, 206
Pearse, Pádraig, 103
Pearson, Allison, 138–9
Perry, Margaret, 158
Pike, Mary, 59–60
plastic bullets, 67, 174, 181
PM, 193, 199
Pomeroy, County Tyrone, 186, 187
pornographic videos, 96–8
Portadown, County Armagh, 61, 164; see also
  Drumcree parades
Presbyterians, 9
Prescott, John, 225
Prevention of Terrorism Act, 43
Price, Lance, 8

Prison Officers' Association, 70
prisoners, 76, 107–8
  Clegg release, 155
  early releases, 51, 145, 167, 216–17
  escapes, 105–7
Provisional IRA see Irish Republican Army (IRA)
punishment beatings, 235

Qin Huasun, Ambassador, 1
Queen's University Belfast, 68, 160–1, 220
Quigley, Martin, 121–2
Quigley, Robert, 73
Quinn brothers (Ballymoney), 187–8, 221

Rabbitte, Pat, 147
Radio Five, 128–9, 139, 144, 212, 214
  Reynolds resignation, 146–7
Radio Four, 54, 129, 140–1, 150, 163, 171, 180,
    199, 228
  From Our Own Correspondent, 203–6, 207–9
Radio Foyle, 155
Radio Scotland, 182–4
Radio Ulster, 21, 85, 110, 113, 172
Rafferty, Seán, 12
Real IRA, 223, 226
Red Cross, Somalia, 93
Red Hand Defenders, 178
Redhead, Brian, 126
Reid, Father Alex, 42, 119, 233
Reilly, Karen, 155
Reilly, Sean, 155
Republican News, 76
Republican Sinn Féin, 52
Restorick, Rita, 193, 227
Restorick, Lance-Bombardier Stephen, 192–3
Reynolds, Albert, 119, 130, 137, 234
  resignation, 145–8
Reynolds, Pauline, 41
right to silence, 51, 67–8
Robbins, Wendy, 93–4
Robert (clergyman), 10–11, 13–14
Robinson, Mary, 84
Rocks, Paul, 97, 247
Rodgers, Bríd, 214
Rogan, Michael, 191
Ross, Willie, 56, 140, 216
Rowan, Brian, 139, 144, 162
Roy, Andrew, 237
Royal Belfast Hospital for Sick Children, 111, 191
Royal Ulster Constabulary (RUC), 8, 12, 19–20, 35,
    39–40, 42–3, 46, 50, 71, 79, 114, 132, 142,
    163, 167, 206, 213; see also Drumcree parades
  Annesley interview, 135–6
  bomb warnings, 22–3
  Brown arrest, 72–4
  crowd control, 60, 67, 154–5, 174
  and decommissioning, 234–5